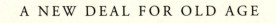

A NEW DEAL FOR OLD AGE

A New Deal
for Old Age

TOWARD A PROGRESSIVE RETIREMENT

ANNE L. ALSTOTT

Harvard University Press

Cambridge, Massachusetts
London, England
2016

Library of Congress Cataloging-in-Publication Data

Alstott, Anne, 1963– author.

   A new deal for old age : toward a progressive retirement / Anne L. Alstott.

      pages cm

   Includes bibliographical references and index.

   ISBN 978-0-674-08875-7

 1. Retirement—Economic aspects—United States. 2. Social security—United States.

 3. Equality—United States. 4. Older people—United States—Economic conditions. I. Title.

   HQ1063.2.U6A436 2016

   306.3'80973—dc23

                                              2015033859

To Johanna and David
with all my love forever

Contents

A NEW DEAL FOR OLD AGE

I

Introduction

NEARLY EVERYONE NOW recognizes that inequality has transformed American life. Americans at the top enjoy secure jobs, stable families, and ample opportunity for their children, while those at the bottom struggle with low wages, disrupted families, and dismal prospects for the next generation. What has largely escaped notice is that the hard-core inequality that has divided America is also undermining our nation's proudest experiment in equality—the Social Security retirement system.

Enacted in the mid-twentieth century, Social Security stood for the proposition that we're all in it together. Along with tax incentives to encourage everyone to save for retirement, the program promised a dignified old age for rich and poor alike. But the sad fact is that we are no longer in it together, and the egalitarian promise of Social Security is failing.

We live in an era of such stark inequality that the experience of old age itself has become increasingly unequal. For the well-off, age 65 now represents late middle age. It isn't until age 80 or so that the average better-off American feels old or faces serious impediments to work and healthy leisure. By contrast, many lower earners struggle to stay in the workforce to age 65. Many face disability in their early 60s, and many more confront limited job options and long-term unemployment.[1]

The last half-century has created a wide—and still-growing—gap in the experience of old age. To be sure, the rich have always enjoyed some advantage: wealth has always bought an easier life.[2] But until relatively recently, the experience of old age was not so very different for the rich and for the poor. Indeed, through the mid-twentieth century, the great majority of people of all income classes aged in a similar way. Most men died in their 60s of heart attacks and strokes, and most women followed in their 70s.[3]

But the past 50 years have wrought a dramatic change in the experience of old age. Public investments in sanitation, medicine, technology, and legal protections for older workers have paid off handsomely in longevity and improved quality of life in old age. Today, the average 65-year-old American can expect to live to her mid-80s, and most of those years will be disability-free.[4] The prevalence of heart disease has fallen dramatically, and advances in treating cancer and strokes have saved lives and reduced disability. Cataract surgery and hip replacements, along with other medical advances, treat debilitating conditions. Disability accommodations, including mobility and hearing aids, have improved life as well. Legal innovation, too, has contributed to the new landscape of old age. The Age Discrimination in Employment Act and the Americans with Disabilities Act have helped change the cultural meaning of old age, and older workers now enjoy a greater array of job options than ever before.[5]

So altered is old age in America that sociologists have coined a new term, the Third Age, to describe the unprecedented range of choices in work, family, and leisure now available to Americans in their 60s, 70s, and 80s. With longer lives and better health, many older people no longer retire in the classic sense. Instead of exiting the workforce permanently in their mid-60s, Americans increasingly remain at work or reinvent themselves, taking on new careers, hobbies, and leisure pursuits. Data confirm the cultural trend: employment among older workers declined from the 1930s to the 1980s but has increased since then.[6]

But the Third Age unfolds very differently for the poor than for the rich. Most obviously, lower-earning workers earn less and accumulate less wealth than their better-off peers, and so they reach their 60s and 70s with far less financial security. But the gap is more than a matter of money: low earners also suffer cumulative disadvantage, which leaves them with a shorter life span, worse health, higher rates of disability, and worse job options. Consider just one metric: American retirees in the top half of the earnings distribution now enjoy 6 more years of life than their peers in the bottom half, a gap that has widened with each successive generation.[7]

A tale of two colleagues illustrates all this at a human level. A Yale faculty colleague of mine—still teaching, writing, and traveling at 71—could pass for 55. He has boundless energy and publishes at a rate that daunts many younger professors. He confided in me recently that he claimed his Social Security benefits at age 65. When I explained that he could have reaped a greater financial return had he waited until age 70, he shook his head. "I know that," he responded, "but I feel ashamed enough already to be collecting what I am."

In another part of the university, a woman in her early 60s is struggling to hold onto her job. After surviving a stroke and a bad fall, she finds her clerical job stressful, but she is too healthy to qualify for disability benefits. She has continued working because she needs the money and the Yale health insurance. She hopes to hang on till age 65, when Medicare begins. Her Social Security benefits and Yale pension will be modest, and she is hoping to find part-time work to make ends meet.

Static Law in a Changing Society

Retirement policy has grown more and more out of sync with the changing experience of old age. Paradoxically, programs originally intended to ensure a decent retirement for all now too often preserve or even worsen the widening gap in the experience of old age.

Social Security is Exhibit A. We progressives like to think of Social Security as a great equalizer. The program's defenders point out, fairly enough, that Social Security keeps millions of elderly Americans out of poverty. The program transformed mid-twentieth-century America by providing a secure safety net for retiring workers and their spouses.[8]

Social Security is, of course, a complex program that incorporates retirement, disability, and survivors' benefits. But the lion's share of spending, and my primary focus in this book, is the retirement program. Accordingly, when I refer to "Social Security," I generally mean the old-age benefits program. (In later chapters we'll see, however, that the components of the program must work together, and that reforms in retirement benefits should motivate reforms in disability and survivors' entitlements too.)

The big problem is that Social Security has remained static despite seismic changes in American life. In 1950, the average American worker was a blue-collar man with a nonworking wife and a high school education (or less). Retirement meant a permanent exit from the workforce at age 68, and he could expect disability and death within a decade.[9] Today, by contrast, the average worker has some college education and a white-collar job. If he (or she) is married, it is to a working spouse, but the average worker is as likely to be unmarried as married. If this person retires at 65, he or she can expect to live another two decades, mostly in good health and disability-free.[10]

The out-of-sync Social Security system increasingly produces perverse results, rewarding affluence and penalizing disadvantage. Consider the problem of early retirement. Even as many older people enjoy the rewards of higher education, white-collar employment, longer lives, better health, and greater work options, Social Security permits workers to claim benefits in their early 60s—and the vast majority do. Until the 1960s, most workers could not claim Social Security until age 65, and most waited longer.[11] Today, workers can collect Social Security as early as age 62, although early retirees pay a lifelong financial penalty in the form of reduced benefits. What is more, nearly half of Americans claim benefits at age 62, and a stunning 75% claim Social Security before today's full retirement age of 66.[12]

The stampede to early retirement is dysfunctional for both higher and lower earners. Most well-off retirees do not need the money in their early 60s. They could remain in the workforce longer, and some (like my Yale faculty colleague) happily remain in their primary career well into their 70s and beyond.[13] For this group, Social Security benefits simply enrich their option set, and the penalty for early retirement doesn't hurt all that much. They can bank the money or count on the extra cash to enable them to choose part-time work, a career change, or time for travel or family or hobbies.

Early retirement looks very different for low earners, but the Social Security rules are no more functional for this group. Many less-educated, low-earning workers have physically demanding jobs, and many are in poor health.[14] Unemployment in this group is high as well. For low earners, early Social Security benefits provide welcome relief from financial hardship. But the financial penalty for early retirement is equally steep for rich and poor. Regardless of income level, early retirees can sacrifice more than 40% of their monthly benefits—for the rest of their lives.

The key point, as economist Alicia Munnell notes, is that Congress has stealthily raised the real Social Security retirement age to 70.[15] Although the program, confusingly, terms age 66 (rising soon to 67) the "full retirement age," the fact is that anyone who claims before age 70 pays a big financial penalty. Thus, for instance, a worker who would receive $1,000 at age 70 would receive only $568 at age 62.[16] The percentage penalty is the same for a highly educated, highly paid college professor as for a low-earning construction worker. But because the low earner typically lacks a private pension and relies mostly on Social Security, the total income hit is substantial, and it lasts for the rest of his life. (That is, the benefit doesn't bounce back to $1,000 once the worker reaches 70—he is stuck with $568 no matter how long he lives.)

Adding insult to injury, the rules on private pensions are stacked to favor the wealthy. The federal government spends more than a hundred billion dollars a year to subsidize private pension savings. These retirement subsidies cost nearly 20% as much as the entire Social Security program.[17] But fully two-thirds of the tax subsidies go to affluent households.[18] And these expensive subsidies have failed to expand private pension coverage to low earners. Only 10% of low-earning workers have any private pension at all, compared with 70% of higher earners.[19]

Social Security is also out of step with the modern family. In the 1950s, nearly everyone married and stayed married. Husbands worked while wives stayed home to raise children, and retirement meant the loss of the family's only paycheck. Today, by contrast, only half of the population is married, and divorce is common. More and more people never marry at all. And women's roles have changed dramatically. The vast majority of wives work, and most work full-time. Single parenthood also is increasingly common.[20]

Yet Social Security's rules presume that Americans still live in "Leave It to Beaver" families. The rules pay an extra 50% of retirement benefits to any worker with a nonworking spouse—without requiring any additional payroll taxes. The result is that two-earner couples lose out, as do the unmarried. Compounding the unfairness, Social Security's spousal benefit increasingly skews to the affluent, who are more likely to have a nonworking spouse.[21]

For decades now, we progressives have turned a blind eye to the perversities of Social Security. The party line has been that any inequity is simply the price of securing a decent retirement for vulnerable Americans. After all, any universal program must include the affluent in order to direct resources to the less well-off. And Social Security's popularity depends on the appearance of universality. Means testing, goes the progressive line, would only torpedo political support for one of the most progressive public policies around.

But the social revolution in the experience of age has been so decisive, and the growth of inequality so staggering, that progressives should reexamine their commitment to Social Security *in its present form*. The hard fact is that the program (together with tax subsidies for private pensions) is becoming less and less progressive, and—worse—less and less functional for workers at the low end of the earnings scale.

Today, well-off Americans not only can look forward to decades of unprecedented prosperity and personal choices during their Third Age but also can augment those choices with sizable public retirement benefits. Social Security and private pensions once represented income substitutes to replace lost wages for those no longer able to work. For the affluent today, though, these benefits amount to a basic income—a cash grant from the government that the recipients can use to supplement their budget, under-write part-time work, or fund ambitious travel and leisure plans.

To be sure, Social Security still awards benefits according to a progressive formula, which replaces a higher percentage of the income of a low earner. The progressive benefits formula marks one of the proudest achievements of American retirement policy, and it still protects low earners compared with, say, a private-accounts scheme like the one proposed by President George W. Bush. But the progressive benefits formula by itself no longer secures a decent retirement for low earners. More and more, Social Security pays substantial benefits to long-lived, affluent workers while imposing heavy financial penalties on low earners who must retire early.

The fundamental problem is that Social Security represents an outdated compromise. Looking back, the period between World War II and 1980 was exceptional, because inequality was low by historical standards. The earnings distribution was compressed, and retirement was predictable and universal. Family life was remarkably homogeneous across social and economic classes. And health outcomes were relatively homogeneous as well. The economic and social patterns of the postwar era presented a gift to policy designers, who could offer universal protections highly valuable to most families.

Today, by contrast, inequality is rampant in education, health, employment, and family stability, and disadvantaged workers typically experience hardship in multiple dimensions of life. Wages at the very top have sky-rocketed, while wages at the bottom have stagnated or fallen. Low-earning, less-educated workers face higher rates of unemployment and greater risks of disease and disability throughout their lives. They are less likely to marry, more likely to divorce if they do marry, and more likely to rear a child as a single parent.[22] These inequalities cumulate over a lifetime. The result is that low-income workers typically live shorter lives and are far more likely to end their lives in poor health and with physical and mental disabilities.

In the broadest terms, social inequality has defeated the universalist promise of Social Security. The ironic and unintended result is that the state now funds a lengthy Third Age for the well-off but leaves low earners in a marginal financial position when they can no longer work. Nor do other programs adequately close the gap. The Social Security disability system plays an important role in insuring workers against total work disability, but the program's disability standard and procedural hurdles can exclude low earners who cannot work and badly need assistance. Unemployment insurance, too, is particularly important for low earners, but current rules do not take into account the difficulties facing older workers who experience unemployment.

Roadblocks to Reform

The financial plight of the Social Security system has prompted scholars and policy analysts in Washington to scrutinize old-age entitlements. Today, 57 million Americans receive Social Security retirement and disability benefits.[23] By 2033, the Social Security trust fund will be unable to pay scheduled benefits.[24] By 2080, nearly one-quarter of the U.S. population will be age 65 or older.[25]

These numbers have generated considerable concern. In light of the longer life spans of today's older Americans, the sensible response, many policy analysts agree, would be to raise the Social Security retirement age.[26] Other developed nations face a similar demographic crunch, and the international trend is decisively in favor of postponing retirement ages.[27]

But the conventional response is that raising the retirement age will be difficult, and perhaps impossible, for three reasons. First is the *egalitarian problem*. Progressives worry—with good reason—that raising the retirement age would harm lower-earning workers, who live shorter lives and suffer early disability due to physically demanding jobs and worse health.[28] This issue is not a trivial one: one-quarter of adults aged 65–74 report some degree of disability, and the rate is 40% for those with less than a high school diploma.[29]

It might seem that the solution would be to offer more generous retirement terms to lower earners, but that move seems to be barred by the second roadblock, the *universality problem*. Social Security has prospered politically and socially because it promises a decent retirement for all workers, rich and poor alike. Introducing new differentials in treatment, no matter how justified, could undermine the political foundations for retirement policy and leave low earners even worse off in the end.

As if the equality and universality problems weren't barrier enough, a third roadblock looms—the *myth of purchased benefits*. Politicians since Franklin Roosevelt have cleverly framed Social Security in terms of ownership: workers, they have insisted, purchase their own benefits via payroll-tax "contributions."[30] Of course, the politicians—like every policy wonk inside and outside Washington—know that the claim is false.[31] Most workers receive more or less than a fixed return on their contributions. But if the political popularity of Social Security is rooted in the myth, then changing benefits—especially cutting benefits—is almost impossible.

Not for nothing is Social Security called the "Third Rail" of American politics, something any sane politician is afraid to touch.[32]

Making the Moral Argument

Competing moralisms complicate the fiscal debate. Some commentators treat the elderly as "greedy geezers," living it up on Social Security benefits that will bankrupt our children.[33] Others argue that the program damages the economy and discourages work, savings, and self-reliance.[34] One critic compares Social Security to a Ponzi scheme, paying windfalls to early claimants and cheating later participants out of a fair return on their money.[35]

Defenders of Social Security, for their part, reject the "greedy geezer" stereotype. The elderly, they say, are mostly hard workers who live modestly and would fall into poverty in large numbers if their benefits were cut. Others invoke society's commitment to deliver the Social Security benefits elderly workers have earned.[36]

But the barrage of competing slogans and stereotypes obscures the serious questions of justice at stake in retirement policy. These moral questions deserve sustained consideration. Take, for example, the ongoing debate over Social Security's solvency. Critics of the present program cite figures to show that the program is bankrupt and unaffordable, while defenders of the status quo cite figures to demonstrate that solvency can be restored with minor tax increases and benefit cuts.[37] Critics point out the increasing longevity of the older population, while defenders emphasize the prevalence of disability among older people.[38] Who is right?

The problem is that the solvency debate dodges the moral issues at stake. Insolvency, standing alone, offers no principled grounds for any policy response. Congress could restore the solvency of the system by raising taxes or by cutting benefits in any of a nearly infinite array of possible ways, with a range of effects on people of different generations, different occupations, and different genders. The goal of solvency cannot justify any particular approach as fair or efficient. Solvency is an accounting concept, a matter of numerical balance, and not a criterion for justice.

Claims about increasing longevity suffer from the same deficit. The fact that Americans are living longer has no necessary normative significance for retirement policy. Some argue that the Social Security retirement age should rise to reflect longevity gains, but one could just as easily argue that older people should simply enjoy longer periods of retirement. The length of the average life span, standing alone, gives no grounds for any particular direction in retirement policy, unless one smuggles in (as analysts sometimes do) hidden normative premises.

The best—and only satisfying—way to gain some purchase on policy directions is to grapple with the values at stake in retirement policy. Claims about solvency and longevity actually implicate one of the deepest and most contested issues in moral and political philosophy: the problem of *justice between age groups,* which addresses how a fair society should allocate resources to individuals across the life cycle. We can know whether a program is "too expensive" only if we have some moral reference point for how much we ought to spend on it. If we think that Social Security pays the right amount to everyone, then, however expensive it is, we should dig deeper and pay the price. But if the public resources now devoted to retirement exceed the fair allotment, then the elderly should reduce their claim so that resources can properly flow to younger age groups.

Is it relevant that society has promised Social Security benefits to retirees? A society, like an individual, should often keep its promises, especially when others rely on the promise in arranging their lives. But it is a serious question whether social insurance legislation represents a promise and, if so, what the promise consists of. Some defenders of Social Security treat any reduction in benefits from the current baseline as an unwarranted "cut."[39] But the program has changed over time, and it is reasonable to expect that Congress will alter it again as society changes. The real question, once again, is what a fair society owes its older and younger members.

The classic answer to the problem of justice between age groups, and one that remains sound today, is that Americans—young and old—should be entitled to look to the state for assistance when they are unable to work. Work disability is, of course, more common as we reach older ages, and it provides a classic justification for state-provided social insurance. Workers often will not or cannot insure themselves against disability in the private market, and so—on a wide variety of theories of justice—the state may properly step in and use its taxing and spending powers to provide disability insurance.

Taking the long view, then, Social Security is a social insurance program that draws on the resources of younger taxpayers to cushion the risks of old age for an older generation. As these risks change, so should the benefits and burdens of the Social Security program. For instance, today's older Americans have benefitted enormously from collective investments in public health, health care, technology, and legal innovation. The result of these social investments is that many of today's (and tomorrow's) over-65s live long, healthy lives, with a set of work, family, and leisure options that would have astonished their grandparents. Retirement policy may fairly take notice of these improvements in allocating resources to the elderly.

The moral problem of justice *within age groups* is significant for retirement policy as well. The experience of age has grown more and more unequal, as we have seen. As a group, today's older Americans enjoy unprecedented levels of education, longevity, and work opportunity. But these benefits have been captured disproportionately by the well educated and the affluent. Disadvantaged workers now face multiple and cumulative hardships, because low levels of education lead to low wages and correlate with poor health and family instability. A just retirement policy should take due care to recognize cumulative disadvantage and unequal flourishing.

These moral propositions motivate this book, and I will argue that it is possible to deploy them to help us move past sloganeering and technocratic jargon. Readers may not agree with the principles I offer; they are, by definition, value-laden, and people may reasonably dispute the values that a fair society should pursue. Even readers who find congenial the principles I offer may not agree with the policy implications I draw and may prefer alternative reforms. But even in these cases, the larger agenda of the book can succeed by prompting policy analysts and legal thinkers to clarify their own policy prescriptions for addressing problems of justice between and within age groups.

From Principles to Policies

Too often, principles and policies occupy separate spheres. Philosophers think deep thoughts about justice but are not trained to design policy. Policy analysts draw on a wealth of facts and experience to offer programmatic reforms, but they seldom ground reforms in first principles of justice. Legal scholars can help bridge that gap, and in this book (as in other projects),[40] I aim to do so. Drawing on literatures in political theory, economics, and law, I show how three principles can motivate concrete reforms that would improve the justice of American retirement policy.

First, the problem of justice between age groups should be guided by principles of *life-cycle fairness* and *social reciprocity*. A just society should allocate resources fairly across the life cycle, ensuring adequate resources for education in childhood, equal opportunity in adulthood, and basic security in old age. But, having secured these basic protections, a society should grant individuals maximum freedom to pursue a life of their own choosing. Concretely, social insurance should provide for those who cannot work due to old age or early disability. But *life-cycle fairness* suggests that it should be the inability to work, and not one's chronological age, that serves as the criterion for entitlement to social assistance.

Justice between age groups implies obligation as well as entitlement, however. When social investments produce large gains to an age group, the *principle of social reciprocity* justifies the state in taking those benefits into account in adjusting resource allocations. In the past one hundred years, the United States has invested public funds in ways that have greatly enhanced the education, health, and work opportunities of people over age 60. These gains enable many (though not all) older people to work longer than ever before, a social fact that should be recognized in the design of public programs.

Second, a fair society should also promote justice within age groups. The experience of age has grown more and more unequal as inequality has widened in nearly every sphere of life—health, education, work opportunity, and family life. These inequalities should be of special concern for justice because they tend to affect the same group of people and to cumulate over a lifetime. Thus, less-educated workers not only earn low wages but also experience shorter lives, higher rates of disability and unemployment, and greater family disruption than their better-educated and more-affluent peers. A fair society should *recognize cumulative disadvantage* and make fair provision for the earlier onset of work disability.

A final principle guides policy design: A fair society should take care not to humiliate its members in the implementation of justice between and within age groups. The *antihumiliation principle* pushes toward reforms that are universal, when possible, and toward procedures that are dignified and unintrusive.

These ideals have strong implications for retirement policy. Life-cycle fairness suggests that we should maintain a combination of public and private pensions that ensure that older Americans do not fall into destitution when they can no longer work. Social Security should remain a pillar of retirement policy, but the retirement age should be raised significantly to reflect the increasing work ability and work options of those over 60.

At the same time, social reciprocity suggests that we should not treat older people as having a moral claim to Social Security benefits fixed at their present levels. It is eminently fair to expect those who have gained from public investments in health and work opportunity to share with the collective some of those benefits by working longer and collecting less from the fisc. Fairness counsels caution in changing the financial entitlements of present retirees, who may have limited capacity to adjust their decisions. Public policy must also take care to ensure adequate work opportunities and legal protections for older workers. But, looking ahead, it is entirely just to adapt Social Security to the abilities and work patterns of the twenty-first century. Doing so does not defeat any defensible moral claim by future retirees.

Policies should recognize cumulative disadvantage by protecting retirement options for low earners and those who experience poor health or disability. Members of these groups should generally be able to retire earlier and on more-favorable terms. Reforms in both Social Security and tax subsidies should ensure that these workers have access to adequate retirement income. Policy design should ensure that these new policies do not humiliate their beneficiaries. Universal entitlements should be used where possible, and any measure of disadvantage should avoid a demeaning means test.

To be sure, ideals of justice do not always yield determinate directions for public policy. Reasonable people might draw quite different conclusions about how exactly to reform Social Security and a host of interrelated programs for disability, unemployment, and pensions savings. Still, this book aims to translate principles into concrete policies. Readers may find these proposals attractive. But even those who prefer another direction may find it useful to see how thinking through the details of policy design can illuminate tradeoffs and synergies that are not immediately obvious.

With this note of humility, I argue that a principled approach suggests five concrete reforms in Social Security and other public programs.

Progressive Retirement: Five Reforms to Restore Fairness to U.S. Retirement Policy

First: *the Social Security retirement age should rise (over time) to 76, but timing penalties in Social Security should be adjusted to permit early retirement on relatively advantageous terms for low-earning workers and those with physically demanding jobs.* At first glance, age 76 may seem high, and indeed it is significantly higher than most conventional proposals to raise the retirement age. But first principles return our focus to work disability and away from chronological age. Studies confirm that the majority of Americans who reach age 65 can work past age 80, so age 76 is, if anything, a cautious number.[41]

Progressive retirement timing would mark a new approach to addressing the egalitarian and universality objections that have, thus far, deterred some progressives from endorsing a higher retirement age. The idea is relatively simple. The range of retirement ages would be the same for all workers, from early retirement at 62 to full retirement at 76. But the financial penalty for early claiming would be based on a sliding scale linked to lifetime earnings. The result is that the system would remain universal in the options it offers: everyone could choose the retirement timing that works for her. But baked into the benefit calculation would be a timing preference for low-earning workers. They would be able to claim Social Security retirement benefits early, as many do now, and with a smaller financial penalty than that imposed today. At the same time, high earners would pay a larger penalty than they do today for early claiming.

The progressive retirement timing rules I propose have major advantages over both current law and proposals simply to raise the retirement age for all.

They achieve the egalitarian objective of securing early retirement on decent terms for workers facing cumulative disadvantage. Progressive retirement timing would also motivate higher-earning workers to claim benefits later, and perhaps work longer—an appropriate result given their longer life spans, increasing health and ability, and greater work options.

An immediate objection springs to mind: If older workers remain in their jobs, won't there be fewer opportunities for younger workers, already hard-pressed by the Great Recession? Economists have studied the issue, and, in a rare bit of happy news from the dismal science, they have found that there is no necessary tradeoff, because the labor market is plastic enough to expand to accommodate a larger pool of workers. It isn't like a musical-chairs game with a fixed number of seats. I will review the evidence for this important claim in a few pages, and I discuss the issue at length in Chapter 4.

Importantly, progressive retirement timing would retain the present Social Security system's commitment to universality. The range of retirement ages offered to every worker would be the same: anyone could claim Social Security between 62 and 76. Each person's choice would be determined, as it is today, by personal circumstances and plans. But the new system would exact a heavier penalty on affluent workers who choose to claim Social Security early. At the same time (as I discuss later) complementary reforms would provide an earlier exit from the workforce (penalty-free) for affluent workers truly unable to work.

Second: *Social Security should create a phased retirement option that would mirror current patterns of work transitions and ease the transition to delayed retirement.* Phased retirement has become more and more common in private industry, and it should become a key part of modernizing the system. Today, most retirees do not permanently exit the workforce all at once. Instead, they cut back their hours, take a less-demanding position, or try a new job. To recognize and facilitate these shifts, the Social Security system should offer three years of half-benefits beginning at age 73, without any reduction in full benefits payable at age 76.

Incorporating phased retirement into Social Security would ease the transition to a higher retirement age. Workers who want or need to slow down could count on the half-benefits from ages 73 to 76 when planning their finances. And the option to retain older workers part-time while they collect partial Social Security benefits could be an attractive perk for employers as well.

Third: *Disability and employment policies should be reformed to protect the interests of older workers.* Progressive retirement timing and phased retirement would protect the great majority of older workers who experience disability and unemployment. Compared with today, low earners could retire early with far less financial loss. And phased retirement would assist even high earners who want (or need) to exit the workforce before age 76.

Still, the state should create additional backstops to protect older workers who find that they cannot work until 76. Feasible changes in Social Security Disability Insurance (SSDI) and unemployment insurance (UI), along with better age discrimination protections and changes in employment law would all anticipate the needs of a new, older workforce.

Fourth: *The spousal benefit for retirees should be gradually repealed.* The spousal benefit is an artifact of family life in the mid-twentieth century, when most wives did not work outside the home. The spousal benefit remains critical for current retirees who lived mid-twentieth-century lives. But the spousal benefit will become far less important for future cohorts of retirees, and it should be phased out, because it no longer reflects the social organization of work. Along with a growing number of policy analysts, I recommend a minimum benefit for low-earning workers to reduce poverty among the elderly generally and to cushion the gradual repeal of the spousal benefit. And I suggest a joint-and-survivor annuity option for people who wish to stretch their Social Security benefit to support themselves and a spouse, partner, or dependent child. Importantly, though, retirees choosing the joint-and-survivor option should pay the full actuarial price for their benefit, as Chapter 9 explains.

Fifth: *Tax provisions related to retirement should be redesigned to serve the interests of the disadvantaged.* Progressive reform should restructure the Social Security financing system to include an equitable tax burden on income from capital. And universal, portable private pensions should be funded by redirecting tax subsidies now captured by the richest workers.

Some of these policies would reduce the budgetary cost of Social Security. The increase in the retirement age (while holding maximum benefits constant) would cut program expenditures dramatically, and the repeal of the spousal benefit would also save money. But some of these proposals would increase government expenditures. The favorable shift in retirement timing rules for low earners and the expansion of SSDI and unemployment insurance would all add to government outlays. As a rough matter, though, the savings seem likely to exceed the additional costs by a wide margin, creating financial capacity in the system to handle a predictable increase in expenditures on SSDI and UI.[42]

The progressive retirement timing proposal is new, as is the phased retirement proposal. The other reforms often build on existing proposals, as noted earlier. But this book's distinctive contribution is to deploy ideals of justice to motivate thoroughgoing reform that extends across social programs and fields of law. It is understandable that Washington policy analysts tend to propose incremental change and to examine elements of the social insurance state in piecemeal fashion. But in this book, I aim to take advantage of an academic vantage point to propose more-ambitious reforms anchored to a moral foundation and spanning a wide variety of programs beyond Social Security. Along the way, I provide principled reasons for rejecting the status quo and other proposed reforms, including means testing and longevity indexing.

Sacrificing Jobs for the Young?

As the economy slowly exits the Great Recession, it might seem that raising the Social Security retirement age takes a leap in the wrong direction. It seems intuitive, after all, that early retirement helps younger workers by freeing up jobs. If we can clear out the Baby Boomers now occupying senior positions, then middle-aged people can move up, and younger people can get a foothold.

But intuition, it turns out, is a poor guide to policy in this case. The most careful studies suggest that raising the retirement age will not harm youth employment. Jonathan Gruber and David Wise conducted a massive, multination study of the relationship between retirement policy and youth employment. They concluded that there is no correlation between later retirement ages and youth unemployment.[43]

Indeed, the researchers found that youth employment and the employment of older workers tend to be positively correlated: that is, holding other factors constant, when more older people are working, so are more younger people.[44] Just as developed economies were able to absorb the influx of women into labor markets in the 1970s, so they can absorb a new group of older workers.[45]

These findings seem especially important once we realize that the United States, like other developed nations, will likely confront a shrinking labor force in the coming decades as the Baby Boom ages.[46] At the same time, gains in the educational attainment of the workforce are projected to slow.[47] These changes will, if anything, tighten demand for workers of all ages.

Seizing the Opportunity

Inequality poses a moral challenge to American retirement policy. When our laws reward lifetime privilege and compound lifetime disadvantage, something has gone badly wrong. Social cooperation in the past century has produced valuable gains in longevity and quality of life for the elderly, particularly those in the top half of the income distribution. We should not hesitate to revisit the public retirement system and to ask them to share some of those gains with younger age groups and with their less-affluent peers.

As the Baby Boom retires, the stakes for the nation could not be higher. The budgetary cost of Social Security retirement benefits and retirement tax subsidies is formidable—more than three-quarters of a trillion dollars annually. But, as I have emphasized, the budget numbers only hint at the real problem, which is injustice between and within age groups. The resources spent to fund healthy retirement for Third Agers cannot also be spent on childcare, on Head Start, on college educations, on payroll tax reductions, or on other measures to ensure just treatment of the young. The resources devoted to healthy retirement for affluent retirees cannot also be spent to cushion the illness, disability, and limited work options of those who bear the burden of cumulative disadvantage.

Funding decades of healthy leisure for the affluent middle-aged simply should not be a social priority. We can and should change American retirement policy so that it insures against work disability and mitigates the outcomes of lives lived in disadvantage.

And we should reject the idea that retirement reform necessarily pits the elderly against everyone else. Older Americans, even affluent ones, have much to gain from a more just retirement policy. Today's policies tempt or force many older workers out of the workforce before they wish to exit. The proposals I outline would support all workers, at every level of income, in crafting a Third Age full of meaningful opportunities.

2

The New Inequality
of Old Age

IN THE MID-TWENTIETH CENTURY, age 65 was old. Only half of men survived that long.[1] Age 65 meant retirement and the looming prospect of a heart attack or stroke.[2] Today, by contrast, many people in their 60s and 70s are virtually indistinguishable—in appearance and lifestyle—from those of us in our 50s. Splashy headlines confirm what we see around us: 65 is the new 45 . . . and 80 is the new 65![3]

Behind the slogans lie real and striking changes in American life. By nearly any measure, people over 65 are, as a group, better-off than ever before. They are better educated, longer-lived, healthier, and wealthier than any preceding generation. And they face an unprecedented array of life options. Increasing numbers of older Americans are choosing to continue in their careers or to reinvent themselves in new jobs in their 60s and 70s. Those who do retire from paid work often have big plans—to travel, to care for grandchildren, or to pursue vigorous hobbies.

At age 65, today's Americans seem more middle-aged than old. Indeed, sociologists have coined a term to describe this extended middle age: the new Third Age, sociologists say, has become a life stage for self-reinvention. With children grown and careers and finances established, older people can reflect on how to spend the two (or three) decades before true old age sets in.[4] The result is that today, retirement no longer marks a social and personal transition to old age. Many people now retire from their full-time jobs in their 50s and 60s and take on new work, sometimes called "encore careers."[5] For these individuals, retirement becomes a midlife transition in which people change some roles (jobs, volunteer work), retain others (as active community members and spouses), and "develop new self-identities."[6] Indeed, a large percentage of older Americans report that they could work but are not working, including 50% of those in their 70s.[7]

But chronological age retains a very different meaning for Americans in the bottom half or third of the income distribution. These less-educated workers have a different experience of work, which brings physical exhaustion and repeated injury. Workers in the bottom half often limp toward their 60s, praying not to be fired and counting the days until they can collect Social Security. They often suffer partial disability—too little impairment to qualify for public disability benefits, but enough to limit their work options and daily lives.

For this group, encore careers and the vast freedoms of the Third Age are terribly remote. Workers at the bottom have jobs, not careers, and they have little (if any) retirement savings outside Social Security, thanks to the decline of unions and the demise of defined-benefit pension plans. They take part-time jobs at retirement to make ends meet, not to fulfill the dream of a new career.

Chronological age, then, has unequal meaning in America today, but it wasn't always so. To be sure, the very richest have always faced better options in old age than the very poorest. But inequality has widened dramatically since the mid-twentieth century. Gaps in education, in earnings, in work options, and in family life have grown in the past few decades.

In this chapter, I explore the paradox of age in America—the combination of enormous gains for the over-65s as a group but high and rising levels of inequality within the group. Looking at four dimensions of well-being (health, education, work options, and family stability), the data sound a repeated theme: large gains for the over-65s as a whole have been captured mostly by the well-off.

Unequal Gains in Health

Begin with the most obvious measure of health for older individuals: life span. In 1900, an American man could expect to live only to age 47. By 1940, he could expect to live to 63, and by 2008, to 78.[8] (Women have longer life spans: in 2008, the expected life span at birth was 76 for a man and 81 for a woman). The gain in longevity is nothing short of stunning: more than 30 extra years of life, on average, gained in just 100 years or so.[9]

The gain in longevity reflects a range of investments in public health and health care. Vaccinations have saved many people from serious diseases. Sanitation and public health measures, including clean water, sewage treatment, and lead abatement—just to take a few examples—have saved lives as well. Access to and advances in health care have saved and extended lives. Although the United States lags behind other developed countries in life expectancy (due primarily to smoking- and obesity-related diseases), the average American can expect a longer and healthier life than ever before.[10]

To be sure, life expectancy at birth is a noisy measure of gains to older Americans. Many major public health measures—sanitation, food safety, and vaccinations—have helped reduce infant and child mortality. And, statistically speaking, reductions in infant mortality would raise the average life expectancy even if the elderly did not live any longer.

To see why, imagine a society with ten people. If five die in infancy and five live to age 100, the life expectancy is 50. If none die in infancy, the life expectancy is 100, with the longevity gain attributable entirely to the decline in infant mortality. So a better measure of the extension of life at older ages is life expectancy at age 65. In other words, how much longer can someone expect to live once he reaches 65? (In the hypothetical, life expectancy at 65 would not change: people reaching 65 would live 35 more years in either case.)

In America in the past 100 years, life expectancy at age 65 has increased substantially (though not as dramatically as life expectancy at birth). In 1900, a 65-year-old could expect to live another 12 years. By 1940, he could expect to live another 13 years—not a major gain. But by 2008, a 65-year-old could expect to live another 19 years.[11] In just over a century, then, the average American gained 7 extra years of life past the age of 65.[12]

But end-of-life gains in longevity have not been evenly distributed. Historically, richer people have lived longer than poorer people.[13] In the first half of the twentieth century, the United States witnessed an equalizing trend as mortality differentials between high and low earners declined. But since the 1950s and 1960s, the longevity gap between rich and poor has widened.[14] By 2008, the gap in life expectancy at birth between high- and low-education groups had grown to 14 years for men and 10 years for women.[15]

The rich-poor gap in longevity also persists when we look at life expectancy at age 65. For example, a Social Security Administration study compared workers retiring in 1977 and in 2006 (at the full retirement age in each case). For workers in the earlier cohort, life expectancy at age 65 was only slightly higher (less than 1 year) for workers in the top half of the income distribution compared with those in the bottom half. For workers in the later-born cohort, however, the life-expectancy gap at age 65 had widened to more than 5 years.[16] Even more troubling are studies showing that the life expectancy of individuals with lower socioeconomic status may actually have dropped in recent years.[17]

To take another example, a recent study found that a 70-year-old man in the lowest tenth of the lifetime earnings distribution is nearly 4 times as likely to die in any given year as a man in the top tenth. The author, economist Hilary Waldron, found that "health and socioeconomic status are positively correlated (the higher the lifetime earnings, the better the health) throughout the entire lifetime earnings distribution."[18]

The causes of inequality in life expectancy are numerous. The National Research Council found that the mortality rate among low-income Americans is especially high by international standards. Lifetime effects of poorer health and life stress can cumulate over time, tending to produce inequality at older ages. And some public health campaigns—notably, the recent campaign against smoking—had a stronger impact on behavior among higher-SES individuals.[19]

Longevity, by itself, cannot tell the whole story of improving health and well-being among those over 65. After all, longer lives might portend more years spent in poor health or with serious disability.[20] But research has confirmed that gains in longevity have been accompanied by gains in health and ability among older people. For instance, Dora Costa found that rates of heart disease, arteriosclerosis, and cerebrovascular disease have fallen substantially in the over-55 population since 1930.[21] Eileen Crimmins and her coauthors found that disability-free life expectancy had increased since the 1980s, so that a typical 70-year-old can now expect to live 14 more years, 12 of those disability-free.[22]

Research has consistently documented the decline in disability among

Americans over 65. To be sure, "disability" can be a slippery concept, and studies vary in their measurements.[23] But what is striking is that, according to a variety of measures, disability rates have fallen enormously in the past few generations. For instance, Manton and Gu find that the share of the population over 65 suffering lengthy spells of disability fell by a quarter between 1982 and 1999, from 26% to 20%.[24]

Rates of disability do increase with age, but the data confirm what the splashy headlines proclaim: a large majority of older people are able to be active until their 80s. For example, Freedman finds that at ages 65–69, 67% of people are either fully able (45%) or can successfully accommodate a disability (22%). That percentage remains high at ages 70–74 (63%) and drops below 50% only at ages 80–84 (47%).[25]

Gains in ability for older people reflect a number of technological and legal changes. On the medical front, some conditions have become less disabling in recent decades: heart disease, visual impairment, and arthritis no longer limit activities as severely as they once did.[26] New therapies such as joint replacement and cataract surgery have improved functioning, as have new drugs for arthritis and heart disease. The Americans with Disabilities Act has dramatically improved access to public accommodations and workplaces since 1990: architectural features like accessible bathrooms, ramps, and handrails are now universal.[27]

But gains in health and ability, like gains in longevity, have been unequally distributed.[28] Lower-income individuals are more likely than their wealthier counterparts to experience hypertension, obesity, diabetes, early stroke, and heart disease.[29] Lower socioeconomic status also correlates with greater severity of disease. A study of patients with serious lung disease found that patients with less income and education suffered poorer lung function and greater physical limitations.[30]

Similarly, a recent study of disability found that 73% of Medicare enrollees in 2011 with incomes of $60,000 or more were either fully able or had successfully accommodated a disability. By contrast, only 42% of those with incomes less than $15,000 and 48% of those with incomes between $15,000 and $30,000 fell into that high-functioning category.[31] Another study found that "more-educated persons have up to a 50 percent lower disability rate than do the less educated," due to several differences between white- and blue-collar jobs: less exposure to toxic materials, lower rates of musculoskeletal injury, and greater cognitive stimulus.[32]

Unequal Gains in Education and Earnings

The past 75 years have witnessed remarkable gains in educational levels in the United States. More and more Americans have attended college, and fewer and fewer have dropped out before earning a high school diploma. In 1940, only 25% of the population managed to complete high school. By 2013, 88% did.[33] At the upper end, only 5% of Americans graduated from a 4-year college in 1940, while in 2013, 32% did.[34]

These trends have already affected today's retirees. Among older Americans born just before World War II, about 20% did not graduate from high school, and just 22% obtained a college degree. By the late Baby Boom, just 12% did not graduate from high school, and 30% graduated from college.[35]

Many of these workers have enjoyed higher incomes thanks to their higher education. The college wage premium, which measures the increase in earnings enjoyed by those with a college degree, has widened substantially since the 1970s, with the result that well-educated Americans now earn far more than less-educated ones.[36]

Once again, however, educational gains—and the higher earnings associated with higher education—have been unequally distributed. Access to college and college completion rates differ markedly for children from affluent and poor families.[37] The increasing value of a college degree has widened earnings inequality between better-educated and less-educated groups.[38]

Wages and earnings have followed the same pattern, with gains for workers as a group amid growing inequality. Since the 1950s, real wages have grown.[39] But inequality has risen dramatically since the 1970s, with notable differentials based on education and occupation.[40] High earners have gained relative to everyone else, while less-educated, low earners have fallen behind.[41] Causes of rising inequality include the rising college earnings premium (and the rising economic return to skill development more generally), as well as declining unionization and growing technological change, including automation.[42]

Unequal Gains in Retirement Options

Gains in health, education, and earning power have also improved opportunities for work and retirement at older ages. Taking the long view, Dora Costa notes that, in 1900, relatively few men retired at all: fully 65% of men older than 64 were in the labor force.[43] By the mid-twentieth century, retirement rates had risen—a product of higher incomes generally as well as the advent of Social Security.[44] Leisure upon retirement gradually became socially acceptable for those over 65, and recreational options expanded.[45]

By the 1950s, retirement had become what sociologists call an institution: a stage of life and a social position with predictable content. A man (and most workers were men) worked full-time until his retirement, often at 65. After a farewell party, the worker traded in his working clothes for casual wear and a decade or so to enjoy travel and recreation with his wife before facing death.

Today, by contrast, patterns of life for Americans in their sixth decade and beyond have become so diverse that it is perilous to generalize retirement as a universal life stage. Most women now work, and both women and men are reinventing what it means to retire. Retirement is no longer a stable institution: it no longer marks a widely-shared life event with a common meaning.

Instead of "retirement," sociologists now speak of a new life stage: extended middle age or the Third Age.[46] There is not yet a set pattern to the Third Age. Instead, sociologists say, it marks a period of self-reflection and self-reinvention as individuals chart a course for themselves. No longer trapped by outmoded retirement rules, Third Agers have unprecedented freedom.

To be sure, older people still begin to leave work in their 60s, and that pattern holds for every educational group.[47] But labor force participation among those over 65 has grown since the 1980s, and the trend is likely to continue.[48] A supermajority of Baby Boomers now say they plan to work past 65.[49]

Longer lives, better health, less disability, and better accommodations help explain the expanding work and leisure options of the Third Age. Higher levels of education and the growth of the service sector also contribute to the trend toward older workers remaining at work. Now that more workers hold white-collar jobs, it is easier to persevere at a job at older ages.[50] Even at lower educational levels, the shift from manufacturing to service employment has reduced the physical demands of some jobs. And the growing service sector has created more-flexible work options and has lowered barriers to entry to employment.[51]

No longer is retirement a one-time exit from the workforce at 65.[52] Some older workers continue full-time at their career jobs into their 70s and even 80s. Many others start new careers, often seeking greater fulfillment by shifting to education, health care, and social services.[53] Most older workers eventually downshift and take "bridge jobs" with lower pay, less prestige, and fewer benefits in exchange for lower working hours and fewer responsibilities.[54] Some find the time, money, and energy to start new businesses; one study reports that 15% of new businesses are started by entrepreneurs over 60.[55]

The law has helped usher in the Third Age. The Age Discrimination in Employment Act forbids employers from disadvantaging older workers based on their age. Mandatory retirement policies, once common, are now illegal (except in narrow circumstances).

But the upbeat story of personal fulfillment in the Third Age overlooks the dramatic inequality in the experience of older Americans. As in other spheres of life, money matters, and it is the affluent over-65s who can choose whether to work and how to reinvent themselves. On average, retirement income has increased and is projected to rise still further, but income inequality will rise as gains go primarily to higher-income retirees.[56]

Lower earners often reach their 60s without sufficient resources to retire. As we shall see in Chapter 3, Social Security benefits are often modest for these workers. And, in contrast with workers in an earlier era, these Americans do not hold union jobs or have defined-benefit company pensions. Today, only half of households have sufficient income to retire at 65.[57]

The result is that the less privileged group scrambles to make ends meet in their 60s, just as they did at younger ages. They continue at their jobs or "retire" but pick up part-time jobs at Wal-Mart for the money. Data confirm that bridge jobs are most common at the high and low ends of the wage spectrum, with very high earners and very low earners most likely to take this path. Although high earners tend to take bridge jobs to improve their quality of life, low earners tend to take such jobs out of financial necessity.[58]

The Third Age, then, is an unequal blessing. For many, it represents the welcome demise of the mid-twentieth-century institution of retirement. No longer are the over-65s forced out of their jobs. And, more and more, they need not look, act, or be treated as "old." But low earners do not partake equally of the new era of longer lives, better health, and expanded life options.

Unequal Families

Major changes in family life have rocked American society since the 1970s, and they will increasingly shape the experience of old age. In the mid-twentieth century, marriage was the central institution that defined the family. Americans married young, had children within marriage, and typically remained married for life. Men and women mostly followed prescribed gender roles, with men in the workforce and women rearing children at home.[59]

Three trends have reconfigured American family life since the "Mad Men" era of the '60s. First, marriage is no longer the dominant site for adult development or childbearing and -rearing. Nearly half of American adults are now unmarried at any given time.[60] The downward trend line is sharp: in 2010, 51% of Americans ages 20–54 were married, compared with more than 80% in the 1960s.[61]

The growing social acceptability of nonmarriage has combined with delayed marriage, divorce, and a striking rise in cohabitation to decimate what was once the expected life pattern for adults—lifelong marriage.[62] The unmarried still have children, however, and two of five children are now born to unmarried parents.[63] Single mothers, and some single fathers, increasingly take sole responsibility for children.[64]

Second, even among the married population, the content of marriage has become heterogeneous and contested. The institution of marriage no longer necessarily implies set gender roles or shared children (or any children at all).[65] Couples now marry later, often with substantial education and career experience, and engage in much less role specialization. Childless couples, blended families, late-in-life marriages, and two-career couples are no longer the exception—they are the new norm.[66]

Third, marital behavior has become stratified by class to an unprecedented degree. Lasting marriage and continuous child-rearing of shared biological children by two parents have become more than ever before the nearly exclusive preserve of the upper class.[67]

As a group, better-educated and higher-income individuals marry later than those in lower socioeconomic classes; over a lifetime, however, they marry at higher rates.[68] Divorce rates also correlate with class: while 46% of marriages end in divorce (or permanent separation) within 10 years among high school dropouts, and 37% end within 10 years for high school graduates, only 16% end in that period for those with a BA or more.[69] By the

20-year mark, the gap in lasting marriages is nearly *40 percentage points* between the more-educated group (78%) and the less-educated group (39%).[70]

Americans debate whether these changes in family life are welcome or worrisome. Changing gender roles have transformed women's lives, opening up new realms of opportunity in work and family life. At the same time, divorce and nonmarital births have shifted child-rearing, to an unprecedented degree, onto the shoulders of single mothers (and, to a lesser extent, single fathers).

Today's older retirees mostly lived mid-twentieth-century lives, and so, for the most part, they are (or were) married for the long term and reared children together.[71] Increasingly, however, older Americans will have experienced these social changes. Some of these changes are positive. For instance, women's income and retirement security will improve overall, thanks to longer periods in the workforce at higher pay.[72] But the unmarried will face retirement with a double burden: low incomes and no spouse to bring in a second income.[73] Single mothers, who tend to be quite poor and to have interrupted careers, will have especially low incomes and precarious retirement security, due to their lower earnings and (as we shall see) to the rules that determine Social Security benefits.

High and rising inequality among older Americans should prompt us to rethink the legal underpinnings of retirement. U.S. retirement policy is built on the assumption that chronological age conveys meaningful information about every retiree. The challenge is to reform the law to recognize the unequal experience of age and to retain our progressive commitments as the Baby Boom and following generations age.

3

Static Law and Growing Inequality

IN AMERICA TODAY, age is less and less a reliable indicator of remaining life span, health, work ability, and career options. For some people, 65 marks middle age, but for others, it represents true old age. By fixing the retirement age in the mid-60s, our public programs err in both directions. As a society, we now fund decades of "retirement" benefits that simply enhance the life options (and household incomes) of active, healthy people. At the same time, our public programs often shortchange the less affluent, who approach their mid-60s bearing the weight of cumulative disadvantage: low wages, little savings, poor health, and disability.

These perverse effects arise because the law of retirement has remained largely static, even as the experience of age has changed and grown unequal. Social Security and tax rules continue to imagine America as it existed in, say, 1950.[1] In that world, men held steady jobs for a lifetime and left work permanently at 65, when illness and disability would soon make it impossible to continue.[2] Women married young and took up the homemaker role. Wives could be left destitute if their husbands died, suffered a disability, or lost a paycheck at retirement.

Today, of course, society looks very different. Women and men no longer obey strict gender roles. Most workers no longer hold a steady job for a lifetime. Lifelong marriage is no longer the norm. And retirement is no longer a one-time withdrawal from the workforce. Instead, people now retire at a wide range of ages and often try a new job or work part-time for some period before retirement.[3]

Although these changes have affected Americans at all income levels, rising inequality has imprinted very different patterns of work and family life for the affluent and the less well-off. Some men and women over 65 enjoy a robust Third Age full of new options, thanks to superior health, work ability, financial security, and job options, as well as a high degree of family stability. But less-affluent women and men often arrive in their mid-60s facing poor health and disability, as well as inferior job options. They typically lack private savings to cushion their withdrawal from work. And more and more, less-affluent Americans are unmarried and have raised children on their own, further compromising their financial well-being at older ages.

This chapter explores the mismatch between Social Security and tax rules, on the one hand, and the inequalities of modern life, on the other. With rules geared to past inequalities, our public laws today increasingly privilege the already privileged. Social Security pays healthy, affluent workers and couples a guaranteed income that improves their financial status, and tax rules subsidize their already-substantial savings. The same programs increasingly leave workers in the bottom half of the income distribution with small retirement checks, little or no private savings, and steep, lifelong financial penalties for those who need to retire early.

Progressives have long made Social Security their emblem of successful social policy. But, together with tax subsidies, the program is becoming less progressive and less able to accomplish its mission—a dignified retirement for all. Without reform, our public laws will continue to address the inequalities of a past era, while ignoring the pressing inequalities of today.

Social Security and the Risks of Mid-Twentieth-Century Life

Social Security, like any public program, was a product of its time. The program combined the appearance of equality with special rules that cushioned the risks of ordinary life, and it treated all recipients with dignity. Although the rules give an advantage to lower earners, the program has none of the trappings of means testing. Everyone claims Social Security benefits easily, in a pleasant office (or, today, online), and based on a record of work. There is no visit to a crowded welfare office, no intrusive interviews with harried workers, and no need to feel humiliated at receiving public assistance.

But the rules of the Social Security program were designed, very cleverly, to award richer benefits to the groups most likely to need them. Brilliantly, the progressive features of the system are buried in the operating rules. The contrast with welfare is stark: a conventional means test highlights the differential treatment of rich and poor, while Social Security buries it. Because the rules that address inequality are hidden in the details, it requires a certain amount of patience to unpack them. But once we lay out those details, we can see how Social Security was constructed to address three key risks of mid-twentieth-century life: low lifetime earnings, outliving one's savings, and the financial vulnerability of wives.

First, Social Security addresses low lifetime earnings via a progressive benefits formula. Put bluntly, the benefits formula is rigged, quite deliberately, to favor poorer workers over richer ones. Lower earners still receive lower absolute dollar amounts than higher earners, but relative to wages, the lower-earning group comes out ahead.

Simplifying a bit, the progressive benefits formula works this way: Social Security collects lifelong earnings data on every worker. At retirement, the program sets a monthly benefit based on the worker's highest-earning 35 years of work. (A worker with a working life shorter than 35 years or who has been unemployed will have some zero years averaged into the calculation, lowering her benefits.)[4] Updated for inflation and general wage growth in the economy, the worker's average earnings determine her benefit level. The formula for the monthly benefit is explicitly progressive, replacing monthly earnings according to this schedule:

> 90% of the first $816;
> 32% over $816 up to $4,917; and
> 15% over $4,917[5]

The result is that high earners receive higher *absolute* benefits but less *relative* to their level of earnings (and relative to the taxes they have paid). For example, in 2014, a low-earning worker with average indexed earnings of $800 per month would receive a benefit of $720 per month (or 90% of her average earnings). A high-earning worker with average indexed earnings of $8,000 per month would receive a monthly benefit of $2,500 (or 31% of her average earnings).

In effect (but never in name), the Social Security progressive benefits formula operates as a means test. An actuarially neutral pension system would offer the same replacement rate to every worker, regardless of her income level. But Social Security offers a better deal to low earners: they receive more in benefits than they would in an actuarially neutral system.

The progressive benefits formula thus responded to a key risk of the mid-twentieth century: the possibility that one might work steadily but earn only low wages over a lifetime. Thanks to unionization and the industrial and social structures of the time, most workers held steady jobs for decades. College attendance rates were far lower than today, and unemployment rates were low as well. The result was that many workers had worked for 45 years or more by age 65. Still, workers at the bottom of the wage spectrum had relatively low earnings, and they might find themselves at retirement with little to show for a lifetime of effort. Social Security deliberately offered (and still offers) those workers a financial boost.

Social Security also addresses a second risk that was pressing in the mid-twentieth century: the disadvantage of a long life span. A troubling risk of old age is that workers may outlive their wealth. Even someone who has saved prudently for retirement may find her money exhausted if she lives to 90 or 95—or beyond.

To address the financial vulnerability of the very old, Social Security benefits take the form of a life annuity—the monthly benefit is guaranteed for the worker's entire life. The life annuity does not link benefits to retirees' present income, and in that sense it avoids a conventional means test. But the life annuity still has a progressive effect if longer-lived people are worse off, generally speaking, than shorter-lived ones. The danger, of course, is that the life annuity becomes regressive if the opposite is true—if, as today, it is the affluent who live longer.

In the mid-twentieth century, most workers had fairly similar life spans and health prospects. An affluent man at 65 could expect to live less than a year longer than a poorer one.[6] Heart disease, strokes, and other serious illnesses shortened lives across the economic spectrum. And women's generally longer lives made the life annuity especially responsive to inequality; long-lived widows often were the most vulnerable of all.

The third risk central to present Social Security rules is the (presumed) financial vulnerability of wives. The program provides a spousal benefit equal to 50% of the worker's benefit.[7] The spouse need not have a work record. She (or he) qualifies simply by virtue of marriage to a Social Security-covered worker.[8] The dollars at stake are substantial: in 2011, the Social

Security system paid an average $613 per month to 3 million wives and husbands solely because they were (or had been) married to a qualifying retired worker.[9]

The spousal benefit responds to the gender roles of the mid-twentieth century, when the vast majority of wives did not work outside the home (or worked sporadically and at low-paying jobs). With only one paycheck per household, the retirement of the breadwinner husband left couples with limited resources at retirement. The 50% additional benefit topped up the worker's benefit with an extra allowance for his dependent wife. The spousal benefit for widows is even more generous: a survivor claims 100% (not 50%) of the worker's benefit.

The spousal benefit, by design, is especially valuable to low-earning workers with a nonworking wife. It is calculated by reference to the worker's benefit, which incorporates the progressive benefits formula. The result is that a low earner and his (nonearning) wife receive a higher replacement rate than a high earner and his (nonearning) wife.

The Social Security spousal benefit is a kind of a mid-twentieth-century cultural artifact. The social assumption, accurate enough at the time, was that wives did not work outside the home, whether they were married to bus driver Ralph Kramden (of *The Honeymooners*) or middle-class executive Ward Cleaver (of *Leave It to Beaver*). The spousal benefit gave both couples a bit extra, and it helped ensure the Kramdens, in particular, a retirement income sufficient to live decently.

Social Security looks very different on the tax side of the ledger, where the rules tend to worsen financial inequality. Two sets of tax rules—the Social Security payroll tax and tax subsidies for retirement—have always been regressive. The 15.3% payroll tax that finances the system applies to every worker, beginning with her first dollar of income. The payroll tax thus taxes even the poorest workers, sending to the government valuable dollars that would otherwise go to buy basic necessities. By contrast, the income tax exempts the poor.

The earned income tax credit (EITC) is sometimes said to offset the regressivity of the Social Security payroll tax. If we analyze the EITC together with the payroll tax, the result is that many low earners receive substantial government payments that offset (or eliminate) their payroll tax liability, especially if they have children.[10] But pairing the EITC with the payroll tax carries a whiff of double counting, because the EITC also serves so many purposes—as an income supplement for the working poor, a substitute for welfare, a work incentive, and a childcare subsidy.

The best way to think about the EITC is to recognize that it adds progressive effect to the overall tax-and-transfer system: it renders the payroll tax, the income tax, the welfare system, and tax expenditures less burdensome to the low-income population than they otherwise would be. But it's arbitrary to bundle the EITC with the payroll tax. The fundamental issue is what the distribution of the benefits and burdens of the Social Security system *should* be. In Chapter 10, I suggest that the payroll tax burden on very low earners during their working years should be viewed as unfair.

And, whatever the significance of the EITC for low earners, the payroll tax clearly is regressive between mid- and high earners, because the tax is capped at $117,000 of wages.[11] The result is that a moderate earner bears a FICA tax of the full 15.3%, while a high earner bears a tax of a much smaller percentage.[12]

Social Security Rules and the New Inequality of Old Age

Social Security addressed three risks of life in the mid-twentieth century: low lifetime earnings, an unexpectedly long life span, and wives' dependency on a breadwinner husband. These provisions remain important for current retirees, many of whom lived the typical patterns of the mid-twentieth century. (As Chapter 11 discusses, reforms in retirement policy should take care to make provision for that group.)

But, beginning with the Baby Boomers and looking ahead, the experience of old age has been transformed. As we have seen, the elderly as a group have experienced unprecedented gains in education, health, and work options. At the same time, new inequalities have grown, and these are not captured by Social Security's outdated rules. The troubling trend is that Social Security increasingly cushions an already-comfortable Third Age for the affluent while failing to serve the needs of low-earning, blue-collar workers.

The Retirement Age

The first, and perhaps the most critical, mismatch, is Social Security's assumption that the chronological age of 65 (now 66, and rising gradually to

67)[13] signals the onset of work disability for most workers. In fact, as we have seen, rising inequality in longevity, health, work capability, and job options has created a sharp divergence in the experience of age for higher- and lower-earning workers. An affluent worker at 65 typically can look forward to two or more decades of healthy life and an array of fairly good job options. A lower-earning worker, especially one who has worked in a physically demanding or stressful job, is far more likely to face illness, disability, and poor job options at 65.

The irony is that the retirement age of 65 was probably outdated even in 1935, when the original Social Security Act came into being. In the 1930s, President Roosevelt's drafters did not study the actual experience of the elderly. Working in the depths of the Depression, the Committee on Economic Security did not inquire deeply into the capabilities of workers in their 60s. Instead, they copied existing public and private retirement plans in Europe and the states, which typically adopted the age of 65 as the time of retirement.[14] Policy makers at the time thought any age older than 65 would serve too few people to address the unemployment crisis, while any age younger than 65 would make the program too expensive.[15]

Even if age 65 made sense in the mid-twentieth century, it is badly outdated now. Economists John Shoven and Gopi Shah Goda have updated the Social Security retirement age for twenty-first-century trends in longevity. Based on a range of metrics for increasing longevity, they find that an updated retirement age would range from 73 to 82.[16]

Perversely, though, present Social Security rules permit retirement even *earlier* than in 1935. Workers can claim Social Security benefits at 62, although there is a hidden—and painful—sting. The rules award maximum benefits at age 70, and they penalize earlier retirement by docking benefits—for life. (Confusingly, the system awards "full" retirement benefits at 66 and offers a "delayed retirement credit" for those who wait till age 70.[17] But, as Alicia Munnell notes, the rules amount to a retirement age of 70 and penalties before then.[18])

The early retirement option was enacted in in the 1950s and early 1960s, first to give wives the option to claim benefits early and then to extend the same option to men.[19] The financial penalty is intended to make the Social Security system whole, so that the value of the (lower) benefit stream at the earlier age is the same (in financial terms) as the (higher) benefit stream at the later age.

In technical terms, then, the cuts in benefits for those who claim before age 70 are actuarial reductions: Social Security technicians have calculated how much the system loses (on average) when a retiree claims benefits early or late (relative to age 66). Sticklers for precision might, thus, object that there are no "penalties" or "bonuses" in the system; instead, the rules insist that everyone bear their own weight by taking less if they claim sooner and getting more if they claim later, so that the total cost per worker remains the same.

But we should be suspicious of averages in an era of high and increasing inequality. The actuarial reductions do not look to the situation of individual workers. Instead, the rules impose the same reductions on high and low earners: both lose a fixed percentage of their maximum benefit for every month of early retirement. And the penalty lasts for the rest of the worker's life. Thus, for example, any worker who claims benefits at 62 receives just 57% of her age-70 benefit. So a high earner would receive a Social Security benefit of $3,000 per month at age 70 but only $1,700 if she claimed at age 62. A low earner would receive $1,000 monthly at age 70 but only $570 at age 62.[20] In this sense, then, the benefit reductions for those who retire before age 70 really *are* penalties: they impose a standard fine on everyone, without regard to health or expected life span.

The early retirement penalty falls hardest on the workers who need public retirement income the most. Affluent retirees can afford to wait. Indeed, the *New York Times* and other publications targeted to the well-off have trumpeted the financial advantages of postponing one's Social Security claim to age 70.[21] But workers struggling with poor health or with disability (short of the total disability insured by the SSDI program) often need to retire early— not to enjoy leisure but because they can no longer support themselves through work.

The mismatch between chronological age and the Social Security retirement age has created a perverse distribution of benefits. Today, the vast majority of Americans claim benefits before age 66, and fully half claim at age 62.[22] Some of these retirees are unable to work, but many can: a 2012 study found that, excluding those already collecting disability benefits, 94% of early retirees reported no health-related work limitations.[23]

The drive to early claiming of Social Security benefits reflects the precarious financial state of many American households. Indeed, early retirees have lower levels of education and lower household income than those who delay retirement.[24] Early retirees without a work disability may simply claim the benefit because it is there—a welcome supplement to household income. Cognitive psychology might explain the behavior: human beings tend to be biased toward present rewards over future ones.[25] Many of us—richer or poorer—feel that we could use a "free" $10,000 or $20,000 per year, and we may not rationally weigh the cost of early claiming for future payouts.

The outdated retirement age means that Social Security errs on both sides.[26] Well-educated, affluent workers could (on average) work far longer than 70, and many have excellent job options. For that group, Social Security amounts to a basic income, a supplement to household finances for workers who, functionally, are middle-aged. At the same time, the program denies retirement benefits to workers under 62 and imposes a high and lifelong penalty on those who cannot wait until 70. Indeed, blue-collar workers are more likely to claim early Social Security benefits, while managers and professionals are most likely to delay.[27]

One result of the mismatch between demographics and the retirement age is that Social Security's life annuity increasingly rewards the privileged. The benefits formula has always, by design, paid higher (absolute) benefits to higher earners. But now, because the wealthy live much longer lives, and because the Social Security retirement age is fixed for everyone, the life annuity confers greater wealth (in expected-value terms) on the affluent simply because they live longer.[28]

The life annuity once protected the vulnerable—typically, long-lived widows whose breadwinner husbands had died and who had no means of self-support. But the same provision now increasingly protects the private wealth of the affluent. The well-off now live long lives cushioned by the Social Security annuity and can pass on more wealth to their heirs as a result.

Average Lifetime Earnings and the Payroll Tax

The second mismatch between Social Security's rules and social reality is the growing inequality in wages and working conditions. Since the mid-twentieth century, real wages for low earners have fallen, and wage dispersion has widened.[29] At the same time, the shift from manufacturing to service work and the rise in single parenthood have created a new class of workers who work at low wages and experience frequent unemployment and underemployment.

Social Security's progressive benefits formula is intended to ameliorate wage differences, but it is becoming less and less functional as high- and low-wage workers experience different earnings patterns. The progressive benefits formula presumes lifelong work at steady wages. In the mid-twentieth century, that presumption was sensible enough: in that era, the primary inequality in working life was one's wage level. Both higher- and lower-paid workers began work in their early 20s and worked steadily, often for a single employer, to age 65. The progressive benefits formula squarely addressed inequality by awarding a higher replacement rate to lower earners.

Today, however, Social Security's rules are becoming less functional in mitigating inequalities in working life. Less-educated, low-paid workers are more likely to experience unemployment and job instability, including involuntary reductions in work hours.[30] These events reduce average earnings over a lifetime, and so benefits fall. When high earners tend to have steady jobs while low earners disproportionately experience unemployment and family disruptions, the 35-year average will tend to reward high earners. (Although high earners often have more education and thus more non-working years, even a worker with a graduate degree typically can work from 30 to 65, filling out 35 years at a good salary.)

For instance, consider two low-income workers. One works at a wage of $1,000 per month (in today's dollars) for a steady 35 years. The other earns the same wage of $1,000 but experiences 10 (total) years of unemployment. The first worker will have a 35-year average income of $1,000 per month. The second will have a 35-year average income of just $714.

Today, due to both low absolute earnings and interrupted work histories, many low-wage workers end up with Social Security benefits below the poverty line.[31] In 2012, for example, the federal poverty line for a single individual over 65 was about $11,000 per year or $917 per month.[32] According to the Social Security Administration, 28% of retired workers received less than that in 2012.[33] To be sure, some of these had incomes from other sources—a pension or a spouse. But even so, the poverty rate among individuals over 65 was 9.1% in that year.[34] Poverty was especially widespread among single Social Security recipients, with 14.5% falling below the poverty line.[35]

Rising inequality in earnings has rendered Social Security's payroll tax even more burdensome to low and middle earners than in the past.[36] In 1937, 97% of workers had earnings below the cap on taxable earnings, while in 2012, 94% did.[37] That change may not seem very significant, but those relatively few workers have very high wages, thanks to the extreme inequality in the U.S. wage distribution. In 1937, 92% of total earnings were taxable for Social Security purposes, while in 2012, only 83% of earnings were taxable, because of the cap on taxable earnings.[38] Self-employment income is especially likely to escape the Social Security payroll tax: in 2012, only 63% of self-employment income was taxable, thanks to the cap.[39]

Of course, it isn't self-evident that the payroll tax cap is unfair. High earners do pay less in taxes than they would without a cap. But their wages are capped for purposes of calculating benefits too, so that (for example) a worker earning $400,000 per year doesn't collect any more at retirement than someone who earns $117,000 (the tax cap in 2014). The issue of fairness can't be resolved without a deeper inquiry into who ought to fund Social Security and on what basis. Logically speaking, the Social Security system *could* operate with or without capped taxes. The question of tax fairness requires its own discussion, which is the task of Chapter 10.

The point for the moment, however, is simply that rising economic inequality alters Social Security outcomes. Growing inequality in wages and working conditions, combined with Social Security's static rules, means that low earners pay relatively more and receive relatively less from Social Security than they did in, say, the mid-twentieth century.

The Spousal Benefit

The third mismatch concerns family status. In the mid-twentieth century, the vast majority of Americans married young and stayed married for life, and very few people had children outside marriage. Most husbands worked outside the home, while most wives did not.

Today, of course, family life looks very different. Most women, including wives and mothers, work—and expect to work their entire lives. Many Americans do not marry at all, and those who do frequently divorce. Many workers are also single parents with sole responsibility for rearing children.

These changes have upended the Social Security rules intended to address the financial vulnerability of families. The spousal benefit is an anachronism today, when the vast majority of women, including wives, work throughout their lives. Baby Boomers and succeeding generations of women have dramatically increased their earnings compared with past generations.[40] Social Security Administration data show that the percentage of elderly women claiming Social Security solely as wives (i.e., with no earnings record of their own) has plummeted since 1960, from about one-third to less than 10%. As of 2011, only 3 million of 36 million retirees claimed Social Security solely as wives (or husbands) rather than as retired workers.[41]

To be sure, many working wives still claim what is, in effect, a partial spousal benefit. This situation comes about when a wife's lifetime earnings are significantly lower than her husband's. For instance, suppose that a husband is entitled to a retirement benefit of $2,000 per month and his wife is entitled, on her own earnings record, to a benefit of $950 per month. Thanks to the spousal benefit, the wife can claim $1,000 (half of the husband's benefit), which is $50 more than she would otherwise receive. These "dually entitled" spouses (who can, technically, be husbands or wives) thus receive some benefit from the spousal benefit.

But government projections indicate that fewer and fewer spouses will rely, fully or partially, on the spousal benefit. By 2080, only a small fraction of female Social Security recipients will claim solely as wives. The great majority will claim as workers only, while a declining percentage will fall in the "dual entitlement" category (i.e., will claim a spousal benefit to "top up" their own earned benefits).[42]

The declining utility of the spousal benefit has a darker side: it translates into a hefty financial penalty on two-earner couples. Every worker pays the Social Security payroll tax at the same rate. But a married worker with a nonworking spouse receives, in effect, 150% of the benefit she paid for. The two-earner couple receives less for their contributions than the single-earner couple does. Over a lifetime, the penalty can amount to hundreds of thousands of dollars.[43]

Eugene Steuerle points out that the spousal benefit also creates other distributional oddities in Social Security. The spousal benefit disfavors working single parents as well as two-worker couples. And the bonus is available to some divorced people but not to others; only those married at least 10 years can qualify.[44]

Looking ahead, then, the spousal benefit will not be needed to ensure wives' retirement security. Generations of social change have transformed the spousal benefit into a regime that, perversely, awards extra money to formally married, single-earner couples, subsidized by harder-pressed unmarried workers, including single parents.[45]

Unequal Tax Subsidies for Retirement Savings

Social Security is not the only feature of U.S. retirement policy that is out-dated. In theory, Social Security is one of three sources of retirement income. The other two are employer-provided pensions and individual savings. The traditional metaphor is the "three-legged stool," with each of the three legs contributing something to workers' retirement security.[46]

But the three-legged stool is badly broken for workers in the bottom half of the earnings distribution. Employers often no longer offer pensions. And those that do now offer defined-contribution plans, which often are less functional for lower-earning workers because they shift the savings obliga-tion and investment risk to the worker.[47]

Tax subsidies for retirement savings are particularly dysfunctional. The federal government spent nearly $130 billion in 2014 to subsidize retirement savings—a sum that equals nearly 20% of the amount spent on Social Security old-age pensions in that year.[48] Of that $130 billion, a whopping 49% of it goes into the pockets of workers in the top 10% of the income distribution.[49] This outcome is the predictable result of the structure of the subsidies, which take the form of exclusions and deductions. These tax pro-visions produce major tax savings for high-income workers in high tax brackets (and little or nothing for low earners).

The result is that low-earning workers (and many middle earners) reach retirement with few pension rights and little personal savings. Only half of retirees now have any pension income at all.[50] Workers with private pen-sions often have sufficient retirement income (together with Social Secu-rity) to retire comfortably, but workers without private pensions often do not.[51]

The big picture is that low and middle earners often do not accumulate sufficient pension entitlements and private savings for a secure retirement.[52] Once workers reach retirement, the bottom 60% rely on Social Security as their primary income source, while the top 40% (and especially the top 20%) can count on substantial income from private pensions.[53]

Is Social Security Still Progressive?

Discussions of inequality in retirement policy sometimes begin and end with one question: whether Social Security is progressive. But that frame is far too narrow to reveal the full range of troubling inequalities in American retirement policy today.

First, when we focus on Social Security, we ignore the other two legs of the three-legged stool: employer pensions and individual savings. These regimes too often fail to support Americans of modest means. Focusing on Social Security obscures the hundreds of billions of dollars now directed at retirement savings by the affluent.

Second, the details of the progressivity calculation matter. Despite the progressive origins and aspirations of the Social Security program, the answer is far from obvious. Social Security's rules, as we have seen, redistribute in a complex and inconsistent fashion.[54] The 35-year averaging period, for instance, disadvantages the unemployed, but the progressive benefits formula advantages those with low earnings. The life annuity increasingly rewards the affluent as a group but extends progressive benefits to a fair number of low earners as well.

Studies typically find that Social Security is, at best, mildly progressive. Studies that lump in disability benefits with survivors' and retirement benefits find that Social Security is "modestly" progressive overall.[55] But disability and survivors' benefits are highly progressive, because lower earners are far more likely to die early or to experience disability. Thus, the retirement system, standing alone, is far less progressive.[56]

Still, the progressivity studies sound two sobering notes, confirming the central message of this chapter. First, the progressivity of the program is declining as retirees who lived in the mid-twentieth century give way to Baby Boomers and their successors, who live very different lives.[57] And, second, the modest overall progressivity of Social Security masks increasingly perverse redistributions due to outdated rules. For instance, Eugene Steuerle and coauthors find that single women fare worse than married ones, all else equal. Male high school dropouts fare worse than male college graduates.[58] And Social Security retirement benefits redistribute to whites from people of color.[59]

Third, and most important, the question of "progressivity" is too flat to capture the multiple dimensions of inequality that now characterize the experience of old age in America. "Progressivity" measures only whether a tax or transfer system effects an overall redistribution of money compared with the initial baseline distribution. It cannot tell us whether the baseline distribution or the final distribution is fair or unfair. Put another way, a progressive system probably moves in the right direction, but progressivity alone cannot tell us whether sufficient resources have reached the disadvantaged.

Progressivity as a metric is too untextured to determine which inequalities a just society ought to address. Perhaps it is enough to satisfy the demands of fairness that older Americans, as a group, have gained in well-being over time. Or perhaps we should be troubled by the increasingly unequal experience of health, work options, and family life.

It will take a normative argument to establish what kind of equality we ought to seek—and what the state's proper role should be in redressing inequality through retirement policy. The next chapter takes up that task.

4

Justice over the Life Cycle

To THIS POINT, I have documented major changes in the experience of old age. Many older people enjoy unprecedented well-being, whether measured by longevity, health, ability, or job options. At the same time, inequality in the experience of age is growing. Disadvantage cumulates for low-earning workers, who experience, relative to their peers, shorter life spans, worse health, fewer job options, and family instability.

But these facts, standing alone, cannot justify any particular change in social policy. It is certainly interesting to know that in 1940 and 1950, the average worker retired at 68 and that, given increases in longevity, an equivalent retirement age would be 76 today and 80 in 2070.[1] But without normative argument, we cannot jump to the conclusion that the Social Security retirement age ought to rise toward 80. Perhaps longer and healthier retirements should be viewed as a social achievement—rather than a reason to rethink the retirement age.

Similarly, without normative argument, we cannot presume that rising inequality among those over 65 requires redress. After all, our society tolerates wide inequalities based on social class, occupation, and age. Without a standard for what justice requires, we cannot assert that those at the bottom merit more—or that those at the top merit less.

In this chapter, I develop the first of two sets of normative principles that, I will argue, should guide reforms in retirement policy. The principles follow from an inquiry into two key problems of justice: *justice between age groups,* the subject of this chapter, and *justice within age groups,* which is taken up in Chapter 5.

Justice between Age Groups

Begin with this foundational question: Why should the state pay special attention to its citizens in old age? Older people, like younger people, may be rich or poor, healthy or ill, able or not, and so on. The challenge for old-age policy, then, is to question whether age ought to be an organizing category for collective concern.

The problem of justice between age groups, to use Norman Daniels' term, is distinct from the problem of justice between birth cohorts.[2] The age group question asks what resources a just society ought to devote to individuals at each life stage. By contrast, the problem of justice between birth cohorts asks about the allocation of resources to particular generational cohorts of people as they pass through all life stages.

As an example of the latter, consider the fact that different birth cohorts received a very different deal from the Social Security system.[3] Social Security was especially generous to the Greatest Generation and to the early Baby Boom and will be far less generous to later age cohorts, due to the pay-as-you-go financing of the system and the sheer size of the Baby Boom.

Theorists have debated how (if at all) the state should respond to the different experiences of birth cohorts.[4] It is difficult, to put it mildly, to compare all the positive and negative experiences of entire generations. The Greatest Generation fought a major war but enjoyed postwar prosperity and family stability. The Baby Boom benefitted from wider access to college but experienced the divorce revolution and the economic uncertainties of globalization.

But here I want to focus on the distinct problem of *justice between age groups.* The human life cycle contains predictable stages of childhood, young adulthood, full adulthood, and old age, and (if we survive long enough) all of us will experience each stage in turn.[5] A just society must take care to allocate resources fairly across the life cycle, which is to say between age groups.

The issues of justice between age groups and justice between birth cohorts can easily be conflated when we debate retirement policy once a particular birth cohort has reached old age. Thus, if we focus on today's retirees, we are (necessarily) thinking about the Greatest Generation and the Baby Boom. But the question of justice between age groups transcends the circumstances of any particular birth cohort. It is both sensible and feasible to carve off the age group question from the birth cohort question: even if a cohort merits extra resources in retirement (or fewer), we ought to know what the just baseline would be. Without a baseline, we cannot know what extra resources (or fewer) would look like at any given age.

Public policy addresses the problem of justice between age groups all the time, if not by its theoretical name. The campaign for early childhood education, for example, is framed in terms of what children need to gain a fair start in life. Proposals for expanded college aid focus on the situation of young people as they enter adult life.

Liberal theorists have argued that justice requires attention both to equality of opportunity and to individual freedom.[6] Equality of opportunity motivates deliberate distributions to children and to young adults one goal of a just society is to break or at least to weaken dramatically the constraints imposed by family background on equality. Public education, most obviously, serves equality of opportunity, but so do publicly funded preschool, health care, and other initiatives to ensure minimum developmental conditions for all children.[7]

Equality of opportunity has also motivated public distributions to young adults, most clearly via higher education. Subsidized student loans, Pell Grants, and public universities aim to broaden access to better jobs and personal advancement. Bruce Ackerman and I have argued for even greater attention to young adulthood as a life stage: we proposed a universal grant or "stake" of $80,000 as a public inheritance for all young adults, including those not headed to college.[8]

When individuals reach adulthood, life-cycle justice looks very different, because individual freedom and responsibility come to the forefront. Liberty requires equality of opportunity, but once opportunities are made available on fair terms, adults choose for themselves the opportunities they wish to pursue and—more fundamentally—the values according to which they will live. Some will pursue worldly success and will succeed (or fail). Others will choose a religious life or a family-oriented life or charity work. All of these are choices open to free individuals in a free society. With some exceptions I will consider shortly, adults should be both at liberty to pursue their own ends and responsible for the choices they make.

These considerations give shape to distributive justice over the life cycle. Younger life stages merit deliberate distribution by the state, because children's development is part of the guarantee of equal opportunity. A just society could not permit children (or their parents) to disclaim equality by skimping on resources during those formative stages. But adults, by and large, should be free to deploy their resources as they choose over their remaining life span. Some may run through their resources in youth and live modestly thereafter. Others might squirrel away resources, anxious about old age or a rainy day. These are value-laden choices and, on the liberal view, should properly be made by each individual according to her own vision of the good.

Old Age and Justice over the Life Cycle

The puzzle, then, is why old age should merit any particular attention from the state at all. Older adults are, after all, adults. As long as their faculties remain intact, it seems that they should continue to take responsibility for themselves, allocating whatever resources they wish to old age.

The libertarian embraces just this approach. Old-age provision, the libertarian asserts, should be a private responsibility and not a matter for public mandate. After all, old age is hardly a surprise. It should be up to each of us, the libertarian says, to save money and plan for the ordinary events of life, including retirement. If some people want to work till they drop in the traces, while others want to retire early at a healthy 60 or 65, then they should plan accordingly.

What the state should not do, according to the libertarian, is use its coercive power to craft a collective program to cushion the predictable events of old age. In a libertarian society, each individual owns her own earnings and other resources, and she should enjoy maximum freedom to use them as she wishes. When the state mandates retirement savings, it unfairly limits her choices: if she would prefer to spend at earlier ages and take her chances in old age, she should be able to do so.

Even a gentler "nudge" toward retirement savings would violate libertarian precepts.[9] Taxing some to offer subsidies to others represents (on this view) an unfair use of the state's power: the tax commandeers resources from people who would rather spend now and confers undeserved resources on those who take up the state's invitation to save for retirement. Nor should the state use tax revenue to rescue people who reach old age in dire straits; the libertarian would view this an unjust redistribution, taking resources from the lives of some to cushion the risks taken by others.

But, by contrast with the libertarian, egalitarian liberals imagine a major role for the state in old-age provision. Old age, the egalitarians point out, brings work disability for many people, at least eventually. But disability of any sort is an unhappy prospect, and many people will discount their own chances of disability. Psychologists confirm that people often have a short time horizon, discounting the needs of their future selves. If the state leaves it to individuals to save for their own old age, many people will fail to do so. Studies of retirement savings confirm that when it is up to individuals to make affirmative decisions to save, they overwhelmingly fail to do so.[10]

The result of this mass myopia, says the egalitarian, would be social chaos, as the state scrambled to deal with large numbers of destitute elderly people. The state, then, has an important role to play in anticipating human cognitive limitations that lead people to undersave for the period of work disability that will (likely) attend old age.[11]

A libertarian might reply that myopia offers only a thin justification for state action. After all, the law leaves many future-oriented decisions to individuals, and we expect them to bear the consequences if they are myopic. People who watch television will be less literate than those with more bookish habits; people who isolate themselves from friends and family may be lonely later in life; and so on.

The difference is that work disability has negative spillover effects on others. When an individual bears the consequences of her own actions, she ought to be free to choose. But when an individual's choices will have negative consequences for others—when her choices spill over, claiming resources properly owned by others—the state may be justified in regulating her conduct.[12] So, for instance, carbon taxes help correct the negative effects of carbon on the atmosphere and climate. Junk food taxes respond to the public health costs associated with poor diet and obesity.

Economists emphasize the inefficiency of negative externalities; for them, the problem is that risky behavior (burning carbon, eating Big Macs) is underpriced.[13] Liberal egalitarians add that negative externalities are unfair as well: they unjustly co-opt the resources of some to address the spillover effects of the actions of others. People who ride bicycles and eat vegetables should not be forced to give up their fair share of resources to fund the social costs produced by people who choose to drive gas-guzzlers and gulp soda. (The situation of people who cannot alter their actions due to low wages and other social conditions poses a different problem, which I address later in this chapter.)

Now, old age itself does not necessarily pose a negative externality in this sense, but *work disability associated with old age* does. To see why, pursue a thought experiment. In a true libertarian society, individuals would be free to save for old age or not. Given myopia and other cognitive realities, many people would reach old age without savings. They would have to work as long as they could, but when illness or disability struck, they would be destitute.

The destitution of the elderly would be depressing, and it might motivate others to respond with charity. But if charity were insufficient, society would be left with the problem of how to feed, clothe, and care for a large number of people no longer able to take care of themselves. A truly hard-hearted society might permit the destitute elderly to starve in the streets, but even that cruel policy would not alleviate negative externalities due to crime, homelessness, and so on.

The law might try to impose a support obligation on the children of the destitute, but filial support laws, if enforced, would be unfair. We do not choose our parents, and we may properly choose not to support them, to treat them like strangers, if that is the treatment they deserve (and some parents do). By definition, the destitute are those whose families have declined to support them, and so it is difficult to justify any state policy that would impose the negative externality of their care on estranged children. In any event, the filial obligation solution would leave a sizable number of destitute elderly people who are childless or whose children will not (or cannot) take on their support.

The negative externality that justifies state action, then, is not old age per se. Healthy people in their 60s and 70s pose no greater social cost than healthy people in their 40s and 50s. But old age eventually brings work disability, except for the few who die before leaving the workforce. In that important sense, work disability in old age differs from work disability at younger ages, which is a (relatively) low-probability event.

The familiar solution to the negative externality of work disability in old age is state-mandated retirement savings. In virtually every developed country, the law requires most people to set money aside in some way so that they do not become destitute in old age.[14] Individual accounts can accomplish this result, but so can an old-age insurance program like Social Security. The payroll taxes that fund Social Security are not literally saved—they go out the door to current retirees. But the program offers a means for the state to require (via taxation) younger workers to protect themselves against destitution in later years.

We have, then, a principled basis for laws that require younger people to set aside resources in anticipation of old age. Critically, though, such policies are fair *only if they correct a negative externality—in this case, destitution due to work disability in old age.*

By contrast, the state cannot fairly require individuals to save for events that might be unpleasant or unfortunate but pose no negative externality. Take vacations, for instance. The lack of an annual vacation is highly unpleasant. Working without a vacation is exhausting. Still, some people do not value vacations; or, at least, they do not value them sufficiently to save ahead of time or to sacrifice earnings when they take time off. (Once again, the situation of people who could not save enough to take a vacation or who would lose their jobs if they took a vacation is a different matter, and one I take up in the next section.)

The lack of a vacation does not pose a significant negative externality on others. People who go without vacation time may be tired, but they typically do not become public charges in the way that the destitute elderly do. It follows, then, that it would be unfair for the state to enact a forced savings program (or a vacation insurance program) to mandate that individuals save for vacation.

The critical distinction is that the inability to work imposes a negative externality, while unpleasant working conditions (that one could avoid but chooses not to avoid) do not. It follows, then, that a public retirement policy should respond to the inability to work in old age and not to the desire for leisure.

Social Insurance for Work Disability

To be sure, many thinkers use imprecise, and sometimes loose, terminology. Writing fifteen years ago, Bruce Ackerman and I discussed pension policy and treated old age, work disability, and retirement as if they were interchangeable. Like other thinkers, we assumed (I am embarrassed now to say) that old age equals work disability and retirement.[15]

But despite the common slippage in terminology, it is work disability that is doing the normative heavy lifting in justifying "old-age pensions" or "retirement policy." People who myopically decline to save and later become destitute impose a negative externality. People who myopically decline to save and later become grumpy because they wish for leisure time in late middle age do not.

The disability insurance component of Social Security can be justified along the same lines. Paying insurance premiums is no fun; neither is saving money for lean times. The result is that some people will not buy disability insurance; they will not save money either. When disability strikes, they may become public charges, creating the familiar negative externalities problem. The state, then, is justified in mandating savings (or in creating mandatory public insurance, such as Social Security) in order to prevent destitution in such cases.

Ronald Dworkin, working in a modified Rawlsian framework, offers a distinct but compatible rationale for social insurance against disability. Dworkin posits that the average person, acting behind a veil of ignorance, would pay something to purchase insurance against disability. He points out (accurately) that real-world insurance markets typically do not function well for disability: some disabilities occur at birth, when insurance is impossible, and others afflict certain segments of society or are subject to moral hazard. The result is that the actual disability market fails to offer adequate insurance, and so, Dworkin concludes, the state is justified in stepping in to provide disability coverage to all.[16]

Both negative externalities and other market failures suggest that society should require individuals to set aside resources to insure against work disability. (Dworkin's rationale might authorize the state to go beyond work disability to other disabilities, but I will not pursue that issue here.) Neither rationale justifies the state in mandating more than that, however; it is work disability, and not the attainment of (say) age 66 that is the insurable event.

To be sure, the notion of work disability poses an administrative challenge, because the state cannot (always) observe work disability, and moral hazard invites individuals to fake or exaggerate disability. We will see (in Chapter 8) that public disability programs have struggled to create fair, accessible, and accurate processes for determining work disability. And we will see that the state can structure a response to disability in different ways: unemployment insurance can take on some of the burden of disability insurance;

and rules keyed to age, employment, and disability can potentially ease administrative burdens (albeit at the cost of some accuracy in targeting benefits to individuals).

But, at this stage, the key point is that in principle the state may fairly require individuals to anticipate their likely inability to work in old age. In principle, however, it should be the inability to work, and not one's chronological age, that serves as the criterion for entitlement to social assistance. And the state may not permissibly require individuals to save for (or otherwise fund) a period of leisure apart from work disability.

Should the Third Age Be a Protected Life Stage?

The conclusion that the state should not fund retirement in advance of work disability merits a closer look. Suppose that I am correct that the liberal tradition supports state action to insure against work disability, not old age. But if the liberal tradition is outdated or inadequate in the face of massive changes in longevity, health, and society, then my conclusion may be narrowly correct but ultimately irrelevant.

Theresa Ghilarducci, for example, opposes reforms that would require older Americans to work longer than they do today. She compares work by the elderly to child labor—a practice still tolerated in developing countries but long ago outlawed by wealthy societies—and suggests that it would be absurd for a rich country to expect older people to work longer than they do today.[17] This is a serious argument, and it deserves sustained consideration. Societies change over time, and it is reasonable to ask whether a longer and more comfortable retirement should accompany social progress.

Taking the argument a step further, the data in Chapter 2 demonstrate that life is very different now than in the mid-twentieth century when writers like Rawls completed their signature work. People now live longer, on average, and older people enjoy wider life options. Perhaps liberal theory should be updated to reflect the dawn of the Third Age, which should offer older (but still healthy) adults a chance to reflect on their lives, pursue new careers and interests, or recommit with joy to existing pursuits. Perhaps the liberal state should not stand on the sidelines but should actively promote and protect a Third Age for all.

This line of argument has some appeal. Indeed, the Third Age has a tantalizing whiff of autonomy about it that seems to evoke the liberal tradition in political theory on which I am drawing. Perhaps it would be autonomy enhancing if state retirement benefits were to support older people as they choose to work less, to change careers, or to take time away from the labor market as they come closer to the ends of their lives.

State support for the Third Age would also seem to enhance equality. If the United States were to provide state benefits only to those experiencing work disability, people could still elect to enjoy a Third Age—but they would have to fund it themselves. The result would be that Third Age freedoms would be available to the affluent but not to the disadvantaged.

The argument for a state-funded Third Age is an argument about justice between age groups; the argument implies that *old age alone* merits additional resources from the state—which is to say, from people of other ages. Thus, the claim must rest on some theory of justice between age groups that would justify privileging healthy people over, say, age 65 by giving them resources not available to younger people.

The strongest case, I think, treats the Third Age as a new phenomenon, a distinct life stage with special developmental needs. Healthy old age certainly is relatively new phenomenon. Some older individuals have always enjoyed good health, but Chapter 2 documented the sea change in longevity and health in the past 60 years. Now that a majority of people over 65 can expect to remain healthy for decades, we may need to reexamine our impressions of the normal life cycle.

As Chapter 2 recounts, sociologists now describe the Third Age as a distinct life phase. Children are typically grown, finances are often secure, and years of healthy life stretch ahead. These features of the Third Age open up new opportunities for exploration, creativity, and change. At the same time, and on a sober note, the Third Age has a clear endpoint in debility and death, prompting serious reflection about individuals' goals for their remaining time.

We might consider the Third Age the happy product of a wealthy society. For the first time in human history, older people can enjoy a significant period of healthy freedom and choice, and they have time to revise their values, goals, and pursuits before confronting death. To put it bluntly, it is the imminence of death that marks the Third Age as distinctive: it is the last clear period of health and ability before true old age begins and the probability of death becomes a daily reality. People facing their mortality, we might argue, deserve special respect and care. They merit an extra share of social resources to create time to reflect, to act, and to devote their last active years to pursuits of their choice.

These considerations suggest that the Third Age is new and perhaps distinctive. But does it justify the use of state power to redirect resources from younger to older individuals? After all, every life stage confronts the individual with difficult tasks of self-reinvention or stagnation. In Erik Erikson's model, for instance, every new life stage presents a crisis of sorts, a drama that individuals must resolve. In Erikson's stages, middle age confronts the individual with the possibility of generativity or the prospect of stagnation. Old age, for Erikson, poses possibilities of integrity or despair as death approaches.[18]

Viewed in this light, the Third Age represents an extension of middle age, as individuals feel freer to explore new kinds of generative activity. Third Agers still healthy and able do not yet face the imminence of death and debility. Indeed, if it were only the imminence of death that merited special resources, then policy should focus on the very old and the very ill—not healthy, middle-aged people with twenty years of ability left.

Even though it is interesting and exciting to witness the creation of a new life stage, the use of law to reallocate resources to Third Agers seems unjustified. Unlike work disability, the Third Age does not seem to pose negative externalities that would justify state action. Absent state funding for healthy retirement, individuals may face fewer Third Age options than they otherwise would. Some will work longer; others will forgo retraining or new careers; others may retire, but on a smaller budget. But these kinds of outcomes are precisely those that attend every adult life stage: when the state declines to redistribute, say, to young adults in their 30s or middle-aged people in their 40s, they too may have to persist at jobs they dislike, forgo a career change, or make do with less.

The broader point is that any age group could, by its lights, make good use of a bigger slice of the social pie. Resources are finite, and many people feel—throughout their lives—that they could accomplish more if they only had more money or time. But unless there is a compelling reason to privilege one age group over others, the state ought to leave it to every adult to decide for herself how best to allocate her money and time over her lifetime.

Indeed, from a life-cycle perspective, the relatively privileged position of Third Agers militates against special treatment. Like others in late middle age, most people in their healthy 60s and 70s no longer have children at home. For many (though not all) workers, wages are at a lifetime peak, and they enjoy seniority in their jobs. The result is that healthy adults in the Third Age often have discretionary time and discretionary income that younger age groups might envy. Public benefits for the Third Age would limit options for younger adults in order to grant greater income and discretionary time to those already relatively well positioned with those resources.

Even if a just society should (and this is debatable) take steps to protect time for self-reflection and self-reinvention, it is not clear that the Third Age is the only appropriate time. A hard-pressed parent in his 30s might benefit from a period of months or years to rethink his career and family choices. A middle-aged worker at 40 might need a chance to retool or change careers if she finds that her skills are likely to become outdated in the coming decades.[19]

Social Reciprocity

Justice between age groups implies mutual obligation as well as entitlement. When equal opportunity, for instance, mandates extra resources for children, then other age groups have an obligation to provide those resources. After all, the state's resources are those of the collective; it must tax one age group (or grant them less) if it is to increase resources to another.

No age group should claim more than its fair share of resources from the collective. Doing so, by definition, deprives another age group of fair treatment. Suppose it were the case, for example, that public education and college subsidies had become unduly lavish, so that public funds provided children and young adults with more than equal opportunity demanded. (Imagine a public education system with a teacher-student ratio of one to one, or publicly subsidized riding stables for all.) In that case, children (and their representatives) should disclaim the extra resources and free them up for another age group.

Justice between age groups, then, implies a *principle of social reciprocity* so that age groups claim only the resources to which they are entitled. When the state makes an investment that improves the opportunities of an age group, that investment may obligate the age group to share those gains fairly with other age groups. Each age group shares a continuing obligation to provide every other age group with a fair share—but not more. When the state invests heavily to improve the life options of one age group, the state may fairly expect any returns to be taken into account in setting reciprocal rights and obligations.

Older Americans, as a group, stand in exactly this position at the moment. Today's older generations have grown up with antibiotics, vaccinations, and cleaner air and water. Public health campaigns have helped reduce smoking and improve the American diet, lowering rates of heart disease and some cancers. Public funding for college has raised college attendance rates and facilitated the shift to white-collar work and away from physical labor. Changes in technology (computers, cell phones, mechanization) have made many jobs physically easier, placing less stress on our bodies over time. And legal change—the rise in antidiscrimination law, particularly age discrimination law—has opened up a range of new options, in part by changing social attitudes.

And these are not fleeting benefits, captured by a single birth cohort. The Baby Boom will not take these gains with it when it goes: Generation X and later cohorts can (generally) expect to maintain these gains as they reach their 50s, 60s, and beyond.

The result is the state of affairs that Chapter 2 depicts: Affluent older Americans now enjoy unprecedented longevity, education, and good health. And they enjoy an array of Third Age options that would have been unimaginable to anyone (even the richest) in earlier centuries. Largely free of disease and disability, many Third Agers can choose how and whether to work and how and whether to retire.

The improving length and quality of old age in America is a critical social fact. It marks a major change from the social conditions that gave rise to New Deal provision for the elderly. But, in this case (as in many), social change reflected the deliberate efforts of the collective, rather than individual achievement. And when gains to a group arise from social cooperation, the collective—the state—has a special claim to recoup some of those gains for the benefit of all.

To see why, consider for a moment a more familiar context in which we debate the division between personal choice and social obligation. If someone makes a fortune selling, say, luxury cars to investment bankers, some would say that her fortune is a purely private asset. After all, she takes on financial risk and puts in long hours on the job. Others, notably Rawls, would point out that her business flourishes in a social and economic context made possible by social cooperation: America tolerates, even fosters, a degree of inequality that helps prop up the market for high-end goods. Even so, the question prompts considerable debate, because it implicates the distinction between choice and chance. Dividing the car dealer's fortune between personal effort and the random luck of the marketplace is a tricky business. Even egalitarian theorists differ on questions such as whether people own their own talents.[20]

Social obligation also arises when citizens make sacrifices for the collective good. Consider the situation of a soldier who fights in wartime. In every major U.S. war, society has taken on special obligations to recognize the sacrifice of veterans and their families. Soldiers in the Revolutionary War and Civil War received veterans' pensions, World War I vets received a soldiers' bonus, and returning servicemen from World War II benefitted from the GI bill. Today, politicians debate whether our society is adequately meeting the just claims of veterans of Afghanistan and Iraq.[21]

A skeptic may be tempted to suppose that gains in longevity and ability are due to individual effort. After all, we all know that our choices about smoking, drinking, diet, and exercise matter for our health. How, then, can I claim that older people enjoying longer lives owe (a substantial portion) of those gains to collective investment?

In fact, longevity, health, and ability gains by older Americans often reflect collective investments and broad technological change rather than individual effort. Some gains in individual health reflect public health measures: think of clean air and water initiatives, public sanitation, vaccination initiatives, antismoking litigation, public investment in teaching hospitals, and so on. And "private" investments in technology and drugs prosper in part because of public subsidies. The federal government has made (and continues to make) massive grants for scientific and medical research, and public subsidies augment private funds for research and development. Legal protections for patents also reflect a public effort to spur private investment in productive ways.

Empirical studies confirm that a range of collective investments have improved quantity and quality of life at older ages. Improvements in medical care (funded massively by Medicare) have extended life span by treating cancer, heart disease, diabetes, and other serious diseases.[22] Public campaigns to reduce infectious diseases have mitigated serious illnesses that shorten lives. It is not so long ago that rheumatic fever, syphilis, measles, typhoid fever, and malaria posed serious threats to wide swaths of the population.[23]

At the same time, new medical technologies like cataract surgery and joint replacement (which reflect public research funding and Medicare spending as well as proprietary knowledge) have improved ability and mobility for many elderly people.[24] Legal changes, notably the Americans with Disabilities Act, mandated architectural changes that benefit the elderly, including ramps, handrails, accessible bathrooms, and accessible transportation.

Even nominally "private" choices are made in a social and economic context shaped by law and by public investments. The choice not to smoke, for instance, is prompted today by antismoking laws, antismoking warnings, and legal sanctions against tobacco companies. An individual's choices to eat a healthy diet and to exercise, similarly, do not occur in isolation but, rather, amid public campaigns and legal regulation (e.g., labeling laws) intended to nudge us toward better behavior.[25]

Society has, thus far, permitted the elderly to keep for themselves the benefits of social cooperation without asking for a readjustment of their social obligations. Today's older people, as a group, enjoy longer lives, better health, and a wider range of life options than ever before. Of course, older people will necessarily capture, in an experiential sense, the extra years of healthy life and the new social options now open to them. But the question should remain whether the extension of healthy middle age among the over-65s should give rise to new financial obligations to the collective. The fixed retirement age for public benefits compounds the inequity: not only do public benefits (paid in de facto middle age) enrich the budgets of individuals capable of working, but those benefits also support them in withdrawing from the workforce, further undercutting their financial contributions to the rest of society.

In the broadest terms, the problem is one of just contribution. Justice among age groups requires us to take notice of the changing experience of old age. It is a social fact that most people past age 65 now enjoy extra years of healthy, disability-free life, including ample work options. This social setting is quite different from the conditions in the mid-twentieth century that motivated old-age benefits starting at 65. Thanks to public health measures including vaccinations, clean air, and clean water, today's Third Agers can (as a group) count on decades of good health and good options stretching from their 50s to their 80s and 90s. Medical research has made major advances in the treatment of serious diseases such as heart disease and cancer that once meant imminent death and now can often be lived with for long periods. And social cooperation, including the Age Discrimination in Employment Act and cultural change in attitudes about work, has ended mandatory retirement and the exclusion of older people from the workplace.

Consider the 76-year-old restaurant owner profiled in the *New York Times* who says he "can't imagine" giving up the "new challenges" he faces every day.[26] Or the retired Wharton professor who first downsized in his mid-50s, pulling up stakes in Philadelphia to move to the country. At age 90, he moved back to the city with his 89-year-old wife to enjoy urban life again.[27]

The significance of social cooperation, on this account, is that the over-65s cannot plausibly claim that their social situation reflects personal choice. They—like all other age groups—benefit from social cooperation. And, like other age groups, they should be expected to contribute to a just distribution of social resources.

The principle of social reciprocity, then, provides a justification for the state to take notice of social change. And it begins to suggest why the myth of purchased benefits should not carry moral weight. We should not understand Social Security as analogous to a private annuity that makes an irrevocable promise of fixed dollar payouts at a fixed age. Individuals who want to buy private annuities to fund a leisurely Third Age should buy them. Social Security should be understood as social insurance: it redeems the promise that a just society will ensure that its citizens, when unable to work, do not become destitute. But older people should also expect society to adjust social insurance entitlements to reflect gains in healthy longevity produced by public investments.

Fairness certainly counsels caution in changing the financial entitlements of present retirees, who may have limited capacity to adjust their decisions. I will discuss justice in transition in some detail in Chapter 6. But first, I want to turn to an important objection to my conclusions about the proper shape of justice between age groups.

What about Jobs for Younger Workers?

It may seem that I have overlooked an important consideration of justice between age groups. Perhaps it is true that, in principle, the state should only address work disability and should not fund years of healthy retirement. But such a policy would likely delay retirement, at least for healthy, able people in the over-65 group. And the consequences of delayed retirement, it seems, could be dire: if older people remain in the workforce longer, then it seems intuitive that younger people would face a longer wait to take on positions of responsibility—and that entry-level workers might not find jobs at all. Instead of serving life-cycle justice, delayed retirement could hinder justice by unnecessarily harming the interests of the young.

This chain of reasoning has supported early retirement initiatives in the EU, and it echoes in Social Security debates in the United States as well.[28] The argument has a great deal of commonsense appeal, but it rests on a questionable economic theory, which economists Jonathan Gruber, Kevin Milligan, and David Wise term the "lump of labor" idea. The lump of labor theory holds that the economy generates only a fixed number of jobs.[29] If that is true, then employment is like a game of musical chairs: younger workers cannot get a job unless older workers leave the game and give up their places.

This lump of labor view of the labor market is plausible ex ante, but so is a competing theory: it is possible that the labor market is dynamic enough to accommodate larger and smaller cohorts of workers. In that case, delayed retirement should not harm the employment prospects of younger workers.

Only empirical evidence can settle the question, and it turns out that the best evidence comes down firmly on the side of the dynamic labor market. Gruber and Wise commissioned a large team of economists to study employment patterns in twelve developed countries over decades. Surprisingly, the researchers consistently *found no correlation between later retirement ages and youth unemployment.*[30]

Indeed, the researchers found that youth employment and the employment of older workers tend to be positively correlated; that is, holding other factors constant, when more older people are working, so are more younger people.[31] Gruber and his coauthors note that the influx of women into labor markets in the 1970s provides considerable evidence to refute the lump of labor theory. When married women starting taking paid jobs in the 1970s and 1980s, the result wasn't mass unemployment in the economy. To be sure, some particular men were displaced by women, and some men fared better than others. Over the same period, wages for men fell (but probably for other reasons as well), and wages for women rose. But in the aggregate, the economies of developed nations were able to absorb the new workers.[32]

The Gruber and Wise researchers also examined a range of early retirement policies adopted in European countries, largely in the 1970s and intended to improve youth employment. They conclude that "there is no evidence that reducing the employment of older persons provides more job opportunities for younger persons."[33]

These findings seem especially important once we realize that the United States, like other developed nations, is facing a static or even shrinking labor force in the coming decades, due to the aging of the Baby Boom. The prime age workforce in the United States is projected not to grow in the 2000s (absent changes in retirement policy).[34] At the same time, gains in the educational attainment of the workforce are projected to slow.[35] These changes will, if anything, tighten demand for workers of all ages.

An Aside: Why Academic Jobs Are Different

Readers who work in higher education may be skeptical of the dynamic labor market story, because it defies our everyday experience of the workplace. Colleges today are sites of generational inequality: Tenured professors are disproportionately Baby Boomers (or older).[36] Young PhDs face a difficult job market, with long tenure tracks if they can find tenure-track positions at all. Many work as contract teachers at low pay or cannot find academic work of any kind.[37]

Universities thus seem to substantiate the lump of labor theory. With older professors occupying privileged positions, there simply aren't enough jobs for younger PhDs who want to teach. Indeed, in a recent (and highly publicized) article, retired professor Laurie Fendrich argued that "[a]cademics who don't retire are greedy, selfish, and bad for students."[38] Polarizing rhetoric aside, many university denizens share Fendrich's concern that the end of mandatory retirement in universities has created a roadblock to the academy for younger generations.

But a closer look suggests that universities are exceptional labor markets in several respects. First, universities tend to impose a fixed number of slots for tenured faculty. Second, universities have resisted expanding the tenured ranks in proportion to the growth in the higher education sector. Instead, colleges have responded to the influx of students by shifting away from tenured jobs for faculty and toward low-paid adjunct positions. Third, tenured professorships are very easily retained by older people, because professors can, de facto, downshift to part-time work (which is highly desired by people nearing retirement) without having to give up their full-time slot (and full-time pay).

To see why these details matter, it's useful to review what Gruber and Wise do—and do not—find. The Gruber and Wise project enlisted more than a dozen economists, who studied a dozen developed countries using a common methodology. The results present findings as to these economies as a whole and may not apply to all sectors or industries. The Gruber and Wise studies find that, in the aggregate, employment is not a zero-sum game; the labor market isn't like musical chairs, where there are a fixed number of seats, and if more players stay in, then there are fewer seats for newcomers. Instead, the studies document that the economy seems to expand when the labor supply grows, so that an increase in the number of older workers (due to a delayed retirement age) doesn't result in youth unemployment.

All this hints at why the three exceptional features of universities matter. The first exceptional feature is puzzling, because the fixed number of tenure slots creates an artificial and unusual zero-sum game. Few (if any) industries would respond to an increase in demand (here, student enrollments) and prices (here, tuition) by holding their payroll fixed! The second exceptional feature explains what is really going on: universities limit tenured positions artificially in order to change their mix of workers, shifting away from tenured faculty and toward lower-paid contract teachers. From 1975 to 2011, the percentage of part-time faculty nationwide grew from less than 25% to more than 40%, while full-time tenured faculty dropped from nearly 30% to about 15%.[39] In effect, universities have changed their business model—not unlike (say) U.S. industry, which has sought to replace union workers with cheaper, nonunion employees.

The third exceptional feature of universities (the ability of professors to work part-time while occupying a full-time slot) explains why older professors are more likely to stay in their positions longer than older workers in more-demanding jobs. An older professor can cut her research hours without having to give up her job to a younger person. By contrast, in business, older workers who want part-time work typically do have to give up their full-time jobs. Put another way, if universities were able to detect when older professors were downshifting, there would likely be more tenured slots available to younger workers.[40]

The takeaway here is that institutions matter, and Gruber and Wise provide strong evidence that on an economy-wide basis, youth employment will not suffer if older workers work longer. (Strikingly, they found this even in Western Europe, which over the relevant period has had more-rigid labor market structures than we have.) Sector by sector, and even firm by firm, certain policies may work to the advantage of the old at the expense of the young. We might tell a political economy story about universities to explain why older, currently tenured people (who hold all the votes) have chosen to protect their own jobs without challenging practices (such as adjunct hiring) that disproportionately affect the young.

Anecdotally, the federal government provides an interesting counterexample that illustrates the economic benefits of delayed retirement. Agencies have actively sought a phased retirement program, which would, for the first time, permit older workers to continue on a part-time basis. Managers are finding that the absence of a part-time option has led older people to retire too early and all at once, taking all their knowledge with them and leaving younger workers in the lurch. A part-time, phased retirement option both accommodates older workers' desire for fewer responsibilities and meets the agencies' need for knowledge transfer.[41]

Principles for Reform

This chapter has developed two principles:

- First is the principle of *life-cycle justice*. Equal opportunity and liberty guide the fair allocation of resources among age groups. Work disability predictably leads to negative spillover effects, and so society may fairly mandate savings (or insurance contributions) against the prospect of work disability.
- Second is the principle of *social reciprocity*. When society invests its resources in ways that benefit an age group, its members have an obligation to share their gains fairly with other age groups, according to the dictates of life-cycle justice.

These principles are, at this early stage, quite general. Still, one proposition is clear enough: a fair society should not devote public funds to supporting retirement well in advance of work disability. To be sure, any real-world policy may operate with some imprecision. The reforms I defend in later chapters do make use of chronological age (along with other information) to approximate the onset of work disability for different groups of older Americans. The result will be that even a reformed system would award public "retirement" benefits to some individuals before they are incapable of working. But it is critical to see that these practical, administrative judgments do not endorse the idea that public policy ought to support a retirement policy that supports the middle-aged.

Moving from principles to policies will require more attention to social facts and to governmental capabilities—a task that will occupy Chapters 7 through 10. But first, I must tackle the problem of unequal age. How, if at all, should a just society take account of the unequal distribution of life options among older Americans?

5

Cumulative Disadvantage
and Unequal Age

To this point, we have focused on the question of justice among age groups. Life-cycle justice, I have argued, supports legal mandates to require each person to save for work disability in old age. And social reciprocity creates an obligation for the beneficiaries of public investments to repay some of their gains to the collective.

Liberal theory suggests that *justice within age groups* is important as well. As Chapter 2 demonstrates, inequality among older Americans is wide and growing. The experience of old age has become unequal, whether we examine life span, health, ability, finances, work options, or family status. And, as Chapter 3 documents, our public institutions have permitted, and sometimes fostered, inequality.

But the simple fact of inequality, once again, does not provide a blueprint for reform. We need a clearer account of justice if we are to determine which inequalities should be addressed, and how to do so. In this chapter, as in Chapter 4, I draw on egalitarian liberalism to frame principles that (in later chapters) will suggest concrete proposals for legal reform.

Economic Inequality and Justice

The problem of inequality in incomes and wages is a familiar topic in distributive justice. Ronald Dworkin, for instance, suggests that a fair society should require individuals to bear the consequences of their own choices but not of "brute luck" or pure chance. The earnings we command in the marketplace reflect brute luck to a considerable degree, because we do not choose our endowments, our families, or the time in which we live. Accordingly, Dworkin concludes, justice requires that the state provide insurance against having capabilities that earn only low returns in the marketplace. Dworkin's income insurance program would tax high earners and award benefits to low earners. Notably, Dworkin's proposal would operate over a lifetime: his redistributive scheme is not particularly aimed at old age.[1]

Philippe Van Parijs also proposes a lifelong program intended to implement a just distribution of resources. He calls for the state to guarantee to each individual the highest sustainable basic income, financed by a tax on income. Basic income grants would be equal for all and payable annually each year. The redistribution in Van Parijs' system enters via the income tax, which ensures that low earners (and the unemployed) receive more resources, on net. Once again, Van Parijs' proposal does not particularly target old age, although lifelong payments would go a long way toward alleviating old-age destitution.[2]

Perhaps most famously, John Rawls formulated the difference principle. In *A Theory of Justice,* he proposes that, once the state has guaranteed equal basic liberties to all, social and economic inequalities should, as far as possible, benefit the least-advantaged members of society.[3]

Who are the least advantaged? Rawls offered, in his initial formulation of the difference principle, only a brief consideration of the content of the "least advantaged" category. He acknowledged a "certain arbitrariness" and suggested that a fair society might target a particular social position (for instance, the unskilled worker) or a level of income or wealth (say, half the median). In later work, Rawls suggested that advantage might best be measured by the origins of disadvantage, particularly family and class origins, natural endowments, and fortune and luck.[4]

Rawls, of course, wrote in the mid- to late twentieth century. His rather bland characterization of the least advantaged should be read against the backdrop of (relative) social homogeneity and economic prosperity in the American 1960s. By contrast, we live today with striking social and economic inequalities, and it is not hard to identify the least advantaged as those who confront compound inequalities extending over their entire lives. Less-educated individuals earn low wages and work under stressful conditions.

They experience frequent unemployment and typically have no private pensions. They often live in areas with poor schools, compounding inequality for the next generation. At older ages, we have seen, low earners confront cumulative disadvantage, with shorter life spans, poorer health, higher rates of disability, and worse options for continuing work.[5]

To be sure, a certain arbitrariness remains in translating these inequalities into sharp-edged categories. Education levels, wages, working conditions, family stability, and health and disability status do not always march in lockstep. Some affluent people suffer ill health at young ages, some with college educations become unemployed, and so on. But the cumulation of disadvantage is significant. It is certainly a terrible event for anyone to suffer (say) a stroke at age 55. But when the stroke victim has a good education, a lifetime of comfortable wages, private health and disability insurance, and a savings account, the circumstances are far less dire than when she is a single mother with no savings and no insurance beyond Social Security.

The cumulating inequalities of our present society represent precisely the kind of social injustice that Rawls meant to target. It is not the case that disadvantage is diffused throughout society. Instead, there is a group—roughly the bottom third of the population—that experiences multiple disadvantages in health, ability, finances, and family life. And these disadvantages tend to cumulate over a lifetime, as poor health and disability compromise job options and family life (for example).

In academic circles, Rawls' difference principle is sometimes treated as a formula to be parsed: Does he really mean that the worst-off person should be better-off than the next worst, and so on?[6] But, taking a broader view, the difference principle reflects Rawls' concern about the moral arbitrariness of the distribution of opportunity and primary goods in society.

Inequality and Old Age

Strikingly, neither Dworkin nor Van Parijs nor Rawls points to economic inequality in old age as a matter of special concern. They focus on the fair distribution of resources during the entire life cycle and, logically enough, propose ongoing redistribution. The less-educated, low-earning young are disadvantaged along with their older counterparts: both groups struggle for the primary goods they need to lead meaningful lives. And policies to address those inequalities would ideally operate over a lifetime, not just in old age: ideal institutions would operate from childhood through adulthood to address underlying inequalities in education, health, work options, and family stability.

But present social conditions and legal institutions are far from ideal. Our society has not met the demands of justice: we have failed to address crushing inequalities in all four dimensions. Even the earned income tax credit (the EITC), widely praised as a progressive means of assisting the working poor, has only modest effects.[7] The result is that the least advantaged suffer across multiple dimensions. The very same people tend to experience the least family stability, obtain the least education, encounter the worst work conditions, and suffer the worst outcomes in health and disability.

Today, then, the case for devoting extra resources to the least advantaged in old age is strong. The failures of our public institutions have compounded inequality, so that low-earning workers arrive at older ages with cumulative disadvantages that shorten lives and hasten work disability. In fairness, the law should recognize and mitigate these inequalities in old age if not before; the law should take notice that the least advantaged may experience work disability at earlier ages due to disability, ill health, and the physical and mental stress of poor working conditions.

Progressive benefits for work disability in old age would both recognize inequality within the group of the elderly and help compensate for the absence of lifelong wage supplements of the kind that Dworkin and Van Parijs recommend. Consider two equivalent programs for insuring low earners against work disability:

- *Lifelong earnings supplements.* Low earners receive a supplemental payment of $x every year during their working lives. Low earners must also contribute $x to a universal work disability insurance program. All workers receive an actuarially accurate payment upon work disability; the payment for low earners is $y, an amount sufficient to enable a decent life without employment.
- *Free insurance.* Low earners are exempt from the forced-savings mandate but, upon the onset of work disability, receive $y (once again, an amount sufficient to enable a decent life without employment).

Either of these programs would provide low earners with work disability insurance on preferential terms. We see variations on these ideas under present law. The EITC provides a partial earnings supplement to workers, and low earners do pay Social Security payroll taxes during their working years. At retirement, workers' Social Security benefits incorporate a formula that awards (relatively) higher benefits to low earners than to high earners.

These programmatic possibilities illustrate that the criterion for justice should not be simple "progressivity"—that is, ensuring that the poor get a bit more than the rich per dollar of contribution. Instead, we should apply a more demanding criterion: we should expect a just state to recognize and address *cumulative disadvantage*. As we have seen, discussions of Social Security sometimes treat simple progressivity as if it is an end in itself.[8] But progressivity is a far less demanding criterion and by itself does not (necessarily) satisfy the demands of justice.

A fair system, then, should pay attention to the timing of benefits and to the living standard they enable. The state should identify those who have suffered cumulative disadvantage and should ensure that they have access to benefits when they can no longer work—even though that is likely to be earlier than for other groups. And the system should ensure that benefits are adequate to live decently.

The Universality Problem

At first glance, the recognition of cumulative disadvantage seems to call for a degree of redistribution that would clash with the value of universalism. Universal retirement has been a core value of Social Security, and the appearance of universalism has helped underwrite the program's widespread popular support.[9] Reforms to improve retirement security for the least advantaged would seem to highlight class divisions that could tear apart Social Security and undermine its achievements. The conventional wisdom has been that paying unneeded benefits to the affluent is simply the price of having any public retirement program at all.

These arguments are familiar in discussions of Social Security. For instance, Virginia Reno responds this way to a proposal to enact a means test:

> Means testing Social Security would fundamentally change it from social insurance (a universal system of benefits earned by all who have paid in) to welfare (a system requiring you to prove you are needy in order to qualify for benefits). . . . Means testing would violate many of the key principles that have made Social Security so effective and popular for 77 years.[10]

And universalism has value beyond political vote-getting. Both theory and empirical studies confirm that universal provision of social benefits tends to build social solidarity and demonstrate social equality.[11] Universalism sidesteps the intrusive procedures and social stigma that attend means testing. Indeed, a large universal program like Social Security can actually transfer more dollars to the disadvantaged than a targeted program can, because means-tested programs (particularly in the United States) tend to be small and to provide meager benefits.

It would seem counterproductive, then, to undermine universalism in the name of recognizing disadvantage. Even if Social Security does not meet ideal standards of justice, perhaps it is the best we can do, given the political and administrative consequences of means testing.

But the framing of the issue in policy debates obscures important issues of justice. What universalism demands is not clear, for instance. Even a means-tested program is universal in some dimensions. SNAP, for example, offers food stamps to all poor households that meet income, asset, and work restrictions. And "universal" programs often are not truly universal. Social Security, for example, is available only to U.S. workers with a documented and substantial work history.

Nor is it satisfying to presume that means testing is the only way to recognize and redress disadvantage. The term connotes humiliating and intrusive procedures and miserly benefits. But, in fact, Social Security beneficiaries already face two different means tests: the progressive benefits formula, which explicitly graduates benefits based on income, and the federal income tax, which taxes benefits at progressive rates. It is not clear, then, when a means test is acceptable and when it is not.

Before we can understand the importance of universalism, then, we should be more precise about what the values at stake really are.

Universalism and Dignity

What, exactly, constitutes universalism? No program (other than a basic income paid in equal sums to every human being) is truly universal. Rather, programs tend to be universal in some dimensions but not others. Social Security, for instance, sets a universal retirement age and has no obvious means test based on current income. But the program's benefits vary with lifetime earnings levels, so that people of the same age can receive very different dollar amounts. And the income tax rules impose tax on Social Security benefits when total income is sufficiently high.[12]

Universalism, then, is not a binary, on-off switch. It reflects, rather, a qualitative judgment against a social backdrop in which certain conditions are objectionable or stigmatizing in ways that reinforce social divisions.[13] Political context matters as well. Whether a program is perceived as universal and whether it reinforces social solidarity depends critically on the political situation. Social Security, for example, was enacted against the backdrop of the Depression and a widely shared sense that the elderly were economically vulnerable through no fault of their own. Welfare programs, by contrast, have foundered on a lack of social consensus about the desert of single mothers and their children.

There is no mechanical formula, then, that will confer on a program the benefits of universalism. Policy analysts sometimes reduce the value of universalism to program design, and particularly to the absence of means testing. Welfare provides the classic example and cautionary tale. In the United States, Temporary Assistance for Needy Families, or TANF—like Aid to Families with Dependent Children, or AFDC, before it—incorporates a means test that reinforces social stigma. Welfare requires members of an already-stigmatized group (impoverished single mothers) to perform, in a relatively public way, the humiliating act of asking for assistance on the grounds of inability to be self-sufficient. Welfare claimants must travel to a welfare office, sit in a public waiting room, and then answer personal questions (How much money do you make? Who lives in your household? Who is the father of your children?) posed by a public official.

But it is not just the means test that makes welfare unpopular and humiliating. The trips to the public welfare office, the posture of supplication before state officials, and the payment of very low benefits valuable only to the destitute—all reflect and reinforce the social isolation of the recipients.

Thus, it is not the means test alone, but rather the political and social context, together with other features of administration, that foster social division and humiliate recipients.[14] Contrast the earned income tax credit (EITC), which targets low earners and employs a means test but is widely popular and does not carry the stigma of welfare. The program differs from welfare in two significant ways: it pays benefits only to workers, and recipients claim their benefits privately via the tax return. The EITC is not universal in the classic sense, and yet it delivers social assistance that enhances material well-being without humiliation.

Social Security itself provides an example of means testing without social division or personal humiliation. The means test is cleverly hidden in two obscure provisions—the progressive benefits formula and the Internal Revenue Code. But despite the happy nomenclature, these provisions impose a means test—of sorts: they cut benefit rates as income rises.

The brilliance of the program's design is that it melds the appearance of universality with the reality of means testing and a host of other conditions, including marital status and history as well as spousal earnings. Social Security appears universal because everyone receives a check. But the amount payable to each individual is a complex function of her lifetime earnings, marital status, retirement age, and the progressive retirement formula.

One might suppose that the means test in Social Security persists only because it is so well hidden. The difficulty with that explanation is that conservative opponents of Social Security have done their best to point out the means test—and to highlight that higher earners receive a very poor "rate of return" on their contributions compared with low earners.[15] And progressive reformers have not been shy about proposing to tilt the formula even further in favor of low-income retirees.[16]

Probably just as important are three key differences between the Social Security means test and the kind of means tests found in welfare. First, as many scholars have pointed out, Social Security is paid only to workers, and it is paid based on their work history. The program thus pays a benefit that appears to be purchased in a dignified way rather than free or a handout.[17]

Second, scholars have also noted that Social Security is administered in an efficient and dignified way. By the time a worker reaches retirement age, the government has already collected all the information it needs: the worker's age and lifetime earnings history. Collecting Social Security is then a simple matter of notifying the government that you'd like to receive your benefits now, please. The program avoids the hassle and humiliation of the trip to the welfare office, the wait in a long line, and the plea to a caseworker to approve your claim.

Third, and less often discussed, Social Security determines benefits based on lifetime earnings, not on a snapshot of current income. The difference is important, because a lifetime earnings test cannot be gamed: 40 years of earnings represents a fairly accurate picture of how a worker's economic life has gone. By contrast, welfare benefits must rely on snapshot income, because they are intended to provide short-term and highly responsive relief. Snapshot income does not necessarily—and is not intended to—capture one's long-term economic position.

These values suggest that Social Security implements what we might term an *antihumiliation ideal.* Many principles of justice counsel against unnecessary humiliation. Autonomous individuals deserve to make decisions and to interact with the state on dignified terms. So it might seem, at first glance, that antihumiliation is implicit in the kind of Rawlsian liberalism I've invoked, and indeed it is. Still, it is worth enunciating an antihumiliation ideal explicitly, because the law has the capacity to adopt more- and less-humiliating modes of administration.

Bruce Ackerman has recently expounded on the antihumiliation ideal in the context of civil rights.[18] Ackerman crystallizes from *Brown v. Board of Education* an antihumiliation principle that counsels against the institutionalization of humiliation. *Brown* and other civil rights initiatives, Ackerman argues, examined the meaning of *humiliation* in different social spheres, according to the "practices and expectations" of each.[19] In education, for instance, the institutional separation of black children "generat[ed] a feeling of inferiority,"[20] and so the *Brown* court properly struck down the legal rules mandating segregation.

Retirement marks yet another "sociological sphere" (to use Ackerman's term)[21] for examining expectations and practices to root out (or avoid creating) institutionalized humiliation. Indeed, the antihumiliation frame helps deepen our understanding of the conventional shorthand of "universalism." Universal programs promote individual dignity and avoid humiliating conditions. Social Security, as we have seen, preserves dignity by framing benefits as earned, by imposing the means test in private and sub rosa, and by avoiding humiliating means of administration.

The antihumiliation ideal appears in classic discussions of universalism as well. Richard Titmuss notes that Britain adopted a universal National Health Service and other programs to provide services "in such ways as would not involve users in any *humiliating loss of status, dignity, or self-respect.*"[22]

Dignitarian concerns explain why the EITC is popular and seems to promote social solidarity even though it is not, in the usual sense, universal. The EITC, too, is an earned benefit (only workers qualify). It administers a means test in private, and (by using the tax return) it avoids the traditional, humiliating procedures of welfare application.

The challenge posed by the antihumiliation principle for Social Security reform is substantial: raising the retirement age while taking note of inequality will require care to avoid humiliating older people with work disability. This is a serious challenge for policy design, and yet we should not mistake the antihumiliation principle as a defense of the status quo. Antihumiliation tells us something about how we ought to implement social benefits, but it is essentially a secondary principle. Standing alone, it cannot justify the current rules on retirement age, benefits, and so on. Instead, it should be consulted in designing the administration of just programs that recognize cumulative disadvantage and promote justice between age groups.

Concretely, the antihumiliation principle does not justify universal retirement at age 66—any more than it would justify universal retirement at age 44 or age 88. Instead, the choice of a retirement age—and the design of a work disability standard—ought to be sensitive to the possibility of humiliation and should consult governmental capacities and social context to avoid humiliation. But nothing in the value of dignity necessarily mandates the public funding of decades of healthy retirement for a majority of the population.

To be sure, the current Social Security Disability Insurance (SSDI) program is probably not a good model for determining work disability in a way that meets the antihumiliation ideal. The program's eligibility rules and procedures set a high bar for proving disability. Workers must come forward with evidence of total disability and (often) undergo a difficult and lengthy appeals process.[23]

But we need not extend SSDI in its current form to tailor public retirement benefits to work disability. Instead, as I will show in Chapters 6 and 7, program design is easier for older people simply because work disability increases with age and correlates with lifetime income and with occupation. For younger workers, disability requires an individual determination: because the vast majority of 25-year-olds, say, are capable of working, the system must provide some means of determining why a particular worker is exceptional.

For older workers, in contrast, we can more readily craft rules that link benefits to likely work disability but retain the privacy and dignity in administration that characterize Social Security. Chapter 7 will show that reforms in Social Security and unemployment insurance can link public benefits more closely to work disability without means testing. Modifications to SSDI could also improve the disability standard and verification process for older workers.

The task for the following chapters, then, is clear: to recognize the unequal experience of old age while also bearing in mind the antihumiliation criterion. We shall see that it is possible to do so while maintaining the eligibility and administrative features of Social Security that have maintained its ability to blur rather than highlight social divisions.

Refining the Principles for Reform

I ended Chapter 4 with two principles for the reform of old-age entitlements. We should now add a third and fourth:

- First is the principle of *life-cycle justice*. Equal opportunity and liberty guide the fair allocation of resources among age groups. Work disability predictably leads to negative spillover effects, and so society may fairly mandate insurance contributions against the prospect of work disability.
- Second is the principle of *social reciprocity*. When society invests its resources in ways that benefit an age group, its members have an obligation to share their gains fairly with other age groups, according to the dictates of life-cycle justice.
- Third is the principle of *state recognition of cumulative disadvantage*. Today, multiple inequalities burden low earners, who have the shortest life spans, the worst health, the highest rates of disability, the fewest (good) job options, and the greatest family instability. A fair society should challenge inequality at every life stage, but while those inequalities persist, retirement policy should take due care to structure policies that take notice of them.
- Fourth is the *antihumiliation* ideal. While not a principle of justice on a par with the others, antihumiliation offers an important criterion for administration: public benefits should adopt administrative procedures that preserve individual dignity and avoid institutionalizing humiliation.

6

From Principles to Policies

It is time to translate principles into policy. Chapters 4 and 5 developed four principles:

- The principle of *life-cycle justice* guides the fair allocation of resources among age groups and justifies state mandates for savings to anticipate work disability, whether during the working years or in old age.
- The principle of *social reciprocity* holds that members of an age group have an obligation to share with others the gains from social investments.
- The principle of *state recognition of cumulative disadvantage* directs state attention to the multiple burdens facing low earners, including illness, disability, low savings capacity, and family instability.
- The *antihumiliation* principle supports administration designed to preserve individual dignity and avoid humiliation.

At first glance, these principles may seem to provide limited guidance for policy design. After all, in policy circles, we typically speak a different language. Policy analysts classify programs as social insurance or public assistance, universal or means tested. They analyze the distributive, behavioral, and efficiency effects of public benefits and the taxes that fund them. Some policy analysts run elaborate regressions to tease out the effects of programs on income, employment, or other economic indicators.

But a closer look reveals that these four principles provide clear directions for policy design and equally clear reasons for rejecting some familiar reform proposals. Life-cycle justice suggests a system of public pensions linked more closely to work disability but also expanded antidiscrimination rules to ensure that able older workers have a fair opportunity to work if they choose. The recognition of cumulative disadvantage supports rules that permit disadvantaged workers to leave work at earlier ages and with adequate support. Social reciprocity suggests that affluent older workers should bear greater costs at retirement, in light of their dramatic gains from public investments. And the antihumiliation principle supports a range of initiatives to provide a dignified exit from the workforce for older workers who experience disability or long-term unemployment before they are entitled to full retirement benefits.

A principled approach also helps clear away roadblocks to reforming retirement policy. A clearer understanding of the deeper purposes of public retirement programs reveals that the egalitarian problem can be addressed without undermining universality, and that the myth of purchased benefits should give way to a more nuanced public discussion about social change and fair transitions.

To be sure, these principles cannot dictate every detail of program design. Some provisions must be crafted according to prudential considerations of cost and administrative capacity. Chapters 7 through 10 extend the analysis, offering a range of possible reforms in Social Security, tax law, disability insurance, unemployment insurance, and age discrimination law.

Democratic politics, of course, will play a large role in determining feasible and attractive reforms. This is (mostly) as it should be: democracy itself is an important value in a fair society. But, as Rawls (in his book, *Political Liberalism*)[1] points out, politics need not mean a crass free-for-all in which powerful interests always win. Chapter 11 draws on Rawls' work to consider how we can—and why we should—meld principles with politics in public discussions of Social Security reform.

The Importance of Principle in Policy Analysis

To translate principles into policies, we must pause for a moment and introduce the core ideas that inform policy analysis. Policy wonks speak what may seem a peculiar language, and yet it expresses useful concepts. Indeed, I will show very shortly that principles of justice provide quite crisp answers to the core questions of policy design. But first, we need a brief introduction to policy analysis.

Policy analysts typically ask (or should ask) three questions about any existing program—or any proposal for reform: First, what is the rationale for state action? Some matters are best left to individual choice and to the operation of market or nonmarket interactions—labor markets or the family, for instance. But the operation of these institutions depends on the configuration of background entitlements and rules, and they sometimes fail badly. Any proposal for change should specify why institutions should be altered.

Second, with this rationale for state action in mind, what—precisely—should the policy change aim to accomplish? For example, a program might attempt to redistribute income, to change behavior, or to improve the allocation of resources. The statement of goals then provides criteria for success. A proposal to redistribute income, for example, should raise the incomes of the target group. A proposal to change behavior should alter the choices people make. And a proposal to increase allocative efficiency should alter prices so that they produce a welfare-improving allocation of resources.

Third, what is the proper pattern of taxation? Some initiatives will raise taxes, and it will be necessary not only to raise sufficient revenue but also to do so taking into account the distributional, behavioral, and efficiency effects of the necessary taxation. Other initiatives will permit tax reductions, and once again, a precise policy design will take into account the distributional, behavioral, and efficiency effects. Critically, the tax side of the equation should not counteract the desired effects of the benefits change. It would be ludicrous to, say, raise Social Security benefits for Group X and fund the change by taxing the Social Security benefits of Group X.

The terms *distribution, behavior,* and *efficiency* have a commonsense sound, but they have precise, technical meanings with subtle content. *Distribution* refers to the impact of a policy on the dissemination of a specified good—usually money or income, but sometimes opportunities or jobs. Policies may be aimed at *redistribution* compared to the status quo, meaning that some groups would receive more or less than they currently do. For instance, a proposal to raise Social Security benefits for survivors might aim to increase the incomes of older widows, who are often very poor.

Behavior refers, of course, to the impact of a policy on the choices individuals make. Policies may attempt to alter behavior to counteract some cognitive bias or to serve some social end. For example, a proposal to enroll workers automatically in employer retirement plans might aim to increase the proportion of workers who save for retirement.

Efficiency is a concept drawn from economics, and it is sometimes misused in popular discussions. Efficiency in its technical sense does not (necessarily) mandate low-cost administration of government programs. Nor does efficiency (necessarily) mandate cutting social programs or taxes. Instead, an economist deems an arrangement "efficient" if it involves a pricing structure that results in an allocation of resources that maximizes the well-being (or welfare) of society. An inefficient market results in a distorted allocation of resources. For instance, the minimum wage may be inefficient because it artificially raises wages for low-wage workers, with the result that the job market is distorted, and too few workers are employed.

These three concepts, used with precision, can provide a rationale for state action and can describe the purposes of a policy initiative, as well as provide criteria for evaluating a program's success. Sticking with the minimum wage example, some have proposed to repeal the minimum wage in order to increase employment for low-wage workers. The goal of the program would be behavioral (to induce employers to hire and retain low-wage workers and to induce these workers to accept jobs and to remain employed). The corollary is that the program's success can and should be measured by increases in employment for low-wage workers due to the program (rather than, say, due to an uptick in the business cycle).

If all this seems complicated and technical, it may be surprising to learn that all these concepts are readily recognizable to any scholar of distributive justice. To be sure, philosophers ponder different questions than policy wonks do: philosophers tend to emphasize the refinement of ideals, while policy analysts translate practical goals into practical policies. But the best policy analysis marries the precision of theories of justice to the details of program design, and for this reason, there should be more than a little shared intellectual territory between the philosopher and the policy analyst.

Efficiency, for example, reflects a utilitarian perspective, typically translated via the discipline of economics, with its emphasis on the maximization of social welfare and its allegiance to market distributions based on accurate pricing. Concerns about distribution and behavior arise in a variety of theories of justice. Even a highly egalitarian theorist such as John Rawls considers the impact of redistribution on behavior; Rawls' well-known difference principle, for instance, incorporates the tradeoff between redistribution and work incentives.

Without a principled foundation, a policy proposal is unanchored, a problem that happens all too often. Complaints about the insolvency of the Social Security system, for example, often do not reflect a clear theory of justice. The result is that the insolvency worry is ambiguous, because it could reflect either the notion that the elderly as a group are receiving too much (so that their benefits should be cut) or that younger citizens are paying too little (so that their taxes should be raised). Without specifying a theory of justice—an ideal—between age groups, there is no way to analyze how Social Security measures up.

For example, some policy analysts have recommended longevity indexing for Social Security benefits. John Turner offers a particularly thoughtful proposal: taking as the goal the solvency of the Social Security system, he suggests that benefits could be indexed to increasing (average) longevity, in order to keep constant the lifetime value of benefits. After reviewing international experience and policy design options, Turner proposes to adjust annual benefits downward to reflect increasing longevity in each age cohort.[2]

Longevity indexing certainly is one way to address the solvency problem. But longevity indexing, as Turner candidly notes, would place the financial burden of increasing life spans on retirees. Lower annual retirement benefits would consign more retirees to poverty. An increase in the payroll tax, by contrast, would place the financial burden of solvency on working-age taxpayers. It is not obvious which solution is fairer, unless we smuggle in the unarticulated premise that retirement benefits are now too high. Solvency, it turns out, cannot be the real goal, because it does not reach the moral issues at stake. The real question is the proper allocation of resources between generations.

Armed with these preliminaries, we can draw on the principles of life-cycle justice, social reciprocity, recognition of disadvantage, and antihumiliation to motivate a set of reforms in present retirement policy.

Life-Cycle Justice and Work Disability

The principle of justice over the life cycle, as developed in Chapter 4, answers all three of the policy analyst's standard queries. First, myopia and negative externalities justify state action—the use of law to mandate insurance for work disability in old age. Second, the government's goal should be for individuals to insure themselves, so that the costs of their work disability do not fall on others. (The state's goal should not be to fund years of healthy retirement.) A fair retirement policy, accordingly, should insure everyone against work disability. Third, the taxation scheme, too, is clear: each individual should pay the costs of insuring herself.

Notably, life-cycle justice mandates intrapersonal but not interpersonal redistribution. The prospect of negative spillover effects justifies the state in overriding individuals' choices about allocating resources over their life spans. Even if I soberly wish to spend all my money now and live out my older years in destitution, that choice is properly foreclosed by the state, and the law may fairly require me to set aside some of my resources to purchase insurance. Justice may require that individuals devote fewer resources to their youth and more resources to their old age than they otherwise would.

But life-cycle justice does not mandate redistribution from rich to poor: it justifies only measures to protect against the negative spillover of the costs of supporting the elderly unable to work. Instead, the proper shape and scope of redistribution must await additional principles—social reciprocity and recognition of cumulative disadvantage. *Ex ante,* then, each person should pay a fair actuarial price for his or her insurance. *Ex post,* the payout of work disability benefits—like any insurance—will differ across individuals.

Concretely, then, the principle of life-cycle justice supports a public retirement program, but one that ties the payment of benefits to any individual to work disability. Today's Social Security system achieves near-universal coverage for work disability at younger ages through SSDI. But at older ages, the program pays benefits at a fixed chronological age, regardless of work ability. The result, as Chapter 3 discusses, is that most Americans begin to collect public retirement benefits in their early and mid-60s, whether or not they are capable of working. As a matter of justice over the life cycle, the program engages in too much redistribution from younger to older workers, compared with the ideal program, which would link payouts to work disability.

A reorientation of Social Security to focus on work disability is consistent with the program's original mission. In the mid-twentieth century, age 65 marked a relatively uniform entry into old age. We can quibble about whether 65 or 70 or some other age would have been a better estimate, at that time, of the onset of work disability. But the larger point is that the experience of old age in that era was relatively uniform. The workforce was mostly male. Most men had limited education and physical jobs, and their health prospects at age 65 were homogeneous. In that era, age 65 marked a reasonable and dignified proxy for work disability.

Today, however, the unequal experience of old age must send us back to the drawing board to confront two major issues for policy design. First, the determination of work disability poses an important and difficult issue, but one amenable to policy design. We need not imagine that all older people must undergo the rigorous, time-consuming, and individualized determinations now used for Social Security Disability Insurance. Indeed, I will argue in a few pages—and at more length in Chapters 7 and 8—that the SSDI model should not be the primary method of determining work disability. Instead of attempting individualized determinations, a better approach would craft new rules based on empirical evidence in order to make plausible judgments, valid for groups, about the likely onset of work disability.

Second is the problem of transition. If older workers must remain in the workforce longer, then society should take seriously the availability and conditions of work. Age discrimination is already illegal, but extending protections to an even older workforce will pose new challenges. Unemployment insurance for older workers, too, will require new provisions. Chapter 8 examines a range of options, including new options for phased retirement.

But, setting aside for the moment these important details, it is critical to see that the ideal of insuring against work disability helps distinguish life-cycle justice from competing notions of fairness sometimes posed in discussions of Social Security. For example, begin with the idea that public retirement benefits should provide equal lifetime benefits per individual. For instance, proposals to raise the Social Security retirement age sometimes draw fire for disadvantaging workers with shorter life expectancies.[3] That criticism imagines Social Security as a kind of retirement savings club, promising members that if they contribute $x, then they are assured of an equal payout $y. But work disability insurance does not and should not promise equal payout to every participant. It is, instead, a contingent entitlement, truly insurance. If a worker is fully capable of work until he dies at 80, then he should collect nothing and presumably will feel happy to have been spared the challenges of illness and disability. If a worker cannot work at 62 and lives to 80, he should collect 18 years of benefits, fairly enough.

The problem with unequal longevity, then, is not that it deprives some people of their fair share of Social Security's payout. The problem is, instead, that some people are burdened by cumulative disadvantage that unfairly reduces their life options.

Taking the opposite tack, and emphasizing gains in longevity for older people as a group, some analysts argue that the Social Security retirement age should rise. Eugene Steuerle points out that in 1940 and 1950, the average worker retired at 68. Given increases in longevity, an equivalent retirement age would be 76 today and 80 by 2070.[4] Steuerle's calculations usefully show the dramatic change in life span since the mid-twentieth century. But it is curious to assume that the goal of a just retirement policy should be to guarantee a retirement of a fixed length, regardless of social changes, including gains in health and ability.

The significance of longevity gains, then, is not that they necessarily authorize a change in the retirement age. Consistent with justice over the life cycle, the state should not attempt to guarantee a standard retirement to all. Instead, evidence about changing longevity, health, and ability is relevant to a prediction about the onset of work disability. Chapter 7 presents empirical evidence suggesting that although the average older person can work well into her 70s, inequality should be taken into account.

Linking public retirement benefits to work disability may, incidentally, return the Social Security system to solvency.[5] Chapter 7 discusses the likely budgetary impact of the specific reforms I suggest, and the savings are substantial. Still, accounting solvency is a by-product of a fair retirement policy, and not an independent rationale for reducing Social Security benefits. Along similar lines, a retirement policy that links benefits to work disability may well induce many older Americans to remain in the workforce longer, but, again, this is an acceptable by-product, not a criterion for success. That is, it would not be a fatal objection if the policies did not increase work—if older people continued to retire at present ages but simply funded their retirement on their own. Life-cycle justice frames that goal not as a matter of discouraging leisure or encouraging work, but instead as a matter of setting the scale of the public pension program at its appropriate level: sufficient to prevent destitution.

Cumulative Disadvantage and Retirement

I will turn to the principle of social reciprocity in a few pages, but first, consider how the principle of state recognition of cumulative disadvantage prompts attention to the problem of unequal age. A fair program of work disability insurance should not presume that the chances of work disability are equally distributed. Instead, a fair program should take notice of cumulative disadvantage, which burdens the same group with limited education, low wages, physical and stressful jobs, worse health, and greater rates of disability.

This principle, too, provides ready answers to the policy analyst's three questions. First, the rationale for state action is that a just society should pay due attention to the multiple burdens facing low earners, including illness, disability, low savings capacity, and family instability. As Chapter 5 discussed, the state should redress unfair inequalities throughout the life cycle, and not just at older ages or in cases of work disability. But a fair retirement policy offers an opportunity to mitigate these inequalities, a task that is important given the state's failure to resolve these inequalities and their cumulative effect on the same group of people.

Second, the goal should be to address the inequalities that pose particular disadvantage at retirement: unequal financial capability and earlier and more-prevalent disability. (As I have throughout this book, I will set aside the topic of health care, but poor health forms a part of cumulative disadvantage and should be addressed.) Third, these initiatives should redistribute from the advantaged, including older people as well as younger ones.

Concretely, a public retirement program should incorporate three elements. The program should ensure adequate income to disadvantaged workers who experience work disability and should expect only token contributions from them. At the same time, the public retirement program should enable—and not unduly penalize—early retirement for disadvantaged workers due to work disability. Penalties for early retirement should thus be progressive, permitting earlier retirement on more-favorable terms for those facing multiple disadvantages. And the program should rely on progressive taxation to reduce the financial burden on the least advantaged during their working lives.

Today's Social Security program unevenly fulfills this ideal. SSDI nominally provides decent benefits for those unable to work, but gaps in coverage and long waiting periods can impose hardship on low earners unable to work.[6] Social Security's lack of a minimum benefit, combined with regressive subsidies for private pensions, leaves many low earners in or near poverty even when they reach retirement age. The early retirement rules offer an early exit from the workforce that is especially valuable to the disadvantaged, but they pay the same hefty penalty (in percentage terms) as more-affluent workers for the ability to retire "early." And the payroll tax base is increasingly regressive as wage and income inequality grow.

The details of these reforms will require examination and elaboration in Chapters 7 and 8. But, even at this stage, it is clear that Social Security's progressive benefits formula alone is insufficient to meet the criteria for justice.[7] The progressive benefits formula, as Chapter 3 explains, provides a higher proportionate payout to lifetime low earners. This feature of Social Security certainly operates to mitigate inequality in lifetime earnings. But the progressive formula is limited in its ability to mitigate cumulative disadvantage. The formula, as we have seen, does not ensure a minimally decent living standard. Nor does it mitigate the hefty financial penalty on early retirement for disadvantaged workers. Nor does it address the increasingly regressive tax structure that funds Social Security.

One clear implication is that a fair retirement program should permit earlier participation on relatively favorable terms for the disadvantaged. In Chapter 7, I consider several options and settle on a system that would enable lifetime low earners to retire early with very little financial penalty. (Penalties on higher earners would be graduated and would be significant for the highest earners.)

The recognition of cumulative disadvantage thus provides a principled ground for addressing what I termed in the Introduction the "egalitarian problem." It is possible both to recognize the increased education, longevity, health, and ability of older workers as a group and to make secure provision for the least advantaged through minimum benefits and progressive retirement timing rules.

One likely objection to this approach is that the correlation between cumulative disadvantage and work disability is strong but imperfect.[8] Some robust people may be able to continue low-paid manual labor into their 70s. Some affluent people may suffer work disability in their early 60s, despite high levels of education and relatively pleasant working conditions. The result is that early retirement rules targeted for the disadvantaged may seem over- and underinclusive.

But that criticism mischaracterizes the foundation for an early retirement program targeted to those experiencing cumulative disadvantage. Low lifetime income is not simply a predictor measure of likely work disability. To be sure, early retirement on relatively favorable terms does have prudential value. It would ease the administrative burden of determining work disability, because such a high percentage of low earners experiences disability in their 60s.[9] But there is a principled rationale for early retirement as well: low lifetime earnings are a reliable marker of cumulative disadvantage, given current social conditions, which heap multiple obstacles in the paths of those with little education and low earning power.

The larger point is that it is entirely fair to offer retirement earlier and on better terms to those facing cumulative disadvantage. At the same time, it is also fair to expect higher earners either to work longer or to take extra steps to document their inability to work. Chapters 7 and 8 will outline a number of alternatives open to higher earners who experience early work disability. They can claim SSDI (on somewhat easier terms than today), they may be eligible for unemployment insurance if they experience long-term unemployment, they can claim early retirement benefits subject to a penalty, or (as Chapter 8 discusses) they can select a new phased retirement option.

The measurement of cumulative disadvantage is, of course, critical to the implementation of these principles and potentially difficult on the ground. One signal advantage is that the Social Security system already collects reliable data on lifetime income, which is the gold standard for measuring disadvantage. Lifetime low income is very difficult for individuals to game or to fake. By contrast, a typical income tax has only one year's information about a taxpayer's economic situation, and it is sometimes too easy for taxpayers to understate their income for a short time.

Still, there are open issues for administration, which Chapters 7 and 10 take up. One is the problem of the part-time worker who has a high wage rate but low total earnings: think of the part-time lawyer or doctor who deliberately chooses to work limited hours. Another is the balance to be struck between public provision via Social Security and subsidized private provision via a reformed 401(k) system.

Social Reciprocity and Justice in Transition

The principle of social reciprocity reinforces the progressive cast of a fair retirement policy. Chapters 2 and 4 discussed the significance of the fact that older Americans, as a group, have reaped gains in life span and in quality of life from public investments, but that gains have not been equally distributed. Social reciprocity calls for affluent older workers to contribute more than they now do to the collective, in order to share their gains with younger age groups and with less-affluent older ones.

Concretely, social reciprocity supports progressive taxation of income, which tends to fall on older and more-affluent individuals. Social reciprocity also provides a powerful reply to what I termed in the Introduction the "myth of purchased benefits." The myth probably contributed—and still contributes—to the popularity of the Social Security program, and it may foster a sense of security. But discussions of retirement policy in the United States are sometimes hampered by claims that workers own their existing state benefits because they have paid for them.

One reply emphasizes that Social Security contributions are not, in fact, set aside in individual accounts or linked to contributions.[10] The pay-as-you-go system uses current tax payments to fund current benefits, and the level of benefits reflects a congressional decision, not a payout of each worker's account. Indeed, some generations as a whole receive far more than they have paid in, while other generations will receive less.

The principle of social reciprocity suggests an additional reason to set aside the myth of purchased benefits. Older workers, as a group, have benefitted from social investments in education, health, disability accommodations, and antidiscrimination. The measure of their "payout" should thus not be limited to their Social Security checks. Nor should their obligation to contribute be exhausted by their Social Security payroll taxes.

Taking a larger view of justice over the life cycle, older Americans enjoying longer, healthier lives with unprecedented work options should not expect that they also have an inviolable right to claim public benefits at a fixed chronological age of 62 or 66. Instead, what they should expect is that society will make adequate provision—in light of changing social conditions—for work disability.

But this reply is not quite sufficient, because it ignores an unstated concern subsumed in the myth of purchased benefits. When older Americans protest, "Hands off my Social Security!"[11] they seem to be staking an owner-ship claim. But they are also expressing a worry about transition, and that worry is a serious one.

Transition is a familiar problem in public policy. Any change in law may shift wealth, defeat expectations, and upset plans. The problem of transition is especially salient for changes in retirement policy, and for good reason. Current retirees who have left work (or have left their primary careers) have a limited capacity to adjust to new rules. Even younger workers have a stake in the transition to a new retirement policy, because retirement planning takes place over the long term.

A principled approach to transition would take seriously the ideal of life-cycle justice in light of current labor market conditions. Older people who have already left work probably have very limited opportunities to return to it, and they likely have made long-term financial and personal plans in reli-ance on Social Security benefits under present rules. In effect, they are not able to work, and so they meet the (transitional version of the) work dis-ability test.

Workers in their 50s have greater flexibility and can fairly be expected to alter their plans, although they have less capacity to do so than younger workers. An appropriate transition policy would give as much notice as pos-sible of changing rules and would take into account age and labor market conditions in assessing work ability. Chapter 8 considers how a reformed unemployment insurance program and a new phased retirement option in Social Security might assist in the transition, helping those unable to find work or to continue full-time.

Antihumiliation and Mass Justice

The antihumiliation ideal informs the administration of justice. Ideally, the determination of work disability would take into account an individual's circumstances, including her education, abilities, and work opportunities. Individuals differ as they age; they differ in their capabilities and ability to accommodate; and they differ in their work options, which depend on training, geography, and demand for their skills. Thus, an English professor who is unable to hear might still be able to do much of her job, while a call-center operator would not. (Whether other feasible work options are open to the call-center operator would depend on her other capabilities.)

Remaining in the ideal world for one thought more, a work disability determination also should not be all or nothing: it is entirely reasonable to anticipate cases in which people can work part-time or take somewhat lesser jobs that add up to partial self-support. An English professor with mild heart disease, say, might be able to work a half-time schedule, an option that is quite common in academia, where courses can be parceled out in easily divisible fashion.

Moving from ideal to reality, though, individualized determinations of work disability prove far less appealing, because they contravene the antihumiliation principle. As Chapter 8 discusses in more detail, the present SSDI program presents a cautionary tale, for several reasons. Individualized determinations are resource-intensive: they are costly for the government and for claimants as well. But cost is not the only reason to take a skeptical view of individualized determinations. Complex legal processes tend to favor the well-off and the well advised and to disfavor the most vulnerable groups. Workers who can hire lawyers, doctors, and other experts can obtain the most favorable interpretation of the law and can pursue their remedies through appeals. Workers who lack the physical, mental, or financial resources to mount a concerted campaign may find themselves excluded—even when their situation is just as meritorious.

These are, of course, good reasons to reform SSDI. The challenge is that SSDI must determine work disability for (relatively) young workers. In this population, permanent disability is exceptional, not part of the expected life course, and many disabled people can ultimately return to work. For this reason, many SSDI reform proposals focus on keeping (younger) people off the disability rolls or returning them to the workforce.[12]

By contrast, the determination of work disability for older workers poses different, and less intractable, problems. When the question is whether people, say, ages 60 and above should be entitled to collect retirement benefits, the disability frame changes. For this group, work disability is far less rare than for younger workers. Just as important, work disability is part of a typical life course rather than a detour. Individuals and the government should face less pressure to send disability recipients back into the labor force, because they are likely at the end of their working careers.

Linking retirement to work disability, then, need not follow the SSDI model of individualized, heavily litigated determinations. A better approach would adopt mass or categorical determinations, with traditional SSDI and its individualized determinations as a backstop for outliers.

The antihumiliation ideal supports a mass justice approach, which stands in sharp contrast to individualized determinations. Lawyers often suppose that justice is best served by individualized determinations, which can take into account the nuances of personal situation. This legal individualism has deep grounding in liberal individualism and the ideal of due process before the law.

And yet, lawyers also know too well the limitations of legal institutions, which raise deep questions about the feasibility and desirability of individualized determinations. Too often, legal processes intended to elicit the nuances of individual situations fail to do so. Instead, they create expensive procedures that invite exploitation by the knowledgeable—but too often exclude the most vulnerable claimants.

For these reasons, we should recognize the potential for what we might think of as mass justice. Mass justice is the already-familiar mode of most social insurance programs: the idea is to use aggregate data to create programs that preserve privacy and dignity and yet do far better than present law in meeting the demands of equality. Categorical rules based on age, lifetime income, and job category permit the government to adopt administrative processes that are easily accessible to all, private, and without the inequities associated with complex, litigation-style determinations.

Social Security itself adopts just this kind of mass justice. The retirement program (technically, Old-Age Insurance) covers most retirees, permitting individuals to qualify based on information the government already possesses (age and earnings history). SSDI, along with Supplemental Security Income (SSI) and unemployment insurance, provide backstops for workers who become disabled or unemployed before old age.

But, as Chapter 3 documented, the present system is dysfunctionally over- and underinclusive because it relies too heavily on chronological age, despite growing inequality in the experience of old age. Chapters 7 and 8 will develop a multilayered approach. Using data on lifetime income and occupation, progressive retirement timing rules will permit workers facing cumulative disadvantage to claim Social Security earlier and on better terms. Workers facing disability but not yet able to claim Social Security will be able to take advantage of new unemployment insurance benefits for older

workers and a new phased retirement option for Social Security. By definition, workers not covered by these rules will be relatively affluent, and they
will always be able to claim benefits under traditional SSDI, with its individualized determinations.

It will take some time to work out the details of these new regimes in
Chapters 7 and 8. But, even at this stage, it is important to contrast mass
justice of this type with traditional means testing. Proposals for means
testing Social Security are familiar, if not terribly popular.[13] The rationale is
straightforward: means testing would reduce the budgetary cost of Social
Security while ensuring that truly poor older people are not left destitute.

But means testing runs counter to two important principles. First, means
testing does not recognize cumulative disadvantage. Means testing implies
that benefit levels should be set based on annual income *at retirement*. This
snapshot of retirement income, though, is an uncertain guide to lifetime
circumstances. A far better indicator of an individual's situation is lifetime
earnings. Accordingly, all the reforms I propose would use the gold standard
of lifetime earnings, and not present "snapshot" income, for determining
advantage and disadvantage.

Second, means testing of the traditional type runs afoul of the antihumiliation ideal. Conventional means testing requires a personal interview and
intrusive questions about the most intimate matters, including household
composition, spending habits, and past consumption choices. And standard
means testing casts the applicant in the position of supplicant. She must
travel to the welfare office, wait in line for the caseworker's attention, and
then conduct herself humbly while answering intrusive questions. This is
institutionalized humiliation.

The antihumiliation ideal captures what I called in the Introduction the
"universality problem," the worry that targeting Social Security to economic
circumstances in any way will undermine the appearance (and reality) of
universal provision. Chapters 7, 8, and 10 will show that the universality
problem can and should be managed. With due attention to the possibility
of humiliation, and by judicious use of mass justice approaches, Social
Security can incorporate attention to disadvantage without imposing a
humiliating means test.

Indeed, Social Security already makes use of just such an approach. The
progressive benefits formula is the model for many of the reforms I propose,
because it uses lifetime income and a progressive formula to make a quiet

adjustment in favor of the disadvantaged. We can, I will show, extend that approach to progressive retirement timing rules as well.

Looking Ahead

The remainder of this book will tackle the task of turning general principles into concrete policy options. I hasten to add that the policies I will propose are hardly set in stone. They represent one—and only one—attempt to tease out the implications of principle for Social Security form. There is surely wide room for disagreement about the practicalities of policy design, and any particular blueprint will provide only a foundation for further discussion.

Even so, I think it is well worth it to push into the world of policy design rather than remain at the level of general principle. Working out some of the details will help reveal pressure points and synergies that are not obvious at first glance. For instance, Chapter 7 wrestles with the problem of how to extend earlier retirement to workers facing cumulative disadvantage. As a thought experiment, I first analyze a system that would graduate the Social Security retirement age based on indicia of disadvantage (lifetime earnings, occupation, and education). But I conclude that this regime could be improved upon with a second proposal that would adopt a universal range of retirement ages—from 62 to 76—but would impose progressive retirement timing rules.

But changing the financial terms of early retirement, it turns out, is only one piece of the puzzle. Rules that would enable some to retire early but encourage others to work longer have ripple effects on a wide range of rules inside and outside Social Security. Chapter 8 tackles the task of reorienting a range of social programs to assist an older workforce, and Chapters 9 and 10 consider the implications of Social Security reform for families and for the tax system.

7

Progressive Retirement Timing

A GROWING CHORUS of policy analysts is calling for an increase in the Social Security retirement age.[1] Even staunch defenders of Social Security concede that the retirement age of 66 is too low, in light of the increasing longevity, improving health, and expanding work options of older Americans.[2] Still, the egalitarian problem has discouraged some progressives from joining the chorus: they worry that the only way to protect disadvantaged workers is to leave the early and full retirement ages as they are.[3]

But we can resolve the policy deadlock by reframing the question. Policy debates tend to focus on how high the retirement age should rise. But age, as we have seen, is a contingent category, with shifting physical and social meaning. Instead of beginning with chronological age, we can and should start with a deeper account of the objectives of retirement policy.

As we have seen, individuals ideally should claim public retirement benefits when they can no longer support themselves through work. And, ideally, the state should pay a basic income or other income supplement to disadvantaged workers throughout their lives. But, as Chapter 6 discussed, the gap between ideal and reality is large. Individualized determinations, as in the case of welfare or SSDI, too often humiliate the recipients and can exclude the disadvantaged. And the United States does not offer an adequate income supplement to the disadvantaged prior to retirement.[4]

This chapter takes up the challenge set by Chapter 6 to craft categorical rules that would accomplish two objectives: to provide a reasonable, yet dignified, means of linking public retirement benefits with work disability and to permit earlier retirement on secure terms for workers facing cumulative disadvantage. The key task, we shall see, is to find reliable indicia for identifying work disability and cumulative disadvantage. Armed with those indicators, progressive retirement timing rules can accomplish both objectives while preserving a high degree of universality and individual choice.

Work Disability and Age

Measuring the extent of work disability among older people is not particularly easy, because data are imperfect, criteria are inexact, and moral hazard may entice individuals to exaggerate (or fabricate) disability. To be sure, age is a strong predictor of work disability. About 16% of people aged 55–64 experience severe work disability—nearly twice as high as the roughly 9% rate for the 45–54 age group.[5] Data on SSDI benefits bear out the correlation between age and work disability: a man aged 50–64 is more than 5 times as likely to receive disability benefits as a man aged 20–49.[6] Today, the SSDI rules make limited use of age in determining work disability, and Chapter 8 discusses how that program might take further steps to accommodate age.

But, as we have seen, there is considerable diversity among older Americans in the experience of old age. Within the group of older people, work disability correlates with lifetime earnings and with occupation as well as health status. And, even within these categories, individual experience differs based on genetic factors, health habits, and luck.

Still, if we bear in mind that the goal is to craft practical rules aimed at mass justice rather than complete precision, data on work disability and age can help us take a cut at measuring the prevalence of work disability among older individuals. As a first cut, consider this question: *At what age can a majority of older people no longer work?* The goal is to help us take a first stab at crafting rules for linking retirement age more closely to work disability.

The answer, it turns out, is not age 65—or anything close to it. In fact, a majority of American workers could work into their late 70s or early 80s. Studies find that about 33% of adults in their late 60s have health problems or serious disabilities that cannot be accommodated successfully.[7] That figure rises to 43% for adults in their late 70s. By ages 80–84, 53% of adults report reduced activity levels, difficulty managing activities despite accommodations, or needing assistance from others.[8]

To be sure, we should interpret disability studies with caution. The concept of disability is slippery and can vary from study to study and program to program.[9] Compounding the measurement problem, most studies rely on self-reporting of disability, and there is no way to check for accuracy of self-reports or consistency across individuals. One person might report, say, walking with a cane as a serious disability, while another might feel that the cane represents a successful accommodation or even removes the "disability" entirely. Studies also differ in how questions for survey participants are framed.

Simple humanity counsels caution as well. Those of us who are older know that aging is felt not only in the onset of obvious disability but also in smaller ways. Older people may have less energy or may need more rest to perform with high energy. Older bodies may need more regular exercise to stay fit, or more sleep to regain energy, leaving less time for work, and so on.

Another important caveat is that work disability data focus on workers' abilities and not job market opportunities. Even though most people can probably work into their 80s, the present job market may not be well organized to accommodate them. Chapter 8 discusses the options for (and the importance of) reforms to combat age discrimination and anticipate unemployment among older workers. Still, at least as a transitional matter, a conservative approach seems wise.

The antihumiliation principle underscores the importance of taking a conservative approach to the disability data. When data show that a majority of older people are unable to work due to disability, it is reasonable enough for public retirement programs to grant the benefit of the doubt to the remainder. Of course, there is no hard-and-fast principle at stake here. We might look, instead, to the age when 60% can no longer work. Or 75%. But 50% represents a cautious first step.

Work Disability and Lifetime Income

Looking beyond chronological age, lifetime income and education level also strongly predict work disability, and they provide a means of identifying cumulative disadvantage.[10] For instance, in 2014, 25% of adults aged 65–74 reported some kind of disability, but the rate was 40% for those with less than a high school diploma and only 15% for those with a BA or more.[11] Rates of disease correlate with income level and education level as well. Heart disease, for example, falls as income rises.[12]

To be sure, these correlations too are imperfect. Liqun Liu and coauthors find that lifetime income is negatively related to disability, especially for men. Still, the relationship is complex, they conclude, and is influenced as well by "gender, race and family structure."[13] Some researchers notice that disability rates tend to converge at much older ages: disability varies negatively with income in the 50s and 60s but much less so by the mid-70s, primarily because of mortality differences: by the mid-70s, many sicker, lower-income people are no longer alive.[14]

It might be possible to refine the correlation between income and work disability further by adding information on job category, because physical occupations tend to produce higher rates of disability. Today, the Social Security Administration does not collect data on occupation type. A reporting system could be designed to capture the degree of physical labor and mental stress associated with particular jobs and informed by data on disability.

Still, as Chapter 6 discusses, the imperfect nature of the income and education correlations does not vitiate the mass justice approach, for reasons both principled and practical. At the level of principle, the state should be concerned about cumulative disadvantage—whether measured by lifetime income, by education level, or by occupation type—throughout the life span. For that reason, it is not unfair if retirement rules based on these indicia permit some disadvantaged workers to claim public benefits while still able to work. The state is, in effect, finally paying an income supplement that should (in an ideal society) have been paid all along.

By the same token, it is not unfair to offer different options to more-privileged individuals. A fair system should provide backstops to public retirement so that anyone experiencing work disability can claim public benefits at the appropriate time. But it is not unfair to expect these workers to go through the additional process necessary to gain access to these programs. Chapter 8 discusses three backstops of this kind: SSDI, unemployment insurance, and a new phased retirement option.

A Progressive Retirement Age?

Before we dive into the details of progressive retirement timing, consider a thought experiment. What if Social Security attempted to recognize the unequal experience of age by adopting graduated retirement ages for different individuals based on their lifetime income, education level, and job type? For reasons I explain next, I find this approach less appealing than the solution I propose, but the thought experiment is worthwhile, because it highlights problems of equality and administration.

Today, the Social Security retirement age is the same for everyone. The "full retirement age," or the age at which full benefits are paid, is currently 66, slated to rise to 67 by 2027.[15] Workers can claim benefits as early as age 62, but they pay a penalty of as much as 25% (30% by 2022) for early claiming, and the penalty is the same (in percentage terms) for everyone.[16] Workers who wait until 70 receive a bonus called the "delayed retirement credit."[17]

But the fixed retirement age ignores the unequal experience of age. A highly paid college professor, for instance, should probably be able to work until 76 or later, reflecting the low-stress nature of her job, the high levels of education needed to attain it, and the high levels of lifetime earnings. By contrast, a low-paid warehouse worker likely will need to retire much earlier in recognition of the multiple disadvantages she has faced: a physically and mentally stressful job, low wages, and little education.

We are so used to thinking of the retirement age as universal that it may seem odd to consider graduating retirement according to progressive criteria. One immediate objection—to which I will turn shortly—is the departure from universalism. But first, it is worth pausing to consider the advantages of a progressive retirement age.

First, as we have seen, the unequal experience of age is well documented. On average, affluent workers can work longer: they have better health, lower rates of disability, and generally more work options open to them. As Chapters 4 and 5 argued, these workers have reaped large gains in longevity and quality of life from social investments, and so it is fair to expect them either to stay in the workforce longer—or, if they want to retire, to fund early retirement themselves.

The option for self-funded early retirement is worth emphasizing. As we have seen, public retirement benefits should be a hedge against work disability, not a pool of money tapped for optional leisure. Affluent workers who want a long period of leisure in late middle age should save to fund early retirement, just as they would save for a vacation, a bigger house, or other consumption items.

By contrast, earlier retirement is not a luxury for many lower-earning workers. On average, lower earners reach their 60s with lower life expectancy, worse health, and higher rates of disability. These workers have often faced relatively harsh working conditions, including higher levels of physical and mental stress, greater unemployment, and less autonomy in the timing and content of their work. The work options open to them at older ages are often quite poor, involving—at best—the same type of high-stress, low-autonomy work.

Second, from an administrative perspective, the good news is that the existing Social Security system already has the data needed to begin to implement a graduated retirement age. Every employer files wage information with the Social Security Administration every year. The result is that the government has an accurate record of lifetime earnings for every worker (setting aside off-the-books work, to which I will return in the next section.)

Lifetime income is the gold standard for justice, because it portrays an accurate picture of an individual's long-term circumstances. Lifetime low earners typically are those who have worked consistently at low wages or who have faced job interruptions for child-rearing or unemployment.[18] Income taxation, by contrast, typically takes a one-year snapshot of income, and tax analysts worry (with justification) that snapshot income can badly over- or understate an individual's true circumstances. A high earner might report a temporarily low income due to a job transition or an extended vacation, but her wealth and other resources mean that she isn't really poor. The mirror-image case can occur too: low earners have volatile incomes and sometimes report temporarily higher incomes that do not accurately reflect their low wealth and (often) high levels of debt.

Mechanically, it would be straightforward to graduate the retirement age based on lifetime income (updated, as under current Social Security rules, to current dollars).[19] For instance, suppose that policy makers decided to raise the retirement age for the top 25% of earners to age 76. The rules could still permit the lowest 25% of earners to retire at 62. The middle 50% would face a graduated retirement schedule between those ages. (Table 1 illustrates the point.) A smooth schedule with no "cliffs" would be relatively easy to design.

Table 1. Linking retirement age to lifetime income

Lifetime income percentile	Full retirement age
Below 25th percentile	62
Between 25th and 75th percentile	Retirement age would gradually rise from 62 to 76 according to a sliding scale based on lifetime income level so that, for instance, a worker at the median income would have a full retirement age of 69.
At or above the 75th percentile	76

Still, a graduated retirement age has two major disadvantages. First, a variable retirement age alters the appearance of universality. Today, the ages of 62 and 67 mark rites of passage for entire generations. The Third Age has brought diversity in retirement patterns, but we all become Social Security claimants together. If the retirement age were income-linked, that social identity would be undermined. Now, some might think it would be a good thing if the political influence of the elderly as a bloc were weakened. Perhaps it would be salutary to reduce the power of the AARP. But, at the same time, there would be dignitarian costs: People receiving benefits in their early 60s would no longer be seen—as they are today—as simply making a choice about early retirement. Instead, they would demarcate themselves as disadvantaged.

Second, retirees could not plan the timing of their retirement with certainty until age 62, when lifetime earnings are computed. Most retirees would have a pretty good idea of their status, and the Social Security Administration could offer a planning calculator. A degree of uncertainty exists today in the benefits calculation: one cannot know one's monthly retirement benefit until age 62, when the calculation of "lifetime" earnings becomes fixed. A graduated retirement age would add a second dimension of uncertainty—timing as well as amount.

A graduated retirement age is worth considering.[20] Still, we can do better, preserving its advantages while addressing its disadvantages, by making use of a lever already in place in the Social Security system—the benefits formula.

Progressive Retirement Timing

The good news is that we can adjust the Social Security benefits formula to achieve much of the upside of a graduated retirement age, but without the downside. The basic idea is that the retirement age would remain universal, but the timing penalties for early retirement would be progressive, permitting lower earners to retire earlier than higher earners with less financial cost in doing so.

Today's benefits formula, recall, imposes the same percentage penalty for early retirement (and bonus for late retirement) on every worker. For workers born in or after 1960, for example, workers retiring at age 62 instead of 67 lose 30% of the full monthly benefit.[21] Thus, a low earner might receive $700 per month instead of $1,000, while a high earner might receive $1,750 instead of $2,500.

Delayed retirement results in bonuses, presently 8% per year for up to three years. Thus, a low or high earner born in 1960 or afterward who can wait to retire until age 70 will receive 124% of her full monthly benefit. Continuing the example, the low earner would receive $1,240 per month instead of $1,000, while the high earner would receive $3,100.[22]

These flat penalties and bonuses ignore the unequal experience of age. Lower earners often need to retire early, with the result that they collect reduced benefits for the long term.[23] High earners often can work longer by virtue of their advantaged position, and they are best positioned to reap the percentage boost in lifetime benefits.[24]

But once we recognize that the retirement timing penalties and bonuses apply equally to low and high earners, we have pinpointed the source of the policy dilemma that opened this chapter. Progressives have worried that raising the retirement age would unduly penalize low earners who must retire early. But that concern reflects the present, flat percentage penalties and bonuses for early and delayed retirement.

The solution, then, is to decouple the retirement timing rules for low and high earners. Earlier in this chapter, I showed that we could do so by varying the retirement age by income. But we can now see that we can achieve a similar progressive effect by *varying the penalties and bonuses for retirement timing based on income.*

For instance, suppose Social Security kept the early retirement age for all workers at 62 but raised the normal retirement age ("full retirement age" in Social Security parlance) to 76, with no further bonus ("delayed retirement credit") beyond that. We could easily craft rules that would permit low earners to collect nearly a full benefit at 62, while imposing a significant penalty on high earners who retire in their 60s.[25]

Table 2 and Figure 1 illustrate variable retirement timing rules based on lifetime income. The lowest earners could retire at 62 with a very modest penalty of 10%, while the highest earners would pay an 80% penalty for retiring so early.

The adoption of progressive retirement timing would require some adjustment of the Social Security benefits rules. Today, the benefit payable at the so-called full retirement age is, in effect, a reduced early retirement benefit (compared with what is available at age 70). The rules should be rationalized so that the amount payable at the full retirement age of 76 is, indeed, the maximum benefit, with no bonuses for late retirement thereafter.

Thus, Social Security would no longer distinguish among early, normal, and delayed retirement ages. Instead, there would be a spectrum of retirement timing options, with one focal point: the maximum benefit, claimable at age 76 and thereafter. The menu of benefits would be set (as under present law) at age 62, so each worker could see the schedule of benefits she would receive at any point. This presentation would not be substantively different from present law, with its penalties and bonuses, but the focal point would be the maximum benefit at age 76 and various penalties for earlier claiming. Along similar lines, the program should also eliminate the present earnings test, which reduces Social Security retirement benefits for workers who earn more than (roughly) \$16,000 per year between ages 62 and 67 and then restores lost benefits later on.[26]

As a transitional (and permanent) matter, it will be important to set benefits and percentages so that low earners retiring at 62 receive no less than today at every age. So, for instance, benefits for low earners should be adjusted so that they receive more than today for early retirement ages but no less than today at later retirement ages. For example, a low earner with an age-70 benefit of \$1,000 under present law might receive \$900 at age 62 under the new system, rising to \$1,000 at age 70 and \$1,042 at age 76. Benefits for high earners, by contrast, should be set so that they receive less at every age until age 76. Middle earners should be, well, somewhere in the middle.

Table 2.   An example of progressive retirement timing: Percentage of maximum Social Security benefit collected at different ages

Lifetime earnings	Age	Proposed benefit (percentage of maximum benefit)
Low	62	90
	70	96
	76	100
Medium	62	45
	70	76
	76	100
High	62	20
	70	66
	76	100

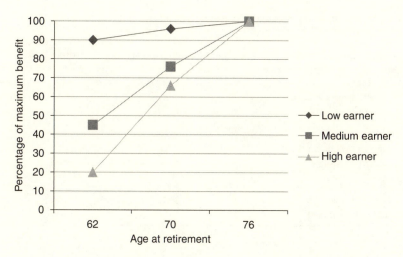

FIGURE I. An example of progressive retirement timing

Table 3 provides an illustration. The table adjusts benefits so that low earners receive at least as much at every age as under present law. Medium and high earners, in this example, receive the same maximum as under present law, and so they receive less at every age until age 76.

Of course, many additional variations are possible. The potential savings to Social Security of delayed retirement benefits are enormous; therefore, benefits for medium and high earners might be adjusted to increase benefits at later ages relative to current law. For example, perhaps at age 76 the medium earner in the example would receive $2,200 instead of $2,000. The key considerations should be to preserve the adequacy of benefits for low earners who must retire early and to implement a progressive system of timing penalties so that high earners receive very little until their 70s.

Importantly, a new progressive retirement timing formula could be designed to provide a gradual transition over time. Indeed, over the past two decades, the Social Security system has accomplished a similar (if less radical) change, raising the retirement age and altering penalties and bonuses for early and delayed retirement.[27] It might also be wise to index age 76 to trends in longevity, so that Social Security automatically captures future improvements in life span. By contrast, indexing the earliest retirement age (age 62) should be approached with caution, because the earliest age is most salient for lower-earning workers, who have not fully participated in longevity gains to this point.

Table 3.   A comparison of progressive retirement timing with current law

Lifetime earnings	Age	Current law	Progressive retirement timing
Low earner	62	565	938
(age-70 benefit is $1,000	70	1,000	1,000
under present law)	76	1,000	1,042
Medium	62	1,129	900
(age-70 benefit is $2,000	70	2,000	1,520
under present law)	76	2,000	2,000
High	62	1,976	700
(age-70 benefit is $3,500	70	3,500	2,310
under present law)	76	3,500	3,500

A system of progressive retirement timing should ideally distinguish between disadvantaged workers and voluntary part-time workers who are not disadvantaged. Even though lifetime income is superior to snapshot income as a measure of disadvantage, it still cannot capture the diversity of individual experience within income cohorts. For instance, a well-educated artist living on $25,000 per year has a different life than a Wal-Mart worker working 60 hours per week for that same annual income. Similarly, it would be unfair, in principle, to treat as "disadvantaged" a lawyer with inherited wealth who takes the occasional consulting gig and averages, over a lifetime, the same $25,000 in earnings.

Although these distinctions are sound in principle, it may not be worth the administrative effort involved to make them in practice. Especially today, with more and more women in the workforce, there are fewer well-educated people capable of high earnings who choose to stay at home. Still, a bit of extra precision might be worthwhile and not too expensive to attain. Hours worked, job type, and education level are all useful refinements. Of these, hours worked and job type might be most easily manipulated; a self-employed worker might exaggerate her hours or misclassify her job. But education level could be reportable to the IRS at, say, age 30 and again at age 50.

Work Incentives and Budget Impact

Increasing paid employment by older Americans is not a principal goal of these policies. Nor is delaying Social Security benefit claims a primary goal.

Still, at least for affluent workers, progressive retirement timing is likely to produce both effects as by-products of progressive reform. To see why, distinguish two stylized groups of people: low earners and high earners.

Begin with the perspective of a lifetime low earner confronted for the first time with the progressive retirement timing rules. Compared with current law, he can claim Social Security benefits at age 62 with far less financial sacrifice. Using the illustrative numbers from the prior section, the new regime would award him 90% of his maximum retirement benefit at age 62, compared with 57% under present law (in comparison with age 70). Financially, then, the payoff to early claiming is higher than it is today, and we could expect more low earners to claim benefits early. The increase in early claiming may not be large, however, because a quarter of low earners today have claimed SSDI benefits by age 62, and many others already claim Social Security retirement benefits at the earliest possible moment.[28]

The effects on work incentives for low earners are less certain, because three effects are likely to operate simultaneously. First, higher Social Security benefits at age 62 alter the relative price of early retirement, making it more attractive. Second, the removal of the earnings test (which appears to beneficiaries as a tax on earnings even though it increases Social Security payouts later) might improve the perceived payoff to continuing to work. Complicating matters is a third effect: the salience of the retirement age. Researchers have found that the present early retirement age of 62 may induce early benefits claiming. Progressive retirement timing rules would have an uncertain effect, because they would both retain the option of retiring at 62 and render salient the maximum benefit age of 76.

Now consider a lifelong high earner. Early claiming of Social Security benefits would be less attractive than under present law: instead of 57% of the maximum benefit, she would (continuing with the illustration introduced in Table 1) receive only 20%. In fact, retirement at every age would be less attractive for the high earner than under present law. At age 70, she would receive only 66% of the maximum (compared with the full maximum today). Financially, then, the high earner would be better off deferring her Social Security claim till age 76 if possible.

Work incentives for the high earner all operate in the direction of working more.[29] The reduction in the Social Security benefits in her 60s and early 70s would encourage her to remain at work. The salience of the new maximum benefit may be strong for high earners, who have the most at stake, particularly if the Social Security system is able to publicize the financial losses—emphasis on losses, which are especially salient in decision making[30]—in claiming early.

The adoption of progressive retirement timing might also change work incentives at younger ages. Like all progressive reforms, the new rules could discourage work for some low earners, because they cushion the financial impact of low earnings. At the same time, however, the new regime could create a positive work incentive for very low earners, because the payoff to working is higher: the new regime would increase Social Security benefits for workers who enter the workforce or who increase their work effort (on the books) sufficiently to qualify for Social Security.

Higher earners would face mixed incentives during their working years. On the one hand, a negative income effect (the prospect of lower Social Security benefits at earlier ages) could induce them to work (and save) more. On the other hand, the progressive nature of the rules could create some disincentive to work, because the consequences of lower earnings are less dire in the more progressive system. The use of lifetime income, rather than snapshot income, would minimize gaming: only high earners willing to live on less for a lifetime could take advantage of the new, progressive regime.

These work incentives would help determine the budgetary impact of progressive timing rules on Social Security outlays. The system would likely pay out more, sooner, to lower earners. Depending on the formula chosen, however, that increase in total benefits paid would likely be swamped by the lower and later payments to higher earners and by greater payroll-tax revenue from increases in work by high earners.

The Universality Problem, Revisited

Despite the advantages of progressive retirement timing, some may worry that additional progressivity could undermine Social Security's universalist appearance. For progressives, Social Security feels, at times, like a fragile achievement that could be shattered by ill-advised reform ideas.

I take the universality problem seriously, but we should be careful not to indulge in what lawyers call a "parade of horribles"—predictions that incorporate the worst outcome at each turn. It is certainly possible that the adoption of progressive retirement timing rules could reduce public support for Social Security, but much would depend on the skill—or lack of skill—with which politicians handle reform. A really inept politician could damage the program by immediately hiking the retirement age and by offering no new benefit (such as the phased retirement option I discuss in Chapter 8) to sweeten the package. And a politician completely unable to count votes could do even more damage by failing to engage younger voters (by highlighting, for instance, payroll-tax relief for that group). But a more likely scenario is that progressive reform would be phased in gradually and bundled carefully with a package of improvements likely to gain broad voter support.

Even so, it is worth thinking through how program design might affect the perception of progressive retirement timing. To begin, we should distinguish substance from perception. In substance, progressive retirement timing is nothing like a "means test." As Chapter 5 discusses, Social Security is distinct from welfare because it is paid only to workers based on their work history, it is administered with care for the dignity of recipients, and it bases benefits on a lifetime income measure. None of these features would change if progressive retirement timing rules were adopted.

So the danger is not that progressive retirement timing would enact a means test, but rather that people might *perceive* (or be persuaded by opponents of reform) that the new rules amount to a means test. Appearances, of course, depend on the perspective of the beholder, and we might distinguish two very different audiences for Social Security: experts and the public.

Experts, of course, will understand the ins and outs of the program, as they already do. They already know that Social Security incorporates a progressive benefits formula and that the myth of purchased benefits is indeed a myth. The progressive retirement timing rules, if adopted, would introduce an additional element of progressivity but without adopting anything like a conventional means test.

For their part, members of the public are unlikely to delve into the details of the progressive timing rules. The strongest evidence to support that prediction is the current Social Security system. People believe the myth of purchased benefits even though the benefits formula is highly progressive. Efforts to persuade the public that Social Security is a "bad deal" for the affluent and middle class have not succeeded; thus, for instance, the second Bush administration failed to persuade Congress or the public to support converting Social Security to a system of private accounts.[31]

At the same time, legislation in the past few decades introduced new progressive features of the Social Security and Medicare systems. In 1983 and again in 1993, Congress imposed income tax on a portion of the Social Security benefits received by higher-income beneficiaries.[32] In 2007, Congress altered the Medicare rules so that higher-income beneficiaries would pay a higher premium for Part B coverage.[33] Premiums for Medicare Part D (the prescription drug benefit enacted in 2003) are higher for high-income recipients and lower (or zero) for low-income participants.[34] These successes suggest that Congress could once again add a new progressive rule, provided that politicians handle the issue prudently and take care to bundle progressive changes with programs with broad appeal.

Good program design can help manage public perceptions. For example, there is no need for the Social Security system to publicize the kinds of charts I provided in this chapter, which highlight differences by income. Experts will want to consider such charts and debate the finer points of phase-in rates and cliffs, but each individual Social Security claimant need only see her own benefits schedule, which shows what she can receive at each retirement age. This kind of individualized presentation is exactly what Social Security uses now.

Pushing the matter one step further, Social Security could even incorporate the progressive retirement timing rules into the progressive benefits formula itself.[35] The appendix to this chapter illustrates how such a plan would work, but the basic idea is easily grasped: the revised benefits formula would add age as a factor and would calculate retirement benefits at any age between age 62 and 76, generating a smooth schedule of benefits for workers based on their lifetime earnings profile.

The Importance of Alternatives to Retirement

Today, with fixed penalties for retiring before age 70, a low earner who retires early sacrifices retirement security for the rest of her life. By contrast, progressive retirement timing would ensure that low earners who claim early receive 90% of their maximum benefit.

High earners who chose to claim benefits early would make a major and lasting financial sacrifice, but this scenario should be of less concern. First, very few high earners capable of working should claim early, given the level of financial sacrifice this decision would involve. Second, high earners not capable of working would have three alternatives open to them, as Chapter 8 describes: enhanced unemployment benefits, enhanced access to SSDI, and a new progressive retirement option.

It is time now to turn to the design of these important backstops to the public retirement system.

Appendix to Chapter 7:
Modifying the Progressive Benefits Formula

Today, the progressive benefits formula is invisible to the public and to Social Security recipients. The formula contains three income brackets but operates behind the scenes to determine each individual's benefit. Progressive retirement timing could be enacted as an adjustment—equally invisible—to the progressive benefits formula.

Today, the progressive benefits formula applies to average indexed monthly earnings (AIME), which represent lifetime income expressed as a monthly amount. For instance, the present benefits formula (in simplified form) looks something like this:

> Full retirement benefit equals . . .
> 90% of AIME up to $1,000
> plus
> 30% of AIME over $1,000 and up to $5,000
> plus
> 15% of AIME over $5,000

Applying this formula, a low earner with lifetime income (AIME) of $1,000 would receive a full retirement benefit of $900, whereas a high earner with AIME of $7,000 would receive $2,400 (which equals $900 plus $1,200 plus $300). Today, the actuarial reduction for early retirement (or credit for "delayed" retirement) then operates as a distinct and visible second step, which shows the worker how much less (or more) she can receive if she accelerates or delays benefits.

It is easy enough, however, to combine the two into a single step: that is, one formula could be used to calculate a schedule of benefits for each worker at each age. The maximum benefit (at age 76) will still be clear, and so will the worker's benefits if she chooses to retire at any given age. What will change is entirely behind the scenes: the actuarial reductions and bonuses will operate together within the three-bracket benefits formula. This approach would render the new progressive retirement timing rules as invisible as the present progressive benefits formula.

The new regime would create a similar benefits formula that would operate to determine the monthly benefit that would be paid (for life) if the claimant retires at any given age. For instance, at age 62, the formula might be:

95% of AIME up to $1,000

plus

20% of AIME over $1,000 and up to $5,000

plus

5% of AIME over $5,000

This formula would award benefits of $950 to the low-earner early retiree (with $1,000 of AIME) and $1,850 to the high-earner early retiree (with $7,000 of AIME).

The formula would change at every age, proceeding along a smooth phase-in schedule, up to age 76. For illustration, the formula might look (roughly) like this at age 70:

98% of AIME up to $1,000

plus

26% of AIME over $1,000 and up to $5,000

plus

11% of AIME over $5,000

The low earner would claim a lifetime benefit at age 70 of $980—a modest bump over the age 62 amount, by design! The high earner would receive $2,240—a significant jump over the age 62 amount but still shy of the $2,400 at age 76. This is probably too generous to the high earner, who should (on average) be able to stay in the workforce beyond 70, but the numbers could easily be adjusted to backload her benefit further.

Critically, these particular numbers are chosen just as an illustration. They incorporate a number of assumptions that might be reexamined. One assumption is that the age-76 benefit under the new rules would equal the full retirement (age 66 or 67) benefit today. That might or might not be the right benchmark. A more likely benchmark would be the age-70 "delayed" retirement amount today. Another assumption—for simplicity of presentation—is that retirees would be grouped into a small number of income brackets and that within each bracket, the age-related adjustment would be the same (in percentage terms). Thus, in this simple example, someone with AIME of $1,500 would face the same age-related *percentage* adjustments as someone earning $3,900. That bracket may be too wide, and a more sophisticated program could adopt a larger number of brackets, with each changing over time.

8

Insuring a Longer Working Life

THE PROGRESSIVE RETIREMENT timing rules proposed in Chapter 7 would give older workers reason to remain employed, but supporting those workers poses new challenges for public policy. Today, a majority of individuals in every educational category exit the workforce by age 67, and only a handful remain in the labor force by age 76.[1] To be sure, employment rates of older workers have risen since the 1980s, but absolute levels of work remain low.[2] Changing work behavior will likely require not only the "push" factor of reforms in Social Security but also the "pull" factor of more-attractive job options and employment protections.

Today, the law presumes that older Americans will not work much past their mid-60s. The Social Security retirement age, the rules on tax-favored pensions, and rules on disability and unemployment all incorporate some presumption that workers over 65 (or so) can retire. The result is that public programs assume that Social Security retirement benefits, including early retirement, will cushion unemployment, disability, and phased retirement for workers in their 60s and beyond. But progressive retirement timing would alter the landscape. Public policy should evolve to anticipate an older workforce and a number of workers in their late 60s and early 70s who cannot yet claim significant Social Security retirement benefits.

The same policy considerations accompany any proposal to raise the Social Security retirement age. Indeed, the task of insuring an older workforce against disability and unemployment would be even more pressing for such proposals: keep in mind that progressive retirement timing would offer nearly full retirement benefits to disadvantaged workers in their early 60s. That proposal has the major advantage of sidestepping disability and unemployment insurance for the population most likely to experience those conditions. Still, the discussion here will be useful even if one has not been persuaded by my case for progressive retirement timing.

In this chapter, I propose three backstops for older workers, corresponding to three obstacles to continued work. First, I propose to modify SSDI eligibility criteria for older workers, to make it easier to obtain benefits in case of work disability. Existing rules permit decision makers to take age into account along with education and retraining ability. Making more explicit the expectations for older workers should help ensure that older workers with disabilities have an exit from the workforce if needed. Once again, it is critical to keep in mind that the progressive retirement timing rules would permit disadvantaged workers to claim Social Security retirement benefits with minimal penalties in their early 60s. Thus, the target group for the new SSDI eligibility rules would be relatively affluent—a group better able to handle the procedural demands of the program and its waiting periods.

Second, and building on work by others, I propose extended unemployment benefits for older workers and other measures to address underlying causes of unemployment. This proposal reflects the fact that older workers typically have low unemployment rates but, when laid off, can take longer to find work. We shall see that the potential for moral hazard for older workers is somewhat less troubling than for younger workers, because an absence from the workforce is less damaging to long-term prospects.

Third, I offer a new proposal to incorporate into Social Security a phased retirement option in order to recognize and mirror Third Age patterns of gradual retirement. Although the details of any real-world program might vary, I illustrate the issues at stake with a proposal that would permit 3 years of half-benefits.

An overarching theme is that the causes of inability to work may seem distinct, but they are often intertwined. Unemployment, disability, and discrimination occupy different legal categories, but many unemployed people have disabilities of some type, and discrimination based on age, disability, and other attributes may foreclose work options. As a result, policies to address retirement, unemployment, disability, and discrimination must be understood as linked. When policy makers cut back on retirement benefits, it is predictable—not pathological—if claims for unemployment and disability increase.[3] The key is to craft policies that insure against true hardship while limiting moral hazard.

Disability and Older Workers

At first glance, it isn't obvious why SSDI would require reform to anticipate an older workforce. The rules, after all, define disability as the inability to engage in substantial gainful employment due to various medical conditions. All of those rules would seem to apply equally well in detecting work disability for both older and younger workers.

At a minimum, however, SSDI would need to alter its rules to take account of the enactment of progressive retirement timing, described in Chapter 7. Today, only workers under the full retirement age (66 today, rising to 67 soon) need SSDI, because older workers can claim retirement benefits rather than disability. Under the proposed progressive retirement timing rules, by contrast, the full retirement benefit would not be payable until age 76, so that workers under that age would have some need for disability benefits. Low earners would have the least need for disability insurance, because they could claim very nearly a full benefit at age 62. But mid- and higher earners in their 60s and 70s could find themselves unable to work due to disability but not yet entitled to anything close to a full Social Security retirement benefit.

A moment's reflection suggests that disability in older workers will differ from disability in the younger population in three ways. First, disability is relatively rare in a younger workforce. Men aged 50–64, for instance, are 5 times more likely to receive SSDI today than are men between 20 and 49.[4] And, as we have seen, disability rates continue to rise at even older ages: Vicki Freedman and her coauthors found that 33% of people report a disability that cannot be accommodated by ages 65–69, and that percentage rises to 37% for those ages 70–74.[5]

Second, for younger workers, it is comparatively reasonable for disability programs to assume that the labor market generates sufficient job options so that willing workers can find employment of some kind. (That assumption may be unfounded in a period of recession, of course, and it may be unfounded for the most disadvantaged workers; but still, it is relatively reasonable.) By contrast, job opportunities may be unevenly available to older workers. Some older workers may be able to continue seamlessly in lifelong careers. But other workers may be subject to pressure to retire, leaving them to search for new employment. Age discrimination may operate illegally but undetectably to disadvantage older applicants and jobholders. Later in this chapter, I suggest that the law should more vigorously enforce prohibitions on age discrimination, but—at least as a transition matter—the law should anticipate that older workers will face barriers to employment not encountered by younger workers.

Third, a critical consideration for policy design is that the problem of moral hazard is far more pressing for younger workers than for older ones. A worker at 30, say, has decades remaining in her working life, which ideally should not be spent on disability if it is unnecessary. A younger worker on disability may fail to establish a work history and thus undermine her capacity to be self-supporting for the long term. Society loses out if disability benefits discourage younger workers from developing their productive capacity, even if their decisions are narrowly rational. For this reason, moral hazard and the rules that "trap" disability recipients on the SSDI rolls have been a preoccupation of traditional SSDI policy.[6]

By contrast, moral hazard for older workers should be of less concern. Workers past age 62 have already established a work history (or not), and their remaining working lives are shorter. Moral hazard still can arise, however, if older workers able to work seek disability benefits for the purpose of retiring prematurely. To prevent an end run around the retirement timing rules, the SSDI system should continue to take steps to forestall moral hazard even for this group. Still, the social stakes on withdrawal from the workforce are lower for older workers.

Today, the SSDI system counters moral hazard by limiting access to benefits in two ways. First is the demanding standard for disability. The system insures workers only against total disability—that is, the inability to work at any job in the national economy. In principle, the program does not take into account whether an applicant could feasibly retrain for new work. Nor does it take into account the business cycle, the state of the local economy, or the availability of suitable jobs.[7]

Second is a set of procedural hurdles to applying for and claiming benefits. The SSDI determination process requires a detailed application, expert input, and, in many cases, a lengthy set of appeals. Even successful applicants must wait for 6 months before receiving benefits, and only a quarter of applicants succeed after their first try.[8] The appeals process, which raises the total success rate to 40%, typically takes more than an additional year and a half.[9] Applicants essentially must not work while their case is pending, because work for more than minimal pay constitutes evidence (obviously enough) of ability to work.

The well-known result is that SSDI denies disability benefits to many workers with real disabilities. For instance, Gordon Mermin and Eugene Steuerle find that less than half of workers aged 51–64 receive disability benefits even when they have significant disabilities.[10]

Present rules do authorize SSDI decision makers to take age into account in combination with education and work experience.[11] The rules provide that workers 55 and over who also have limited skills and education will be considered to have a limited ability to retrain for new work.[12]

Still, some have made the productive suggestion that the SSDI eligibility criteria should be further eased for older workers.[13] The Simpson-Bowles Commission, for example, recommended that the Social Security Administration should design a "hardship exemption" for older workers unable to work.[14] A number of OECD countries already have age-related rules that ease disability qualification for older workers, and so models exist that the United States might adapt.[15]

Disability standards for older workers should not pathologize old age but should take notice of research on the effects of age on capabilities. Studies suggest that older workers can, overall, be just as productive as younger ones, but their skills and capacities are not identical. On average, older workers tend to have greater knowledge and experience but somewhat reduced learning speed.[16] These differences are not universal and should not be exaggerated, and yet they are relevant to a disability determination for an older worker. SSDI rules should recognize that older workers may not match the speed of learning of younger workers, and so it may not be feasible for an individual to retrain for any new job in the economy. Relaxed rules could also take note of unemployment in the local economy and in the applicant's field of work and could provide a partial payout in cases of partial disability.[17]

In addition, the SSDI rules might adopt a streamlined procedure for older claimants. A simplified and quicker procedure would implement the antihumiliation principle and would acknowledge the greater prevalence of disability at older ages and the shorter remaining work lives of older workers.

Concretely, the rules might offer a shorter waiting period—say, 3 months instead of 6. And continuing disability reviews, normally every 2–5 years, might be less frequent for older disability recipients.

Along these lines, David Stapleton suggests that workers over 55 might be entitled to special protections in case of adverse circumstances, including the onset of lasting health problems or disabilities that limit work, adverse changes in employment options, and substantial increases in care needs of a spouse or dependents. Older people whose earning prospects diminished due to such events could enter a program designed to provide employment support for the transition to retirement. Benefits would include streamlined and expedited SSDI determinations. Beyond that, the program could offer a wage subsidy to boost earnings and permit part-time work, could subsidize dependent care, and could offer a Medicare or Medicaid buy-in to reduce health insurance costs. Stapleton estimates that, depending on the eligibility criteria, such a program would serve 150,000 to 300,000 new claimants between ages 55 and 62 each year and would cost roughly 5 to 10 billion dollars per year.[18]

Another proposal would target workers in physically demanding jobs, who are especially likely to encounter physical disability in the years just before retirement. Eric Klieber suggests that SSDI could add a new, second-tier disability benefit that would protect a worker unable to perform the "essential duties of his or her occupation."[19] This kind of proposal would, de facto, target workers in physical jobs: for instance, a UPS driver in his early 60s who could no longer do the heavy lifting required by his job could receive SSDI benefits.

Anticipating Moral Hazard

In recent years, the SSDI program has grown in size and expense. Between 1989 and 2009, David Autor points out, the proportion of American adults on SSDI doubled from 2.3% to 4.6%.[20] This phenomenon has triggered concern among some policy makers that the program is paying benefits to workers who are not truly disabled.[21] But it is not clear that moral hazard is the underlying cause of the program's expansion. Economists agree that population growth, the entry of women into the workforce, and the aging of the Baby Boom have all contributed.[22] There is more debate on the relative importance of changing legal standards for disability and the role of those standards in awarding an increasing share of benefits to claimants with mental and musculoskeletal disorders.[23]

Delayed retirement, combined with rules that readily recognize disability in older workers would, predictably, increase the SSDI disability rolls still further. Some increase in the disability rolls would inevitably accompany any increase in the retirement age.[24] The Simpson-Bowles Commission, as we have seen, correctly anticipated a greater demand for disability benefits when proposing an increase in the retirement age.

But at this point, two key advantages of the progressive retirement timing rules (outlined in Chapter 7) come to the fore. First, the progressive retirement timing rules would put less pressure on the SSDI system than an across-the-board increase in the retirement age. A rise in the retirement age would leave many lower earners in need of disability benefits, while the progressive retirement timing rules would ensure lower earners immediate access to retirement benefits, leaving them secure without recourse to SSDI.

Second, the proposed progressive retirement timing rules ensure that older workers in need of disability benefits will—in sharp contrast with today—be relatively well-off. In contrast with an across-the-board increase in the retirement age, the progressive retirement rules would ensure that older workers are relatively affluent and thus have relatively good work options, as well as the resources to navigate a proof-based system. Middle- and upper-class workers would have better access to doctors, disability advocates, and lawyers to help prove their cases.

It is also wise to keep in mind that the adoption of progressive retirement timing rules would likely produce budgetary savings in Social Security retirement benefits, which would offset the increase in disability benefits.

None of this implies that SSDI should dispense with all safeguards against moral hazard among older workers. SSDI should continue to offer an exit from work only for those unable to work, and it should not open a back door to early (healthy) retirement. Past policy proposals intended to limit moral hazard in SSDI have focused on the problem of keeping younger people at work and off the disability rolls. Reforms might include tax changes to discourage employers from firing people with disabilities[25] and expanded in-work supports including rehabilitation and workplace accommodation.[26]

These proposals would help older workers as well as younger ones and should be part of the discussion as policy makers anticipate the disability needs of an older workforce. But disability benefits should not be the only backstop for older workers unable to work full-time. The task of disability, as Matthew Diller points out, is to evaluate medical conditions and relate them to social facts about work.[27] A complementary approach focuses on the availability of work and the responsibilities of older workers in seeking new work. This is the task of the unemployment insurance system, to which I now turn.

Unemployment and Older Workers

Older workers, like younger ones, experience unemployment, but typical patterns of work are somewhat different. To begin with, older people are less likely to work than younger ones. In 2012, only 41% of individuals aged 55 and older were in the labor force, compared with 81% of those aged 25 to 54. And work participation drops sharply at even older ages: only 19% of individuals 65 and over were in the labor force in 2012, and only 11% of those 75 and older.[28]

Still, as Chapter 2 noted, there has been a substantial upward trend in work at older ages. In 1992, just 30% of the over-55s were in the labor force, compared with 41% in 2012. The data show the same upward trend for workers over 65 and over 75.[29]

Older people who are in the workforce are less likely than younger workers to be (involuntarily) unemployed. In 2013, for instance, the unemployment rate was 5.4% for those age 65 and over, compared with 6.3% for workers aged 25 to 54. Unemployment in 2013 was highest for young workers: the 20-to-24-year-olds, for example, had a nearly 13% unemployment rate.[30]

But older workers who lose their jobs and wish to continue working often experience longer spells of unemployment. The Congressional Budget Office reports that reemployment rates for men age 62 or older are about half those for men between 25 and 34, and more older men leave the labor force after they lose their jobs.[31] Analysts debate the reasons for the difference. Age discrimination may play a role, but the availability of retirement benefits (public and private) also facilitates exit from the workforce.[32]

One cautionary note is that the present pool of older workers may not reflect the composition or ambitions of the older workforce after the enactment of progressive retirement timing (or an increase in the Social Security retirement age). Improvements in the adequacy of Social Security benefits and private pensions (as discussed later) might lead lower earners to leave the workforce, thus exiting the pool of the unemployed. Middle-class and affluent earners, by contrast, would be more likely to remain in the workforce rather than retire early. Indeed, many middle- and especially upper-income workers would adopt a new time horizon, remaining in the workforce into their 70s instead of retiring or cutting back work in their 60s. Thus, it is difficult to predict the overall employment experience of older workers as a group.

Still, whatever the aggregate unemployment rate, it seems likely that the pattern of longer spells of unemployment for older workers will hold, because of age discrimination, difficulties in retraining (actual or perceived), and a relatively short remaining career span before retirement. That is, some older workers may not seek work as vigorously when they have a short time before they can claim adequate retirement benefits.

Policy makers might consider three approaches to anticipate an increase in the older workforce and potential causes of unemployment. The first, and most obvious, policy tool is the unemployment insurance system. It would be possible to offer extended unemployment benefits to older workers, in light of their longer (average) unemployment spells and the somewhat lower stakes for moral hazard, as discussed earlier. At the limit, extended unemployment benefits begin to shade into conditional early retirement for the unemployed, an approach with international precedents.[33]

At the same time, extended unemployment benefits for older workers would have the added advantage of taking pressure off the SSDI program. The unemployed often turn to disability benefits when work is scarce, as in the 2008 recession.[34] Expanding UI benefits for older workers would give them a longer grace period to seek work before turning to disability.

Moral hazard is, of course, a traditional concern of unemployment insurance (UI) design, but just as in the case of disability insurance, moral hazard is somewhat less problematic for the older workforce. First, the progressive retirement timing rules would likely pull many lower earners, who are most likely to be unemployed, out of the unemployment pool and into full retirement. Second, unemployed older workers—unlike unemployed young workers—already have an established work history and are not in danger of missing their footing in the labor market entirely.

And, just as in the case of disability insurance, the UI program's existing features would combat moral hazard. UI benefits have a relatively low replacement rate, and they are available only to those fired or laid off, not to those who voluntarily quit. Further, the same innovations that could limit moral hazard for older workers in SSDI would operate for UI as well.

A second policy approach to unemployment among older workers would address age discrimination. Despite the federal law prohibiting age discrimination in employment, David Neumark and coauthors find that age discrimination remains prevalent.[35] They point out that older workers often leave their career jobs and take bridge jobs, so that fighting age discrimination in hiring is as important as combatting it in the more traditional arena of discharges. Still, they point out, hiring cases are legally difficult, because damages are smaller and cases are hard to prove.

A key problem is that age discrimination protections themselves may, perversely, discourage hiring if employers perceive that it is too difficult to fire older workers who do not work out.[36] Given this complicating factor, the net effects of age discrimination legislation remain uncertain. Some economists find that the Age Discrimination in Employment Act has promoted employment among older adults.[37] Others point out the limited effectiveness of rights enforcement[38] and debate possible perverse effects on employment.[39] The Americans with Disabilities Act provides another avenue for protecting employment for older workers with disabilities, but economists have also debated whether that legislation has reduced employment.[40]

One promising approach to reducing age discrimination against older workers would, perhaps counterintuitively, limit legal protections against age discrimination. The problem arises because it is often rational for employers to prefer younger workers, even when they don't hold animus or negative stereotypes about older ones. In purely economic terms, older workers tend to be relatively expensive, because they have higher wages and because their health care costs are (on average) greater. It isn't irrational for an employer to prefer a younger worker who costs (say) $20 per hour and whose health insurance is cheap to an older worker who has earned $35 per hour and whose health insurance is expensive. The fear of an age discrimination lawsuit may, in itself, deter some firms from taking a chance in hiring an older worker.

Michael Harper has suggested that the law could address hiring discrimination by permitting employers to hire older workers on a probationary basis, so that if they do not work out, they can be let go without fear of a discrimination suit. Another idea, along similar lines, is to permit workers to waive age discrimination protection for some period (or altogether).[41]

Thinking more broadly, additional reforms could directly reduce the cost of hiring (and keeping) older workers. For instance, a number of economists have noted that high health care costs for older workers can discourage employers from hiring. Making Medicare the primary (rather than the secondary) payor for workers aged 65 and over would relieve employers from bearing the extra health care costs.[42] Repealing the Social Security retirement earnings test, which is often misperceived as a permanent tax on earnings, might also remove a work disincentive from workers' perspective.[43] Several economists have also noted that the Social Security payroll tax on older workers discourages work, and that many long-career workers receive little or no boost in Social Security benefits for marginal payroll taxes paid. Reducing the payroll tax on older workers could remove the disincentive.[44]

A third, and complementary, approach to unemployment, to which I now turn, is the introduction of phased retirement in Social Security.

Phased Retirement and Social Security

SSDI and unemployment insurance represent targeted approaches to the problems of disability and unemployment. Both are traditional forms of social insurance, and both can be adapted to the needs of older workers. Still, both have well-known limitations. The total disability standard and the procedural requirements of SSDI exclude some people unable to support themselves through work. Unemployment insurance provides only modest income replacement for a limited period. Critically, beneficiaries cannot work while collecting either SSDI or UI: neither program is designed to support those who can work to some degree but cannot work full-time. This gap is particularly problematic for older workers who, as we have seen, tend to exit the workforce gradually.

A complementary approach, in the spirit of mass justice, would create a universal entitlement directed at older workers and intended to facilitate part-time work and a gradual exit from the workforce. To that end, I propose that Social Security should incorporate a phased retirement benefit that would permit retirees to receive half their retirement benefit for 3 years in advance of age 76 without financial penalty.

Phased retirement is a growing trend in the private sector. The term has variable meanings but typically connotes a gradual retirement arrangement in which older workers cut back their working hours and receive an income supplement to make up for lost wages.

Yale University, for instance, offers faculty who are between ages 65 and 70 the opportunity to work half-time at gradually reduced pay. Retirees who opt for phased retirement receive a full salary their first year, 75% in the second year, and 50% in the third year. The Yale plan incorporates both a phased retirement option and an incentive for faculty to retire by age 72: it requires faculty to agree to retire permanently at the end of the 3-year phased period.[45] To take another example, the federal government is poised to adopt a phased retirement plan that will permit retirement-eligible workers to draw half-pensions while working part-time.[46]

Phased retirement serves a number of purposes for employers and for workers. For employers (such as Yale) seeking to reduce their senior workforce, phased retirement is a lure to older workers to exit in a predictable way. Phased retirement is also useful for employers seeking to retain older workers, however: a part-time schedule with an income supplement may keep some senior workers in their jobs longer. The phased retirement program for federal workers is intended, in part, to encourage senior workers to remain long enough to train their successors.[47]

For workers, phased retirement mirrors the patterns of the Third Age described in Chapter 2. Workers can make a planned and gradual exit from their career jobs. Phased retirement payments prevent a precipitous income loss, giving them time to try new employment or begin education, leisure, or charity activities.

Other countries have accommodated phased retirement and other flexible work options for older workers. A number of EU countries have introduced some form of phased retirement that permits workers to reduce working hours and receive income support to make up for reduced pay. Phased retirement has been introduced by law or by collective bargaining or by a combination of both. Some countries have designed phased retirement to discourage early retirement in full; others have phased retirement that encourages workers to remain in the workforce in some way past the full retirement age.[48]

In the United States, many private employers have introduced phased retirement, and removing legal barriers to phased retirement could enable more employers to do so.[49] The enactment of legal mandates for phased retirement is probably an inferior approach, however. For one thing, private pension coverage in the United States is extremely uneven, as Chapter 3 notes, and so any phased retirement scheme relying on private-pension payouts would be unavailable to many workers. For another, the cumulation of employer mandates (including health insurance) may have perverse effects on the employment and hiring of older workers; it would be unwise to add a new and potentially costly mandate that would raise the cost of employing older workers.

Phased retirement could be readily adapted to the Social Security context. The idea would be to provide income support that would ease the transition to a bridge job or out of the workforce. Payments should not, however, be conditioned on part-time work; they should be available unconditionally, to minimize administrative cost.

It is important to note that the proposal for phased retirement in Social Security is entirely prudential and not required as a matter of principle. The goal is to fill the gaps left by SSDI and UI and to do so in a way consistent with the antihumiliation principle. But phased retirement does represent a compromise: it would fit uneasily with the principle of insuring work disability, and it would fund healthy retirement or other Third Age choices for some workers.

Still, on purely prudential grounds, the case for some kind of phased retirement option is appealing. Phased retirement would be especially valuable during a transition period, because it would soften the full retirement age of 76 to a partial retirement age of 73. Phased retirement would raise the budgetary cost of Social Security relative to a program without it—but it would relieve pressure (and reduce costs) in the SSDI and UI programs.

9

Families and Retirement

JUST AS THE PAST CENTURY has witnessed the transformation of old age in America, so have the past 50 years marked a revolution in American family life. The influx of women into the workforce, the decline in marriage, and the rise of single parenthood have altered the meaning of family and the texture of family life. At the same time, however, inequality in family life has widened. Affluent men often marry affluent career women, and (on average) they rear children together in lasting marriages. Poor Americans marry rarely and often bear and rear children outside marriage. And the middle class is somewhere in the middle, with rising rates of nonmarriage and single parenthood.

The result is that Social Security's family provisions are badly outdated. In the mid-twentieth century, most families of all classes followed a traditional pattern of lifelong marriage, traditional gender roles, and child-rearing within marriage. For retirees from that generation, the major risks of family life were the retirement, death, or early disability of the breadwinner. And, as Chapter 3 documents, Social Security responded to those risks. Spousal benefits and survivors' benefits ensured that a breadwinner's dependents— his wife and children—would not be left destitute.

Today, however, the spousal benefit is less and less functional. More and more, it rewards privileged families at the expense of ordinary and less-privileged ones. In this chapter, I argue that cultural change—the changing meaning of "normal" in America—requires a rethinking of what family security means in the twenty-first century. I show that reorienting Social

Security family benefits toward children and away from spouses would best serve the core functions of social insurance against work disability.

The Increasing Arbitrariness of the Spousal Benefit

Providing for family security has been a core mission of the Social Security system. So-called derivative benefits were enacted to provide financial security for wives and children who depended on the breadwinner's paycheck. In 1939, the architects of Social Security estimated that 80% of retirees were husbands in single-earner couples.[1] The homogeneity of family life in the mid-twentieth century was a gift to Social Security's designers, who could craft universal rules that would meet the needs of the vast majority of families.

These family rules still exist today. Retirement-age spouses can claim a benefit based on the retired worker's earnings history: the spousal benefit is 50% of the worker's benefit, so that a married couple receives 150% of the amount the worker alone would receive. A divorced spouse can claim his (or her) own spousal benefit at retirement age if the marriage lasted at least 10 years. A spouse under the retirement age can claim a spousal benefit if the worker retires, becomes disabled, or dies, provided she (or he) has minor children living at home. Children under age 18 (or children who experience disability during childhood) are entitled to benefits as well.

For instance, suppose that a worker retires at the full retirement age with a Social Security benefit of $2,000 per month. His wife, if she has also reached full retirement age, will receive $1,000, whether or not she has ever worked for pay. If she has worked, she will claim the larger of her own earned benefit and the spousal benefit. A divorced wife at full retirement age would receive the same $1,000 (or her own earned benefit if greater), provided the marriage lasted at least 10 years and she has not remarried. If the worker dies, the surviving wife will receive the full $2,000 worker's benefit (and will no longer receive the spousal benefit).[2]

These examples begin to hint at the arbitrariness now built into the Social Security spousal benefit. The single-earner couple receives, in effect, a free 50% increase in Social Security benefits. A two-earner couple pays more in taxes (on the wife's earnings) but may receive no additional Social Security benefit if the wife, in the end, claims only the spousal benefit (because her earnings are low relative to her spouse's). Even if the two-earner couple collects more than $3,000 in the end, they will have paid proportionally more in payroll taxes for the marginal benefit.

As Gene Steuerle points out, the arbitrariness of the spousal benefit does not end there. A single parent, never married, receives no spousal benefit at all. A spouse married less than 10 years, similarly, receives no spousal benefit—and more and more marriages fall short of the 10-year mark.[3] In addition, the many Americans who divorce and remarry will find that their Social Security benefits bounce up and down based not only on their own earnings record, but on those of their former and present spouses as well.[4]

The Supreme Court's *Windsor* decision in 2013 brought a measure of parity to the spousal benefit rules: same-sex married couples can now claim spousal benefits.[5] But the Social Security system's focus on formal marriage and the assumption that wives do not work outside the home are badly out-dated. Rates of cohabitation are growing, and the rate of single parenthood has skyrocketed. By 2009, 70% of married women worked outside the home, and 77% of married mothers of children aged 6–17 did so.[6] Among all women with children, 71% worked in 2011, compared with 47% as recently as 1975.[7]

Equally out-of-date are the assumptions that women often work part-time and that wives earn less than their husbands. The vast majority (74%) of adult female workers worked full-time in 2011, for instance,[8] and 38% of working wives in 2010 earned more than their husbands.[9]

The result is that the spousal benefit is increasingly arbitrary when measured against the social reality of the family. In 1969, 54.2% of couples had a working wife, whereas by 1998, 82.2% did.[10] Today, the most vulnerable families, economically speaking, are single-parent families, especially single-mother families because of women's generally lower earnings. Single parents face the day-to-day stress of rearing children alone and can encounter job interruptions when children are ill, have special needs, or have ordinary needs that are incompatible with the demands of employment. In 2011, for example, the poverty rate for American families with children was 18%, but for single-mother families it was 42%.[11]

By contrast, married couples tend to be relatively well-off. In 2012, for example, the median income of married couples was $76,000, the highest (by far) for any family type.[12] As a group, better-educated and higher-income individuals marry later than those in lower socioeconomic classes; over a lifetime, however, they marry at higher rates.[13] Divorce rates also correlate with class: while 46% of marriages end in divorce (or permanent separation) within 10 years among high school dropouts and 37% end within 10 years for high school graduates, only 16% end in that period for those with a BA or more.[14]

Data from the Census Bureau illustrate the close association of cohabitation with lower-income groups and marriage with higher-income status. In 2011, more than half of unmarried-couple households had incomes at or below the 40th percentile of the income distribution. In neat symmetry, more than half of married couples had incomes at or above the 60th income percentile, and nearly one-third had incomes at or above the 80th percentile.[15]

Economists and sociologists debate whether marriage makes couples better-off or if better-off couples are more likely to marry.[16] But in either case, marriage—and especially lasting marriage—is increasingly the province of the affluent. The result is that spousal benefits are growing regressive in their distribution.[17]

Rethinking the Principles of Family Assistance in Social Security

The changes in family life require a principled rethinking of the role of family benefits in Social Security. Bracketing current law for a moment, the question is how, if at all, social insurance should recognize family ties. It turns out that the principles developed in Chapters 4 and 5 suggest a reorientation of family benefits away from formal marriage and toward the protection of children, particularly children with disadvantaged parents.

The principle of life-cycle justice, as we saw in Chapter 4, justifies social insurance mandates so that the inability to work does not leave workers destitute. Today, men and women both engage in lifelong work. Society is no longer organized to deny women the ability to support themselves or to relegate them to a subordinate role. This is not to say that gender discrimination has been eliminated—just that the sweeping changes in the organization of family life have largely eliminated the institutionalized role of dependent wife.

There are, to be sure, a minority of families that still pursue traditional gender roles. Indeed, some have reverse-traditional roles, with a stay-at-home father. These stay-at-home parents could find themselves severely disadvantaged if their spouse becomes unable to work or dies. It might seem, then, that the negative-spillover rationale would support the continuance of spousal benefits, at least for these families.

But there is a key difference between present-day stay-at-home parents and mid-twentieth-century wives. In the mid-twentieth century, society was organized around the breadwinner husband and at-home wife, and gender was determinative. Employers expected men to conform to work roles incompatible with child-rearing, and many employers would not hire women, especially married women. Gender discrimination in employment was legal, explicit, and widespread. The distinction, then, is that the dependency of wives was built into the social structure in the mid-twentieth century.

Today, by contrast, the dependent wife (or husband) is no longer an involuntary and institutionalized role. The choice typically reflects either affluence (think of the high-earning couple in which one spouse "takes time off" because the demands of a high-level job are too great)[18] or religious commitment. In either case, the context is transformed: in the mid-twentieth century, the death of a husband would typically leave a wife without education, without job experience, facing widespread prejudice in the job market, and with few childcare options. Today, by contrast, a typical at-home parent has worked for some time, often is educated, and, should the need arise to work, will face a very different labor market and childcare options.

Children, however, do merit special consideration under the principle of life-cycle justice. Equal opportunity marks childhood as a period of special concern for a just state and, as Chapter 4 discussed, the state should take care to ensure minimally decent economic conditions for all children. It follows, then, that the death, disability, or retirement of a parent should trigger special attention by the state. But it should be children—and not formally married spouses—to whom assistance is targeted.

The recognition of cumulative disadvantage adds to these directives. Low-earning single parents are arguably the most disadvantaged group in our society. Their financial situation and the stress of solo child-rearing put them—and their children—at risk in multiple ways.

Putting these principles together, the social insurance system should insure individual workers against work disability. Family benefits for non-workers should focus on workers' children and on the children of single parents and low-earning parents in particular. The antihumiliation principle suggests that aid should be, as far as possible, distributed in a dignified way.

One might argue—and Jerry Mashaw and Michael Graetz have done so eloquently—that the United States should ensure the economic well-being of families with children even before death or disability strike.[19] A respectable case might also be made for a children's allowance, a basic income payable to children, or other child-centered reforms.[20]

Even short of more sweeping reforms, however, these principles have strong implications for the reform of derivative benefits.

Reforming Social Security Derivative Benefits

Concretely, three reforms would realign Social Security derivative benefits with the contours of twenty-first-century family life: repeal of the spousal benefit, preservation of children's benefits, and enactment of a minimum benefit.

The three proposals are linked. Children's benefits would provide economic security for children when a parent is unable to work. Just as today, children's benefits are particularly important for the families of low-earning workers, who are more likely to experience disability during their working years or to die early.

Repeal of the spousal benefit would reflect the changing nature of family life. Each spouse in a married couple would retire or collect disability (if applicable) based on his or her own earnings record. A widow or widower, similarly, would be left with his or her own retirement benefit (rather than succeeding to the deceased spouse's benefit, if higher).

A serious concern is whether these changes would adversely affect women as a group, given their generally lower earnings and (still) greater childcare responsibilities. In 2012, for example, the average male retired worker, aged 66–69, received an average benefit of $1,885 per month, whereas the comparable female worker received $1,483. The average monthly benefit for women claiming as wives was only $634.[21]

Women's situation merits attention, but retention of the spousal benefit is a relatively poor solution. For one thing, the spousal benefit will gradually disappear even without formal action. Women's earnings have risen dramatically over time, and so have their years of employment. Late Baby Boomers, for instance, will have a median work history of 40 years, compared with 30 years for women born between 1936 and 1945.[22]

This sea change in women's work behavior will transform Social Security as well. Fully 66% of women born during the later Baby Boom, for example, will claim retirement benefits on their own earnings record alone, and only 11% solely as spouses. The comparable figures for women born between 1936 and 1945 are 44% and 38%.[23]

Projections indicate that these trends will continue: by 2080, only a small fraction of female Social Security recipients will claim solely as wives. The great majority will claim as workers only, while a declining percentage will claim as dually entitled (i.e., on the basis of their own earnings record, "topped up" by the spousal benefit).[24]

What would be ill-advised, of course, would be to repeal the spousal benefit for today's retirees. Older retirees lived mid-twentieth-century family lives, and the spousal benefit remains functional for them. Younger retirees adopted more mixed patterns, but they relied on the spousal benefit in planning for retirement, and it is difficult to justify altering the system midstream. For these reasons, a gradual transition seems sensible.

Over the mid- and longer term, a minimum benefit is a better way to address women's vulnerability, as a number of scholars and policy analysts have concluded. A minimum benefit would enhance the economic security of disadvantaged workers by ensuring them a decent living standard not conditional on formal marriage.[25]

Minimum-benefit proposals vary, but they typically provide an annual benefit at or above the poverty level for workers who have clocked at least a minimum number of years of work. The Simpson-Bowles proposals, for instance, include a minimum benefit set at 125% of the poverty threshold for workers with a 30-year work history.[26] Melissa Favreault proposes a minimum benefit set at 60% of the poverty threshold for those with at least a 20-year work history and at 110% of the poverty level for those with a 40-year (or longer) work history.[27]

The design of the minimum benefit reflects a tension between two objectives. On the one hand, Social Security is designed to be available only to people with a work history. On the other hand, a minimum benefit will be useful to caregivers only if "work history" is defined in a manner consistent with care work. Thus, the Favreault proposal, which kicks in for those with a 20-year work history, likely would assist more caregivers than the Simpson-Bowles proposal, which requires a minimum 30-year work history.

The key is to keep in mind the target of the minimum benefit. Some proposals seek only to ensure that long-term, low-wage workers have a decent minimum income. That is a worthy goal, consistent with the principle of recognition of cumulative disadvantage. But when society—as it should—also seeks to aid caregivers, the target audience changes to include workers with children (or other dependents) who have shorter working lives and lower earnings due to interrupted work.

Social Security once incorporated a minimum benefit, but it was repealed in 1982 in part because of concerns about double-dipping by military and government retirees.[28] The Supplemental Security Income program (SSI) provides a minimum benefit of sorts, but benefit levels are extremely low, and the means test is draconian.

Any proposal for a minimum benefit must confront a design issue first introduced in Chapter 7: potential inaccuracies in the measurement of life-time income. As discussed in more detail in that chapter, lifetime income is typically a sound measure of advantage and disadvantage, because it is hard to fake a lifetime of low earnings. Still, lifetime earnings may be a poor indicator of economic well-being for an individual who has voluntarily earned little.

But this problem is less worrisome in the context of the minimum benefit than in the context of the retirement timing rules. What kind of person—today—voluntarily works part-time and relies on a partner for support? The vast majority are mothers and fathers who cut back working hours (or quit entirely) for periods during their child-rearing years. These mothers and fathers might, in theory, be able to earn more if they worked more hours, but instead they are caring for children. To the extent that the minimum benefit assists these individuals by giving them a higher retirement or dis-ability benefit than otherwise, it is a good outcome rather than a defect.[29]

To be sure, there are less-appealing cases. There are rich trust fund kids who work little because they do not need to (and not because they are caring for children). There are also affluent people who choose low-paying careers in the arts because they love their work. But, in the spirit of mass justice, the minimum benefit fits fairly well with its objectives.

A complementary approach to the situation of caregivers, also widely endorsed by scholars and policy analysts, would directly increase the Social Security benefits of parents with care responsibilities. Some proposals would create childcare "dropout" years, which would improve average earnings by permitting workers to exclude zero years attributable to parental (or other dependent care) responsibilities. Other proposals would give Social Security earnings credit to caregivers during childcare years, including (depending on the proposal) time spent on parental leave and years while children are young. Still other proposals would adopt a supplemental benefit payable to caregivers.[30] A number of developed countries provide some kind of credit for caregiving work, and so there are several models that the United States might follow.[31] At-home parents and parents taking leave from work, for instance, might receive Social Security credits at a flat rate or at a percentage of their past salaries.

To be sure, proposals of this type can be more administratively demanding than a minimum benefit. It has proved tricky in the EITC context, for example, to identify which parents are present in a child's home.[32] Identifying caregivers years later, when retirement looms, would be difficult. Giving both parents credit automatically would amount to a flat increase in benefits for parenthood (rather than care), which seems to have little advantage over a minimum benefit.

Survivors and Family Security

To gain a sense of how the reformed system would work, return to the example of a worker who retires at the full retirement age with a Social Security benefit of $2,000 per month. Under the proposed rules, that worker would collect only his own benefit based on his own earnings record. His wife would collect her own benefit based on her earnings. If the worker died, the wife would have her own benefit to live on, even if it is lower than his.

This scenario may seem worrisome, compared with current law. If the widow's earnings record is modest, she will have less to live on than she would today. But the perception of unfairness shifts if we take as the baseline an unmarried woman with the same earnings record: under both present law and the new system, she will have only her own earnings record as the basis for a claim. The difference is that formal marriage confers no advantage under the new regime.

It is important to bear in mind, too, that the minimum benefit would set a floor on each individual's benefit, raising benefits for those with lifetime low earnings. Children's benefits, also, would be available (as under present law) when an individual loses a co-parent during the child-rearing years.

Still, it may seem that my proposals eliminate, too lightly, the life insurance for spouses that present Social Security provides. (Children's benefits would continue to provide life insurance for children.) Many workers, if they thought about the matter, would like to insure a spouse, a partner, or the mother or father of their children. Life insurance is, of course, available in the market, but prices are steep over age 40, and some combination of budget constraint and myopia may prevent people from buying insurance.

But these considerations do not add up to a defense of the spousal benefit. Given today's heterogeneous family patterns, it would be indefensible to limit public life insurance to formally married spouses. A fairer model might extend the kind of minimal marriage ideal discussed by Elizabeth Brake to the Social Security context and permit each worker to designate one beneficiary in addition to children.[33] (To be clear: this is not Brake's proposal but rather my thought experiment based on Brake's conception of minimal marriage.)

It would be possible to replace survivor benefits for spouses with survivor benefits for partners. Although I tend to think that doing so would be unwise, it is worth considering, if only to see the challenges it poses. One's partner could be determined by election or by a factual determination based on cohabitation. Obviously, any factual determination would be difficult, and it would involve the government in delicate inquiries into living arrangements. The liberal alternative would be to allow each worker to designate a survivor, who might be a romantic partner, a parent, or a friend—but each person would only have one beneficiary.

In essence, then, such a system would provide life insurance for each worker above and beyond the existing life insurance for children. The advantage of such an approach is that it would recognize the diversity of family forms, providing equal benefits to married couples, unmarried partners, adult siblings living together, adult children living with parents, committed friends, and so on.

The defect in this extended scheme (which does not affect Brake's own proposals for minimal marriage) is that the prospect of no-marginal-cost life insurance might induce unwelcome commercial bargains. That is, people might be tempted to monetize their life insurance entitlements, selling the insurance payout to others for current cash. Although the law could prohibit such sales, they might well take place sub rosa.

A better alternative, proposed by several policy analysts, would be to replace the spousal benefit with an *optional* joint-and-survivor annuity.[34] Joint-and-survivor annuities are common in the private pension world, where they permit retirees to trade a lump sum for a stream of payments that will last for the life of the retiree plus one other person (usually a spouse). In the private-pension context, the choice is typically between a single-life annuity, which pays out over the retiree's own life, and a joint-and-survivor option. A given lump sum produces a higher monthly benefit if spread out over one person's life rather than two, but the tradeoff is worth it for some couples, because the joint annuity ensures a lifetime income for both.

In the Social Security context, the key innovation would be that retirees electing a joint-and-survivor option should, just as in the private market, pay full price for it. That is, a retiree collecting the standard, single-life annuity would receive more than a retiree choosing the joint-and-survivor option. The difference in benefits should reflect the higher actuarial cost of the joint-and-survivor option.

To take a simple example, suppose that Johanna reaches age 72 and decides to file for Social Security benefits. The standard Social Security benefit, payable during her life alone, would be $2,000 per month. She could also choose a joint-and-survivor option that would continue benefits for her spouse's life. The tradeoff is that Johanna would receive a smaller monthly sum, based on the higher actuarial cost of the joint-and-survivor annuity. So, depending on her spouse's age, Johanna might receive only, say, $1,600 per month—but she would know that her surviving spouse would receive that amount for her lifetime even if Johanna dies first.

In principle, joint-and-survivor annuities could be extended beyond formally married couples to any two (or perhaps more) people. For instance, suppose that Johanna isn't married but that she has a child with a significant disability. A joint-and-survivor annuity would permit Johanna to use her Social Security benefits to add to her child's lifetime security, albeit at the cost of reducing (perhaps significantly) the monthly payout, depending on the child's age and life expectancy.

Perhaps this idea seems confusing: After all, isn't Social Security *already* a joint-and-survivor annuity program? The key difference is that today's rules provide a joint-and-survivor option that is (a) mandatory, (b) limited to formally married couples, and (c) provided at no extra cost (in the form of higher premiums or lower benefits) to retirees. An optional system would permit retirees greater flexibility, and actuarially sound pricing would ensure that—in sharp contrast with today—those who benefit from a joint-and-survivor option pay full freight for it.

In the mid-twentieth century, the repeal of spousal survivor benefits would have been outlandish and cruel, because it would have left many widows destitute, often without an earnings record or job experience, and well into middle age or more. For this reason, spousal survivors' benefits, like the spousal benefit, should be phased out as discussed earlier.

Today, however, the vast majority of survivors who are adults have their own earnings record. The new minimum benefit would enhance the position of low earners, and survivors with minor children would receive additional income as well.

10

Reforming the Taxation of Retirement

THE PRINCIPLES DEVELOPED in Chapters 4 and 5 have concrete implications for taxation. The principle of life-cycle justice implies that the state should mandate intrapersonal redistribution: ideally, each person should pay taxes during her working years to insure herself against work disability over her lifetime, including at older ages. The principle of social reciprocity supports the taxation of affluent individuals, including older people who have accumulated wealth and are enjoying longer and better lives due to social cooperation. The recognition of cumulative disadvantage suggests that the state should reduce taxes and underwrite savings by low-earning individuals working toward a variety of goals, including a secure retirement. And the antihumiliation principle tends to endorse the use of tax subsidies—rather than welfare payments—for retirement savings, thanks to the (relatively) dignified and private character of interactions between individuals and the state.

Expanding on these ideals, we can imagine a range of institutions. Ideally, Social Security should provide a baseline public retirement benefit financed by progressive taxes on working-age individuals and supplemented by taxes on affluent retirees. Income and wealth taxes are the most familiar progressive taxes, but the state might reach for additional criteria in order to target cumulative *advantage*. Bruce Ackerman and I suggest, for instance, that a public pension system might justly be funded by a tax keyed to privilege during childhood. That is, adults who had enjoyed a privileged childhood would be expected to contribute more, as adults, to public retirement than their peers from disadvantaged backgrounds.[1]

Ideally, too, the state should assist low earners in accumulating additional savings over their lifetimes. Low wages make it difficult for individuals to save for any of the many goods that today's society requires individuals to purchase in the private marketplace. Individuals may have very different preferences: some might place top priority on, say, saving to buy a house or start a business, whereas others might value saving to fund a child's college education or to set aside a rainy-day fund. But the combination of low earning power and the market commodification of such goods leaves low earners at a significant and cumulative disadvantage.

Still working in the realm of ideals, a just state should weaken the link between market earnings and such aspirational goods by providing an outright capital grant—as Bruce Ackerman and I propose in *The Stakeholder Society*[2]—or by subsidizing savings in a progressive manner. Ideally, the state should remain neutral toward individuals' life plans but should recognize that capital is a crucial foundation of life planning in a capitalist society. Savings fund life choices, whether the goal is to purchase a house, finance a child's education, fund a period of unemployment, or create a nest egg to supplement public retirement.

Mindful of the antihumiliation ideal, the state ideally should secure these goods to its citizens without resorting to means-tested programs. Progressive savings grants run through the tax system, for instance, would permit individuals to accumulate funds in a private and dignified manner, without proving destitution to the state in any public way.

From Ideal to Reality: How Present Tax Rules Fall Short

Measured by these standards, current institutions fail miserably. The payroll tax that funds Social Security is regressive and increasingly so, and the government pays enormous tax subsidies to the rich to underwrite their private pensions.

Today, the federal government devotes nearly $130 billion every year to subsidies for private pensions, including employer plans and IRAs.[3] But high earners are more likely to work in stable jobs with pension benefits, and tax subsidies direct the largest dollars to high-earning workers—and nothing at all to low earners. The result, as Chapter 3 documents, is that the affluent retire with ample private pensions, while low earners rely heavily on Social Security alone.

Stepping back from the details, the larger point is that reforms in taxation and private pension subsidies should go hand in hand with Social Security reform. The frustrating fact is that the dysfunction of the private pension system is well known to policy analysts but has not penetrated the political shield that protects entitlements for the affluent. The good news is that policy analysts have advanced several exciting and effective options for promoting pension coverage for lower earners, including universal, subsidized retirement savings accounts and progressive funding for Social Security.

Reforming Tax Subsidies for Private Pensions

Subsidies for pension savings are ingrained in the laws governing taxation and retirement. The tax code devotes hundreds of pages to employer pensions, 401(k)s, 503(b)s, IRAs, Roth IRAs, and so on. Union contracts and nonunion salaries are set on the assumption that pension contributions are tax-advantaged. The investment industry competes hard for IRA investment dollars, and some tax specialists spend their entire careers (truly!) on the intricacies of pension taxation.

But it is worth asking whether we should have such subsidies at all. The principles of life-cycle justice, social reciprocity, and the recognition of cumulative disadvantage could all be satisfied by public retirement programs. Why, then, should the government also create public-private hybrids?

Tax subsidies for private pensions predate Social Security. In the 1920s, Congress sought to reward and to encourage employers that had begun to establish pension funds. Ultimately, however, these pension funds provided only limited pensions to relatively few workers, and the solvency of the funds depended on the solvency of the employers, so the experiment was something of a failure.[4] The enactment of Social Security marked a public solution to the pension problem. But tax subsidies for private pensions remained on the books.

Policy analysts sometimes compare U.S. retirement policy to a three-legged stool (as discussed in Chapter 3). The idea is that Social Security was not intended to be the sole vehicle for retirement provision, and that the other two legs (employer pensions and private savings) should be important as well. But, as Gene Sperling, Michael Lind, and others have pointed out, if retirement policy were a three-legged stool, two of its legs would be badly broken, because too many people of modest means lack employer pensions and private savings.[5]

As Chapter 3 documents, both employer pensions and private savings skew heavily to the affluent, and many low-earning workers reach retirement without either one. Older Americans in the top 20% of the income distribution receive substantial income from savings and employer pensions; just 17.3% of their income comes from Social Security. By contrast, older Americans in the bottom 40% receive more than 80% of their income from Social Security.[6] Forty percent of tax expenditures for retirement savings are captured by high-income taxpayers.[7]

One might suppose that tax subsidies for private pensions serve some other function—say, increasing national savings. But no. A number of studies have established that current subsidies do not do much to increase net savings. Instead, they simply encourage the affluent to shuffle money from one pocket to another: the wealthy know that they can garner tax benefits by stashing their savings in retirement accounts.[8]

We might, then, adopt either of two approaches to tax subsidies for private pensions. One is simply to repeal them and use the $130 billion per year to enrich Social Security for the disadvantaged via a substantial minimum benefit and, perhaps, larger children's benefits in Disability Insurance (DI) and Survivors' Insurance (SI). This idea is a serious one, and it is most consistent with life-cycle justice and the focus of public provision on work disability. If people want to save for retirement, fine. But a truly adequate Social Security system could provide a fair foundation for personal choice.

If the United States is to continue subsidizing retirement savings, at a minimum the rules should be reworked to the benefit of the disadvantaged.[9] For instance, Gene Sperling proposes a universal 401(k) program. Workers would be automatically enrolled, and payroll deductions would fund the accounts. The government would match contributions dollar for dollar up to $4,000 annually.[10]

Other variants of the universal 401(k) are possible. Bill Gale (and, in an earlier proposal, Gene Sperling) has suggested refundable tax credits deposited directly to savers' accounts. The match rate could even be increased for lower earners to increase the progressivity of the system.[11]

Other sensible and progressive proposals abound. Andrew Biggs recommends universal, automatic enrollment in an employer-sponsored 401(k), with each worker contributing a minimum of 1.5% of pay, matched by employers.[12] He proposes to combine that system with a universal, flat Social Security benefit set at the poverty level. Michael Lind and his coauthors also recommend a universal, flat minimum benefit in Social Security. They recommend collateral reforms including contribution limits for tax-advantaged private pensions on the order of $5,000 per worker per year.[13]

Reforming Social Security Funding

Present payroll taxes for Social Security are regressive, thanks to the tax cap on earnings. A low earner and her employer pay FICA tax on every dollar of her wages, but an affluent worker (and her employer) cease to pay any FICA tax at all on earnings over $117,000 (in 2014).

Progressives sometimes suppose that the regressivity of the FICA tax is unobjectionable, because the progressive benefits formula for Social Security outweighs it. That is, on a lifetime basis, low earners still come out ahead, because they receive a far higher "return" on the tax dollars they pay. (As Chapter 5 discusses, whether this statement is true is subject to some debate.)

But life-cycle justice suggests that the level and distribution of taxation during the working years matters. That is, even if Social Security taxes plus benefits are progressive on a lifetime basis, we should be concerned about the taxes faced by working-age people. It is little comfort to the single parent struggling to pay the grocery bill that she (may) someday collect Social Security benefits that are high relative to her tax payments. She needs the money now.

In more-formal terms, Chapters 5 and 6 suggested that the recognition of cumulative disadvantage implies that the state should heavily subsidize or even excuse low earners' contributions for work disability insurance. At the same time, however, the antihumiliation principle counsels retaining some tax contribution for every worker. Universal taxation has well served the perception (and reality) of Social Security as a universal program. But the present system imposes a heavy burden: taking into account the employer and employee FICA taxes, low earners pay far more in Social Security taxes than in income taxes.

Policy analysts have proposed two sensible, incremental reforms that would relieve the increasing tax burden on low earners while recognizing the obligations of the affluent in accordance with the principle of social reciprocity. First, Congress should eliminate the cap on earnings subject to the Social Security payroll tax. The cap on earnings has already been lifted for Medicare tax purposes, and a number of policy analysts, including the Simpson-Bowles Commission, Michael Lind, and others, have recommended lifting or eliminating the cap for Social Security.[14]

Second, Congress should raise additional revenue by taxing capital income. The Affordable Care Act created a new tax on investment income, now taxed at a rate of 3.8%.[15] Raising the rate of tax would fund a substantial reduction in the Social Security payroll tax, redirecting the tax burden in a progressive fashion.[16]

Two objections are worth anticipating. Some may object that raising the Social Security tax cap would be unfair to high earners, who will pay more into the system without a corresponding increase in benefits. This notion reflects the myth of purchased benefits, which (incorrectly) treats Social Security pensions as linked in some actuarially fair way to FICA taxes paid. As we have seen, the myth of purchased benefits ignores the many ways in which the system separates contributions from benefits. For instance, lower-earning workers receive proportionally more thanks to the progressive benefits formula, while higher-earning workers receive a disproportionately high lifetime payout because they live longer (on average) and because the rules do not reduce their benefits on that account.

The myth of purchased benefits is not only descriptively incorrect but morally flawed. Individuals who want to invest their private assets and reap a market return can do so, but that is not the task of the Social Security system. Instead, Social Security should work toward justice between and within generations. High earners have benefitted disproportionately from social and economic structures that have increased wage inequality and created a new class of extremely highly paid professionals. In light of this increasing social inequality, it is appropriate and fair to expect higher earners to contribute more without receiving more.

A second potential objection invokes, once again, the universality problem. As I discussed in Chapter 7, it is critical to recognize that Social Security already incorporates income-related distinctions without undermining its universal appeal. And in recent years, Congress has taken steps to increase the progressivity of the tax side of the program—without notable public objection on universality grounds. In 1993, for instance, Congress lifted the Medicare tax cap, and it has not been reinstated. In 1983, and again in 1993, Congress acted to impose income tax on middle- and higher-income Social Security recipients. And, most recently, the Congress enacted new Medicare and health insurance–related taxes on high-income Americans.

And, once again, program design can promote sound politics. Policy makers might, for example, consider earmarking (that is, linking) new, higher taxes to benefits that will be attractive to many voters: say, the phased retirement option. Earmarking has proved useful in a range of public programs (including Social Security and Medicare), because it helps remind voters that tax increases fund benefits they want.

Facing the Political Problem

To this point, I've concentrated on the substance of policy planning, giving no consideration at all to politics. This focus reflects my comparative advantage, which lies in linking moral principles to policy design. But a principled approach can also, I think, point the way to a more effective political strategy. I turn to this point in the next, and final, chapter.

II

Principles and Politics in Retirement Policy

As I speak to colleagues and friends about retirement policy, I hear a common concern: "I'm with you on the substance. But how on earth can we get around the politics of Social Security?" What they mean, of course, is that the political forces that support current law are powerful. They include, presumptively, anyone over 60, the AARP, and any politician (of either party) seeking to win votes by scaring older people with the prospect that their Social Security will be cut.

The political barriers to reform are, indeed, formidable. Making any changes in Social Security will be difficult in Washington's toxic atmosphere— light on facts and heavy on scare tactics. It may be even more difficult to attempt, as I have argued we should, holistic reforms in a wide range of laws affecting retirement policy. Not for nothing is Social Security called the "third rail" of American politics, as George W. Bush discovered when he attempted (and failed) to enact a private accounts program.[1]

Making political predictions is not my field, and so I won't attempt any. I cannot predict whether the political forces in favor of Social Security reform will be able to prevail. It remains to be seen how effectively reformers will organize and how their efforts will interact with party politics, the presidential election of 2016, and the state of the economy. But, short of making predictions, it is possible to reflect on the political context for Social Security reform, and so I offer two suggestions, one principled and one practical.

Democracy and Justice among Age Groups

John Rawls, whose early work I first invoked in Chapters 4 and 5, wrestles mightily in later work with the problem of how to construct a principled politics. Rawls argues that a just society could structure its political affairs to preserve democratic decision making while also ensuring justice for all. The thorniness of the problem is apparent on a moment's reflection: democracy has moral value because it permits self-government, and yet, unfettered democracy will not always produce just results, particularly for disadvantaged groups. It is far too easy for powerful or well-organized groups to grab resources at the cost of weaker, dispersed groups.

Rawls' take on the problem of democracy has clear implications for Social Security reform.[2] What Rawls calls *political liberalism* retreats from the attempt to craft a "comprehensive doctrine" that everyone would accept. Instead, political liberalism aims to accommodate reasonable pluralism of views and to incorporate reasonable public bases of justification on key political questions.[3] Rawls' ideas provide a deep and compatible framework for the approach I take in this book. I have pointed out wide and growing inequality in the experience of old age, and I have argued for corrective policies grounded in social cooperation and justified by public reason.

Although Rawls does not focus on Social Security, it isn't hard to extend his theory to retirement policy. Rawls posits that the basic structure should include institutions that adjust for society's tendency to deviate from background fairness.[4] Social Security—and, more broadly, public subsidies for retirement—do just this. As I argued in Chapters 4 and 5, a just society ought to make provision for people when they can no longer work and should take due note of cumulative disadvantage. And my argument, like Rawls', rests in part on an ideal of social reciprocity.[5]

To be sure, we might debate whether Social Security falls within Rawls' category of constitutional essentials—or whether, instead, it belongs to the realm of what he terms "ordinary politics." Constitutional essentials, in Rawls' theory, should be founded on principle and should constrain democratic politics. The right to free expression, for instance, qualifies as a constitutional essential, meaning that no majority vote could legitimately overturn it. Other matters, however, Rawls consigns to democratic politics and majority rule, and in this camp Rawls includes most ordinary tax and transfer policies.

It is not obvious where Social Security should fall in Rawls' classification. As a first approximation, I think there is a sound argument that Social Security marks a (small *c*) constitutional commitment of the United States. Although the written Constitution does not, of course, include any commitment to old-age pensions, legal scholars including Bruce Ackerman and Bill Eskridge have suggested that Social Security, like civil rights legislation in the 1960s, marks an enduring shift in the relationship between state and citizen.[6] If we view Social Security as a constitutional essential, then democratic politics should hold only limited sway when it comes to debating reforms.

But even if Social Security is not a constitutional essential in this sense (so that democratic politics are the proper forum for reform), it seems to me that discussions of old-age provision should be conducted according to principles of what Rawls terms "public reason"—that is, a reasoned debate invoking principles rather than raw self-interest. Rawls, for instance, concludes that policies implementing the difference principle would fall outside the constitutional realm, but he anticipates, even so, that public reason would be the appropriate mode of discourse.[7] This book fits the model closely: it aims to elucidate the principles at stake in Social Security reform and to encourage discussions of principle—rather than discussions grounded in budget balance or raw interest group bids for money and power.

Building a Political Coalition

Turning now to practicalities, suppose that Social Security is to be left to the realm of ordinary politics and that—regrettably—public reason may not carry the day. With those assumptions, we are deep into the weeds of practical politics and coalition-building. But even here, there is room for optimism that Social Security reform can muster broad support.

Of course, older Americans are a large and growing segment of the population, and they do vote at high rates.[8] And perhaps they will vote selfishly to preserve present law, despite the need for reform. But even if we suppose that everyone votes according to self-interest, so that everyone over 60 will be dead set against reform, we should not forget that the remaining 80% of the population[9] has a considerable interest in reform. The present retirement system no longer just supports older people unable to work. Increasingly, the system devotes public funds to a lengthy Third Age for healthy older people.

Those public funds are unavailable for schools, for tax relief, or for anything else. The excess funding should be understood as a resource claim that should be measured against competing claims—and not as a bedrock moral entitlement.

This brings us to a second political observation. Framing the case for change in explicitly moral terms may pay off in the political arena by building support that looks beyond narrow self-interest. Research has shown that people filter new information based on the ideologies and cultural world-view they hold.[10] Whatever one may think of the Tea Party (and I disagree with nearly every position it stands for), its members have crafted a libertarian moral agenda, depicting the IRS as tyrannical and government as wrongly interfering with personal liberty via "excessive taxes."[11]

By contrast, progressive reformers too often shy away from moral language. Instead, they couch the case for Social Security reform in technocratic terms. They warn of the insolvency of the trust funds and counsel prudence. But the technocratic story buries the moral lede and, in the process, fools no one.

Solvency warriors are, most likely, trying to build consensus by avoiding potentially divisive moral issues. They may be trying to avoid taking a position on which age group should get more, and which less. They may hope to avoid bitterness over redistribution and the defeat of settled expectations.

But any reform in retirement policy implicates moral issues, and there is no way of avoiding them. Some defenders of Social Security insist that there is no crisis and that a few incremental reforms will suffice. But even incremental reforms will inevitably redistribute from some individuals to others, and the only square way to meet their objections is with a moral argument based on justice between or within age groups.

Policy analysts, with some reason, tend to attribute Social Security's political popularity to the myth of purchased benefits. And yet, we should remember that Franklin Roosevelt, who insisted on contributory financing for Social Security, also described the program as a moral initiative, a commitment to its older citizens that a just society should undertake. A complex modern society, Roosevelt argued, creates economic insecurity, which the state should address: "The millions of today want, and have a right to, the same security their forefathers sought—the assurance that with health and the willingness to work they will find a place for themselves in the social and economic system of the time."[12]

More recently, the Great Recession has motivated renewed attention to the inequalities that are eroding the life chances of ordinary Americans. The new populism has found expression in grassroots movements like Occupy Wall Street and in elite institutions like the new Consumer Financial Protection Bureau. But it is not just Wall Street that needs thoroughgoing reform. Demographic and economic change have transformed American society in ways that endanger Social Security's ability to mitigate inequality and to provide security to those who cannot work.

And we should not assume that Americans over 60 will be a roadblock to principled reform. Today's older generation enjoys unprecedented well-being. They are living longer, healthier, and richer lives. When we ask them to rebalance generational obligations in light of these gains, we may find a receptive audience if we lay out the moral issues at stake in terms of life-cycle justice and social reciprocity.

NOTES

REFERENCES

ACKNOWLEDGMENTS

INDEX

Notes

1 Introduction

1. For subjective statements about the experience of old age, see, e.g., Hamm (2010); UBS Investor Watch (2013). The UBS report offers poll results: a majority of their investors "do not feel 'old' until they are in their 80s." For objective evidence, see the discussion in Chapter 2, which documents the rising well-being of older people as a group but wide and growing inequality.

2. Waldron (2007) (discussing historical differentials in mortality by socioeconomic status).

3. See Centers for Disease Control (2012), p. 46 (Table 21); Munnell (2013), p. 2.

4. Centers for Disease Control (2012); Crimmins et al. (2009).

5. Chapter 2 documents these facts.

6. Chapter 2 documents these facts.

7. Waldron (2007) (finding that male Social Security–covered workers in the top half of the earnings distribution born in 1941 live 5.8 years longer than those in the bottom half; the gap was 1.2 years for those born in 1912).

8. See Van de Water et al. (2013).

9. Steuerle (2013), pp. 1–2 (noting that in 1940 and 1950, the average worker retired at 68); Social Security Administration (2014i) (noting that in 1940, a 65-year-old man could expect to live 13 more years).

10. Centers for Disease Control (2013) (reporting that, in 2010, an American man or woman at 65 could expect to live 19 more years); Crimmins et al. (2009) (noting that a 70-year-old can now expect to live 14 more years, 12 of them without disability).

11. Early retirement at age 62, with actuarial reduction, was introduced in 1956 for women and 1961 for men. Social Security Administration (2013), Table 2A.20.

12. National Academy of Social Insurance (2014) (reporting that 74% of Social Security claimants in 2011 had benefits reduced for early retirement and that "just under half (41 percent of men and 47 percent of women)" first claimed at age 62).

13. See Munnell (2013), p. 4 (Table 3) (reporting that 62% of workers with advanced degrees remain in the workforce at ages 62–64, while only 42% of high school graduates do; by ages 65–67, the proportions are 47% and 29%, respectively).

14. See General Accountability Office (2014), pp. 7, 15–16; Leonesio et al. (2003).

15. Munnell (2013).

16. Munnell (2013), p. 4 (Table 4).

17. The Joint Committee on Taxation (2013) predicts that tax expenditures on employer pensions and IRAs will amount to $126 billion in 2014. The White House Office of Management and Budget (2014), Table 11.3, estimates that Social Security OASI outlays will be $708 billion in 2014.

18. Marmor et al. (2014), p. 183 (noting that "two-thirds of federal tax expenditures for retirement saving go to those in the top fifth of the income distribution").

19. Marmor et al. (2014), p. 185 (Figure 10.2) (noting that 70% of workers with incomes of $75,000 and above had private pensions, while less than 10% of low earners [earning less than $10,000] had pensions).

20. Alstott (2013).

21. See Chapters 2 and 9.

22. See Chapter 2.

23. OASDI Trustees (2013), p. 2.

24. OASDI Trustees (2013), p. 4 (OASDI trust fund, which includes retirement and disability).

25. Reznik et al. (2005–2006), p. 37.

26. See, e.g., Simpson-Bowles Commission (2010) (recommending an increase in the Social Security retirement age); Marmor et al. (2014), pp. 194–201 (recommending a gradual increase in the Social Security full retirement age to 70). See also Shoven and Goda (2010) (estimating age inflation since 1935 and projecting that the retirement age in 2050 should range from the mid-70s to late 80s, depending on the adjustment method used).

27. Siegel (2014); OECD (2013), ch. 1.

28. Marmor et al. (2014); Burtless (2013a); Ghilarducci (2005); Reznik et al. (2005–2006); GAO (2014); Leonesio et al. (2003). But see Mermin and Steuerle (2006) (pointing out that the large percentage of low earners who claim SSDI would be unaffected by an increase in the Social Security retirement age).

29. American Community Survey (2014) (based on 2012 data).

30. Diller (1996), pp. 383–384 (quoting Roosevelt's claim that contributors have a "legal, moral, and political right to collect their pensions").

31. See, e.g., Steuerle and Rennane (2011) (comparing Social Security benefits and taxes over a lifetime for different retirement cohorts and finding that earlier cohorts,

on average, received more than later ones); Beach and Davis (1998) (pointing out the low rates of return to some low-income and minority households).

32. For a recent example of the "Third Rail" metaphor for Social Security politics, see Keane (2013).

33. Geiger (2012) (reporting Senator Alan Simpson's use of the "greedy geezer" phrase); Gokhale (2013) (arguing that Social Security and Medicare overpay today's elderly at the expense of future generations).

34. Biggs (2013a).

35. Tanner (2011).

36. See Kuttner (2012) (criticizing the "greedy geezer" notion and contending that economic growth, not cuts in Social Security, are the best way to secure the economic future of today's children); Van de Water et al. (2013) (reporting that Social Security benefits keep 15 million retirees out of poverty); Ruffing and Van de Water (2011) (criticizing Simpson-Bowles for cutting expected Social Security benefits).

37. For an example of news coverage of the most recent Social Security Trustees Report, see Prial (2013). For an example of the argument that Social Security is affordable, see Reno and Walker (2013), p. 32–36 (arguing that expenditures will remain stable at about 6% of GDP).

38. See Favreault and Johnson (2010) (discussing budget and longevity issues); Ghilarducci (2005) (pointing out that disability rises with age).

39. See, e.g., Ruffing and Van de Water (2011).

40. See Alstott (2008); Alstott (2007); Alstott (2004); Ackerman and Alstott (1999).

41. See Chapter 7.

42. For the substantial revenue gained by more-modest increases in the full Social Security retirement age, see CBO (2012).

43. Gruber et al. (2010), pp. 9–14.

44. Gruber et al. (2010), p. 10.

45. Gruber et al. (2010), pp. 4–5.

46. Hill and Reno (2005), p. 12.

47. Hill and Reno (2005), p. 13.

2 THE NEW INEQUALITY OF OLD AGE

1. Social Security Administration (2014i) (reporting that, in 1940, 54% of men survived to age 65).

2. Hoyert (2012), Figure 3 (showing declining rates of death for those over 65 since 1935).

3. See, e.g., Union Bank of Switzerland (2013) (reporting that investors do not feel "old" until they are in their 80s); Hamm (2011) (headlined "Retirement at 65? But It's the New 45!").

4. See Moen (2003); Han and Moen (1999); Moen and Spencer (2005).

5. Freedman (2007).

6. Kim and Moen (2001). See generally Freedman (2007); Olson (2014).

7. Weir (2007).

8. Centers for Disease Control (2012), p. 46 (Table 19).

9. See also Shoven and Goda (2010), p. 144 (in 1935, a 65-year-old had a 3% chance of dying within a year; today it's 1.5%); Social Security Administration (2014i) (noting that, in 1940, only 54% of men survived to age 65; by 1990, 72% did).

10. National Research Council (2011).

11. Centers for Disease Control (2012), p. 46 (Table 21).

12. See also Munnell (2013), p. 2. Women typically live longer than men, whether measured at birth or at age 65. In 1900, the gender gap was less than 1 year: a 65-year-old man was expected to live slightly less than 12 years, while a women could expect to live slightly more than 12 years. By 2008, women had gained 8 years of life after age 65, while men had gained just 6. CDC (2012), p. 46 (Table 21).

13. Waldron (2007).

14. Waldron (2007) (citing a number of studies confirming widening inequality in the second half of the twentieth century).

15. Olshansky et al. (2012), p. 1806. See also Cristia (2009).

16. For the earlier-born cohort, workers in the top half of the earnings distribution expected to live 15.5 more years at age 65, while workers in the bottom half expected to live 14.8 more years at that age. For the later-born cohort, the comparable life expectancy is 21.5 for the top half and 16.1 for the bottom half. Waldron (Table 4). See also Congressional Budget Office (2008); Duggan et al. (2008).

17. Olshansky et al. (2012), p. 1806 (finding that white, female high school dropouts had a life expectancy at birth of nearly 79 in 1990 but only 74 in 2008); id., Exhibit 2, p. 1806. See also Tavernise (2012) (discussing four studies reaching similar conclusions).

18. Waldron (2013), Table 1 (67–71-year-old men).

19. National Research Council (2011); Ho and Fenelon (2013).

20. For a discussion of this hypothesis, see Costa (1999), pp. 61–63.

21. Costa (1999), pp. 62–63.

22. Crimmins et al. (2009), Table 2. See also Schoeni et al. (2008).

23. Houtenville et al. (2009) (discussing the difficulties in measuring disability with survey data); Mashaw and Reno (1996) (discussing the variety of legal and statistical definitions of disability).

24. Manton and Gu (2001). For estimates of current rates of disability, see Johnson (2012), p. 3 (Figure 1) (finding that in 2008, 42% of adults aged 62–69 reported moderate disability, while 18% reported serious disability); Leonesio et al. (2003), p. 2 (Table 1) (finding that, in 1990, 27% of individuals aged 62–64 were "severely disabled"; an additional 22% reported "one or more health problems" but were not severely disabled). For a note of caution regarding the pace of future improvement, see

Fuller-Thompson et al. (2009) (finding that disabilities in activities of daily living either remained constant or increased modestly between 2000 and 2005).

25. Freedman (2014), p. e92 (Table 3).

26. Martin et al. (2010), pp. S20–S21.

27. Hill and Reno (2005), pp. 11–12.

28. Braveman et al. (2010) (finding a negative relationship between health outcomes [including diabetes, heart disease, and obesity] and income and education levels); Centers for Disease Control and Prevention (2005) (finding that lower levels of education and income predicted that individuals would have a greater number of risk factors for heart disease and stroke); Eisner et al. (2009) (finding, in a study of individuals aged 40–65 with chronic obstructive pulmonary disorder [COPD], that lower educational attainment and household income were related to "greater disease severity, poorer lung function, and greater physical function limitations"); Schoeni et al. (2008) (finding that "disparities in disability" have increased over the past 20 years, because the gains in ability over that period have been largest for the high-income, the married, and the educated).

29. Avendano and Glymour (2008); Braveman et al. (2010); Centers for Disease Control and Prevention (2005).

30. Eisner et al. (2009).

31. Freedman et al. (2014), p. e92 (Table 3).

32. Cutler (2001).

33. U.S. Bureau of the Census (2014), Table A-2.

34. U.S. Bureau of the Census (2014), Table A-2. See generally Hout et al. (1993).

35. Favreault (2012), p. 2 (Figure 2); Autor et al. (2008).

36. U.S. Department of Education (2012a) (documenting inequality in preparation for, access to, and completion of higher education); U.S. Bureau of the Census (2014), Figure 10 (showing increasing earnings premium for bachelor's and advanced degrees); Mitchell (2014), p. 5, Table 1 (showing increasing college education among later birth cohorts).

37. U.S. Department of Education (2012b), Table 1.3 (showing that college students with less-educated parents are more likely to be older, to attend community college, and to attend a for-profit four-year college).

38. Mitchell (2014), p. 10, Figure 6 (showing increasing college earnings premia); see also Campbell et al. (2005), p. 14 (finding that "the increase in family income and wealth inequality leads to greater dispersion of educational attainment, primarily because those at the bottom of the educational distribution have fallen further below the average level of education").

39. Favreault (2009b), p. 4, Figure 2.

40. See Autor et al. (2008); see also Social Security Administration (2012a) (showing increasing inequality of earnings from 1989 to 2013); Spletzer (2014) (reviewing the literature on earnings inequality).

41. Piketty and Saez (2003) (noting the rise in the share of earnings and income going to the top decile); Autor (2014) (documenting inequality among the bottom 99%).

42. Autor (2014).

43. Costa (1999), p. 1.

44. Costa (1999), pp. 2–3.

45. Costa (1999), pp. 133–152.

46. Gray (2005).

47. Munnell (2013), p. 4, Table 3 (portraying labor force participation from 1999–2012 and noting that less-educated workers are most likely to leave the labor force, with only 29% of high school graduates working by age 65, while 47% of those with advanced degrees remain in the labor force).

48. Waldron (2004), Table 3 (noting increase in labor force participation of men and women over 60 since 1985); Quinn (2005), p. 32; Johnson et al. (2009), p. 1 (noting increasing workforce participation between 1993 and 2008; men over 65 increased from 25% to 36%, and women over 65 increased from 16% to 26%).

49. Quinn (2005), p. 34.

50. Banerjee and Blau (2013), p. 7.

51. Johnson et al. (2009), p. 5–6.

52. Cahill et al. (2006), p. 523; Johnson et al. (2009), p. 4.

53. Johnson et al. (2009), p. ix; Ellin (2014).

54. Johnson et al. (2009); Cahill et al. (2006).

55. Hannon (2014).

56. Butrica et al. (2012), pp. 54–55.

57. Munnell (2012), p. 3.

58. Cahill et al. (2006), p. 523; Quinn (2005), p. 34.

59. Cherlin (2009), pp. 63–86. See also Bergner and Kellner (1964) (describing the expectations and social development of married couples in mid-twentieth-century America).

60. See U.S. Bureau of the Census (2011), Table A.1 (52% of adults were married in 2011).

61. The 2010 figure represents the author's calculations based on U.S. Bureau of the Census (2012b), Table 57. The 1960s figure is reported in Yamaguchi and Wang (2002), p. 441.

62. U.S. Bureau of the Census (2009), Table 6 (reporting that 33% of men aged 15 and older had never married, 42% remained in a first marriage, 20% had been divorced at least once, and 20% had been married at least twice); U.S. Bureau of the Census (2013), Table HS12 (showing a rise in nonfamily households, which include single people and cohabiting couples).

63. Hamilton (2011), p. 4 (41% of births in 2009 were to unmarried women).

64. U.S. Bureau of the Census (2012a), p. 8, Table 3 (noting that, in 2010, 7.2% of all households were headed by single mothers, and 2.4% were headed by single fathers).

65. See Bianchi (2006); Sweeney (2002); Fry and Cohan (2010).

66. Cherlin (2004); Alstott (2013).

67. Harden (2007); Alstott (2013).

68. Cherlin (2010), p. 404.

69. Cherlin (2010), p. 405; see also Bramlett and Mosher (2002), p. 55 , Table 21 (noting that marriage rates rise with income).

70. Copen et al. (2012), Table 5.

71. Social Security Administration (2013), Table 3.E4 (showing that in March 2013, 62.8% of adults over 65 were married, but only 35.4% of the poor were married).

72. Butrica and Smith (2012a), pp. 2–3.

73. Favreault et al. (2012), p. 2, Figure 1 (compared with prior cohorts, Baby Boomers will have fewer widows but more never-married individuals).

3 STATIC LAW AND GROWING INEQUALITY

1. Eugene Steuerle also notes that Social Security was "designed for a different era." Steuerle (2013), p. 1.

2. Moen (2003).

3. Moen (2003).

4. Social Security Administration (2014e). The maximum benefit is computed at the age of first eligibility (generally age 62); future earnings are irrelevant. Social Security Administration (2013).

5. Social Security Administration (2014a, 2014c).

6. For the earlier-born cohort, workers in the top half of the earnings distribution expected to live 15.5 more years at age 65, while workers in the bottom half expected to live 14.8 more years at that age. For the later-born cohort, the comparable life expectancy is 21.5 for the top half and 16.1 for the bottom half. Waldron (Table 4); see also Congressional Budget Office (2008).

7. Social Security Administration (2013).

8. Divorced spouses are entitled if the marriage lasted 10 years. Social Security Administration (2012b).

9. Social Security Administration (2013), Table 5.C1.

10. For data on tax liability and EITC payments, Marr et al. (2014).

11. The $117,000 figure is for 2014; the amount is updated each year. See Social Security Administration (2014f).

12. The total payroll tax (employer plus employee) is generally considered to be borne by workers.

13. Legislation enacted in 1983 raised the retirement age gradually from 65 to 67, beginning with workers retiring in 2000. Social Security Administration (1983).

14. Costa (1999), p. 1 ("[T]he use of sixty-five as the age of retirement has a long history and was not an invention of the Commission on Economic Security. After

becoming synonymous with work incapacity in Bismarck's Germany in 1883, it was adopted as a retirement age in the United States"). Costa notes that Civil War pensions began at age 65. Costa (1999), p. 11. Wilbur Cohen's history confirms that the Committee on Economic Security did not consider any alternative to age 65, but that "there was no scientific, social, or gerontological basis" for selecting age 65 other than its wide use in state and foreign pension systems. Cohen (1957), pp. 3, 17, 21, 24.

15. Cohen (1957), pp. 3, 17.

16. Shoven and Goda (2010).

17. The delayed retirement credit was introduced in 1972; the actuarial adjustment for delayed retirement has increased over time and now stands at 8% per year. Munnell (2013), p. 2.

18. Munnell (2013), p. 2.

19. Munnell (2013), p. 2.

20. Munnell (2013), p. 4, Table 4.

21. Wasik (2014).

22. National Academy of Social Insurance (2014).

23. Knoll and Olsen (2014), p. 27.

24. Knoll and Olsen (2014), pp. 24–25.

25. See Behaghel and Blau (2013) (finding that the full retirement age frames workers' benefit-claiming decisions); Hill and Reno (2005), pp. 21–22 (noting that wealth illusion and money illusion may lead people to retire early).

26. Baker and Rosnick (2010), p. 2, Figures 1 and 2 (showing increasing divergence in life expectancy at normal retirement age between the top half and bottom half of the income spectrum).

27. GAO (2014), pp. 15–20.

28. Baker and Rosnick (2010).

29. Kopczuk et al. (2010) finding that earnings inequality in the United States decreased from 1937 to 1953 and increased thereafter).

30. U.S. Department of Labor, Bureau of Labor Statistics (2014), Table A-4 (showing that in May 2014, the unemployment rate was 9.1% for high school dropouts, 5.8% for high school graduates, and 3.3% for BAs and higher); Steuerle (2011), p. 9 (pointing out that two groups have low lifetime earnings: consistent work at low wage or interrupted careers due to child-rearing).

31. Favreault et al. (2007). Jack Vanderhei finds that, taking into account health care costs, many lower-earning workers would not have sufficient retirement income even if they delayed retirement into their 70s or 80s. Vanderhei (2012). But cf. Munnell et al. (2009) (finding that more than 80% of low-income households would have adequate retirement income if they worked till 70).

32. Social Security Administration (2013), Table 3.E1.

33. Social Security Administration (2013), Table 5.B6.

34. Social Security Administration (2013), Table 3.E2.

35. Social Security Administration (2013), Table 3.E6.

36. Kopcke et al. (2014); Whitman and Shoffner (2011).

37. Social Security Administration (2013), Table 4.B2.

38. Social Security Administration (2013), Table 4.B4.

39. Social Security Administration (2013), Table 4.B2.

40. Favreault et al. (2012), p. 3 (Figure 3): compared with earlier cohorts, late Baby Boomer women will have a median of 40 years of employment, compared with a median of only 30 years for women born in 1936–1945.

41. Social Security Administration (2012a), Table 5C1 (data for 2011). See also Butrica and Smith (2012a), p. 4 (finding that married women's rising earnings will make more wives eligible for retired-worker benefits and fewer wives eligible for spousal benefits).

42. Social Security Administration (2012b).

43. See Schieber (2012), p. 285 (Table 24.3).

44. Steuerle (2011), pp. 8–9. Butrica and Smith (2012b), p. 15, point out that the duration of marriages ending in divorce has declined among "more recent cohorts of women," with the result that Social Security divorced-spouse benefits may not be available: among women born 1936–1945, 80% had at least one marriage lasting 10 years, while among late Boomers (born 1956–1965), the percentage is projected to be 68%.

45. See Biggs et al. (2009) (finding that "the progressivity of auxiliary (spouse and dependent) benefits is projected to decline significantly more than the progressivity of worker benefits").

46. See Lind et al. (2013), p. 3; Marmor et al. (2012).

47. Lind et al. (2013), pp. 4–5.

48. Office of Management and Budget (2014), Table 11.3; Joint Committee on Taxation (2013), pp. 39–40.

49. Sperling (2005), p. 5.

50. Reno and Walker (2005), p. 8.

51. Reno and Lavery (2007), p. 8.

52. Lind et al. (2013), p. 7, Figure 3.

53. Lind et al. (2013), p. 3, Figure 1; Reno and Lavery (2007), p. 6.

54. Steuerle et al. (2013), p. 2 (pointing out the complex redistributions in Social Security).

55. Social Security Administration researchers report that Social Security old-age, survivors', and disability insurance, taken as a whole, is "modestly progressive on a lifetime basis." Biggs et al. (2009).

56. Congressional Budget Office (2006) (finding that retirement benefits are less progressive than OASDI as a whole; the progressivity of the benefits formula is offset, but not entirely, by the shorter lives of low earners, which reduce the value of the life annuity); Lu et al. (2012) (finding that income-related differentials reduce but do not eliminate the progressivity of Social Security retirement benefits).

57. See Biggs et al. (2009) (finding that "progressivity has declined in recent decades" and that progressivity will decline for cohorts retiring in the 2010s).

58. Steuerle et al. (2004).

59. Steuerle et al. (2013), pp. 1–2.

4 Justice over the Life Cycle

1. Steuerle (2013), pp. 1–2.

2. Daniels (2006), p. 28; Daniels (1988), pp. 11–16.

3. For calculations of net benefits from Social Security for different birth cohorts, see Steuerle and Quackenbush (2012).

4. Rawls (1971); Ackerman (1981).

5. Daniels (1988), p. 41 (noting that everyone will age, and so everyone will experience consistent differential treatment by age).

6. In the following discussion, I draw broadly on the approach taken in Rawls (1971), Ackerman (1981), Van Parijs (1998), and Dworkin (2002). Daniels (1988), pp. 119–124, offers a somewhat different—though broadly compatible—approach, which he terms the prudential life span account.

7. Alstott (2008).

8. Ackerman and Alstott (1999).

9. Cf. Thaler and Sunstein (2008) (articulating a rationale for policies that nudge individuals toward retirement savings but permit opt-out).

10. Thaler and Sunstein (2008).

11. Bruce Ackerman and I recommend a state-paid old-age pension justified by the myopia of the young. Ackerman and Alstott (1999).

12. See Ackerman (1981).

13. For an economist's free-rider argument for compulsory old-age pensions, see Posner (1995), pp. 262–263.

14. See OECD (2013).

15. Ackerman and Alstott (1999), pp. 133–142.

16. Dworkin (2002), pp. 76–83.

17. Ghilarducci (2005), pp. 36–45.

18. Erikson (1959).

19. See generally Offe and de Deken (2013) (proposing universal sabbatical grants).

20. Dworkin (2002), pp. 87–92 (endorsing redistribution to those with lesser talents); Kronman (1981) (opposing "talent pooling").

21. The inadequacy of medical care for veterans sparked a major scandal in 2014. See, e.g., Hulse (2014) (discussing political fallout from the resignation of the Secretary for Veterans Affairs. Some veterans themselves understand their entitlements as a matter of reciprocity. Slear (2014).

22. Costa (2005), pp. 23–24.

23. Costa (2005), p. 24.

24. Hill and Reno (2005), pp. 9–24.

25. Thaler and Sunstein (2008).

26. Ellin (2014).

27. Strauss (2015).

28. Dalton (2013) (reporting discussions of early retirement initiatives in the EU); Anton (2013) (reporting the "astonishing" fact that most experts reject the tradeoff between youth and elderly employment).

29. Gruber et al. (2010), pp. 4–5.

30. Gruber et al. (2010), pp. 9–14.

31. Gruber et al. (2010), p. 10.

32. Gruber et al. (2010), pp. 4–5.

33. Gruber et al. (2010), pp. 13, 41.

34. Hill and Reno (2005), p. 12.

35. Hill and Reno (2005), p. 13.

36. The number of professors who are 65 or older doubled between 2000 and 2011. Williams (2012).

37. Woolf (2010).

38. Fendrich (2014).

39. Curtis and Thornton (2012–2013), p. 7 (Figure 1).

40. There are, of course, multiple factors at work in determining academics' work behavior. For instance, the end of mandatory retirement has prevented universities from forcing older professors to retire, with the result that faculty now work until older ages. See Ashenfelter and Card (2001). The shift to defined-contribution pensions from defined-benefit pensions probably also helps explain why this generation of tenured faculty now continue in their jobs past what was once a standard retirement age.

41. Yoder (2012).

5 Cumulative Disadvantage and Unequal Age

1. Dworkin (2002), pp. 92–109.

2. Van Parijs (1998).

3. Rawls (1971), pp. 75–80.

4. Rawls (1975), discussed in Weatherford (1983).

5. See Quadagno (2008), p. 64, 314–315.

6. See, e.g., Tungodden and Vallentyne (2006) (considering whether the difference principle reduces to leximin).

7. Alstott (2010).

8. See Chapter 3.

9. Graetz and Mashaw (1999), pp. 156–158.

10. John and Reno (2012).

11. See, e.g., Skocpol (1991), Lester (2011).

12. IRC section 86.

13. Titmuss (2006), p. 46 ("The challenge that faces us is not the choice between universalist and selective social services. The real challenge resides in the question: what particular infrastructure of universalist services is needed in order to provide a framework of values and opportunity bases within and around which can be developed socially acceptable selective services aiming to discriminate positively, with the minimum risk of stigma, in favour of those whose needs are greatest.")

14. Titmuss (1968), p. 46, also emphasizes the importance of context and discounts the simple distinction between universalism and means testing: "The challenge that faces us is not the choice between universalist and selective social services. The real challenge resides in the question: what particular infrastructure of universalist services is needed in order to provide a framework of values and opportunity bases within and around which can be developed social acceptable selective services aiming to discriminate positively, with the minimum risk of stigma, in favour of those whose needs are greatest."

15. See, e.g., Tanner (2012); Beach and Davis (1998).

16. See, e.g., Weller (2010), pp. 38–39 (proposing to make the formula more progressive).

17. Skocpol (1988); Handler (1995), p. 27.

18. Ackerman (2014), p. 13.

19. Ackerman (2014), pp. 129–130.

20. Ackerman (2014), p. 131.

21. Ackerman (2014), p. 133.

22. Titmuss (1968), p. 40.

23. See Chapter 8.

6 FROM PRINCIPLES TO POLICIES

1. Rawls (1993).

2. Turner (2011), pp. 41–69.

3. See, e.g., Turner (2011), pp. 73–74.

4. Steuerle (2013), pp. 1–2.

5. In general, a delay in the payment of Social Security benefits would reduce the program's cost. See generally CBO (2012), p. 10 (finding that a gradual increase in the full retirement age to 70 would reduce social security outlays by 13% by 2060).

6. See Mermin and Steuerle (2006) (noting that workers with disabilities may not qualify for SSDI and that less than half of workers aged 51–64 receive disability benefits even when they have significant disabilities).

7. For instance, Lu et al. (2012) argue that because Social Security remains progressive overall, there is no need to link retirement timing to income levels.

8. See Lu et al. (2012) (noting that the relationship between lifetime earnings and longevity is complex; noting also that factors such as gender, race, and family structure affect the correlation; and arguing that it would be difficult to justify denying early retirement to a high earner in poor health).

9. Mermin and Steuerle (2006) point out that 25% of workers without high school diplomas claim SSDI and so would be unaffected by a change in the Social Security retirement age; Leonesio et al. (2003), pp. 6–7 (estimating that raising the retirement age could leave 25% of early retirees facing a severe work disability, but that only 8% would qualify for SSDI or SSI because they do not meet SSI means test or SSDI work test or do not meet total disability test).

10. See Graetz and Mashaw (1999), pp. 41–42.

11. See, for example, American Federation of State, County, and Municipal Employees (2012).

12. Marmor et al. (2014), pp. 164–169 (discussing a number of reforms).

13. See David John's defense of means testing in John and Reno (2012).

7 Progressive Retirement Timing

1. See Simpson-Bowles Commission (2010), Business Roundtable (2013).

2. See Marmor et al. (2014), pp. 194–201.

3. See Ghilarducci (2005). Leonesio et al. (2003) point out that early retirement serves as a de facto disability program for a significant percentage of workers. But see Mermin and Steuerle (2006) (pointing out that so many low-earning workers claim disability benefits that they would be unaffected by an increase in the Social Security retirement age). GAO (2014) also points out that workers with physically demanding jobs or who are unemployed may claim early retirement benefits despite any increase in the full retirement age.

4. See Alstott (2010).

5. Marmor et al. (2014), p. 154 (Figure 9.1).

6. Duggan and Imberman (2009), p. 338.

7. Freedman (2014), p. e92, Table 3 (at ages 65–69, 67% are either fully able or can successfully accommodate a disability). See also Leonesio et al. (2003), p. 2, Table 1(reporting that, in 1990, 27% of individuals aged 62–64 were "severely disabled," while another 22% reported "one or more health problems").

8. Freedman et al. (2014), p. e92, Table 3, found that 53% of Medicare enrollees at ages 80–84 reported having reduced activity, experiencing difficulty despite accommodations, or needing assistance from others due to disability). By contrast, 43% of those aged 75–79 fell into those categories. Similarly, data from the 2012 American Community Survey, available at http://www.census.gov/acs/www/data_documentation /pums_data/, and tabulated by my research assistant, Jesselyn Friley, show that 51.5% of people report disability by age 82. In this dataset, people are considered to have a

disability if they have difficulty with any one of several activities or instrumental activities of daily living: hearing, cognitive, ambulatory, self-care, and independent living. See Freedman et al. (2013) (finding that, between ages 75 and 84, about half of individuals have difficulty or are unable to perform activities or instrumental activities of daily living).

9. For a paper discussing the difficulty of measuring disability with survey data, see Houtenville et al. (2009). See also Mashaw and Reno (1996) (explaining more than twenty definitions of disability used in government benefits and statistical analysis). For a discussion of the American Community Survey's methods of measuring disability, see U.S. Bureau of the Census (2010).

10. Freedman et al. (2014) p. e92, Table 3; Ghilarducci (2005), pp. 44–45.

11. U.S. Bureau of the Census (2010–2012).

12. Sabbah et al. (2008) (noting that controlling for allostatic load [factors such as obesity] reduces but does not erase the income correlation).

13. Liu et al. (2012).

14. Dupre (2007).

15. That is, workers born in 1960 or later have a full retirement age of 67. Social Security Administration (2014g).

16. Social Security Administration (2013).

17. Munnell (2013).

18. Steuerle (2011), p. 9.

19. Social Security Administration (2013)

20. Natalia Zhivan and her coauthors consider a variant of this idea: they explore a proposal that would link the Social Security *early* retirement age to lifetime income (AIME as calculated for Social Security purposes). They find that this rule would protect the ability of low lifetime earners to retire early, but because the proposal does not change the penalties for early retirement, these low earners would also continue to face large penalties for early retirement. Zhivan et al. (2008),

21. Social Security Administration (2014g).

22. Social Security Administration (2014b).

23. See Waldron (2004) (noting that early retirees have, on average, poorer health and higher mortality risk); Rutledge et al. (2012), pp. 2–3 (noting that before the Great Recession, those who claimed Social Security benefits at 62 tended to be less educated and have lower incomes; the Great Recession increased claiming among all income groups).

24. See GAO (2014), p. 7 (reporting that factors influencing early claiming include health status, spouse's health status, other income, and psychological factors including loss aversion).

25. Melissa Knoll and Anya Olsen usefully explore varying early retirement penalties in Social Security for the purpose of discouraging early claiming, but they examine

only lockstep changes in the terms of early retirement. Knoll and Olsen (2014), pp. 29–31.

26. For present rules, see Social Security Administration (2014c). For an explanation of the earnings test, see Olsen and Romig (2013) and Gruber and Orszag (1999).

27. Social Security Administration (2013), Table 2.A.20.

28. Mermin and Steuerle (2006).

29. Compare CBO (2012), pp. 9–10 (raising the full retirement age would increase work and delay benefits claiming); Behaghel and Blau (2012) (finding that the increase in the full retirement age led to delayed claiming of Social Security benefits); Mastrobuoni (2009) (finding that the mean retirement age has risen in response to the increase in the Social Security full retirement age).

30. Kahneman and Tversky (1984) motivated many studies by social psychologists on loss aversion.

31. Galston (2007) provides one account.

32. Social Security Administration (2015).

33. Klees et al. (2014), pp. 12–13.

34. Klees et al. (2014), pp. 7, 13–14.

35. Dan Halperin suggested this idea, which is brilliant.

8 Insuring a Longer Working Life

1. Munnell (2013), p. 4 (Table 3).

2. Munnell (2013) p. 4 (noting that labor force participation has risen since 1985).

3. See Milligan and Wise (2012), pp. 1–2 (finding that international experience has shown that countries that raise the retirement age can expect rising disability rolls). See also Bingley et al. (2012); Jönssen et al. (2012).

4. Duggan and Imberman (2009), p. 338.

5. Freedman et al. (2014), p. e92 (Table 3).

6. Autor et al. (2011).

7. 20 CFR 404.1505, available at http://www.ecfr.gov/cgi-bin/text-idx?SID =fc3384da9d6d803b0745e8e086dc956c&node=20:2.0.1.1.5.16.188.6&rgn=div8 (defining disability as "inability to do any substantial gainful activity"). For a description of SSDI eligibility rules and procedures, see Marmor et al. (2014) pp. 154–168.

8. Marmor et al. (2014), p. 160.

9. Mermin and Steuerle (2006) (SSDI applicants wait 132 days, on average, for an initial review of their claims, and appeals take an average of 485 days more).

10. Mermin and Steuerle (2006).

11. 20 CFR 404.1563, available at http://www.ecfr.gov/cgi-bin/text-idx?SID =fc3384da9d6d803b0745e8e086dc956c&node=20:2.0.1.1.5.16.197.58&rgn=div8 (persons

age 55 or older are in a category in which "age significantly affects a person's ability to adjust to other work.")

12. 20 CFR 404.1568(d)(4) provides that if a worker is 55+ and has a "severe impairment that limits [him] to sedentary or light work, we will find that [he] cannot make an adjustment to other work unless [he has] skills that [he] can transfer to other skilled or semiskilled work." See also Appendix 2 Medical-Vocational Guidelines, available at http://www.ecfr.gov/cgi-bin/text-idx?SID=fc3384da9d6d803b0745e8e086dc956c&node =20:2.0.1.1.5.16.202.102.12&rgn=div9 (providing tables that give preference to those with advanced age, limited education, little or unskilled work experience, and nontransferable skills).

13. Mermin and Steuerle (2006) point out the importance of disability to low-income, older workers and suggest briefly: "If policymakers wish to further protect those in poor health or in strenuous occupations while raising the retirement age, disability eligibility could be made more lenient at older ages." CBO (2012), p. 9 points out briefly that SSDI could be made easier to claim at older ages if the Social Security retirement age were raised.

14. Simpson-Bowles Commission (2010), p. 51.

15. OECD (2003), pp. 78–83.

16. Struble and Sullivan (2011).

17. See OECD (2003), pp. 65–67, 78–83.

18. Stapleton (2009).

19. Klieber (2009), p. 50–51.

20. Autor (2011), pp. 5–6.

21. Joffe-Walt (2013). For a discussion of the increasing size and cost of SSDI and its causes, see Marmor et al. (2014), pp. 166–168.

22. Pattison and Waldron (2013); Ruffing (2012); Ruffing (2014).

23. Autor and Duggan (2010); Duggan and Imberman (2009); Ruffing (2014).

24. See Milligan and Wise (2012) on the interaction between retirement policy and disability benefits.

25. Burkhauser and Daly (2011).

26. Autor and Duggan (2010); Autor (2011); Liebman and Smalligan (2013). See also MacDonald and O'Neil (2006); Lipman (2003).

27. Diller (1996), pp. 366–388.

28. U.S. Department of Labor, Bureau of Labor Statistics (2013), Table 303.

29. U.S. Department of Labor, Bureau of Labor Statistics (2013), Table 303.

30. U.S. Department of Labor, Bureau of Labor Statistics (2014).

31. CBO (2012), p. 9.

32. Rutledge (2014).

33. Gruber et al. (2010), p. 24, report that France had a policy that permitted early retirement for people 60 and over who lost their jobs.

34. Merline (2012).

35. Adams and Neumark (2006).

36. Neumark (2008).

37. Neumark (2008); Neumark and Song (2011); Adams (2004).

38. Neumark (2013) (finding that older workers did not fare better in the Great Recession in states with stronger age discrimination laws and suggesting that the effect may be due to the difficulty of detecting and proving discrimination amid major disruptions in the labor market).

39. Lahey (2006) (finding that age discrimination laws reduce employment of older workers by discouraging their hiring).

40. Neumark (2008), pp. 19–21.

41. Harper (2012) and Harper (2013).

42. Neumark (2008), pp. 18–19; Goda, Shoven, and Slavov (2007); Johnson et al. (2006); Munnell and Sass (2008), pp. 135–136.

43. Johnson et al. (2006), pp. 22–23; Olsen and Romig (2013); Gruber and Orszag (1999); Biggs (2013a).

44. Johnson et al. (2006), pp. 20–22. Biggs (2013a) also proposes elimination of the payroll tax on older workers to lessen work disincentives. Goda et al. (2009) point out that current Social Security rules also penalize long careers, and that establishing a "paid up" category of workers could boost net earnings for workers with long working lives.

45. Yale University Faculty Phased Retirement Plan (2012).

46. Details of the program will be filled in by regulations that have not yet been issued. Hicks (2014).

47. Hicks (2014); Yoder (2013).

48. Pedersini (2001).

49. U.S. Department of Labor Advisory Council (2008) (noting demand by employers and workers for phased retirement but also noting legal impediments).

9 FAMILIES AND RETIREMENT

1. Meyer (1996).

2. Social Security Administration (2013), Table 2.A21.

3. Butrica and Smith (2012b), p. 15 (pointing out that the duration of marriages ending in divorce has declined among more recent cohorts of women, with the result that Social Security divorced-spouse benefits may not be available; among women born 1936–1945, 80% had at least one marriage lasting 10 years, while among late Boomers (born 1956–1965), the percentage is projected to be 68%).

4. Steuerle (2011), pp. 8–9. See also Steuerle (2013).

5. *U.S. v. Windsor*, 570 U.S. 12 (2013), available at http://www.supremecourt.gov /opinions/12pdf/12-307_6j37.pdf.

6. U.S. Bureau of the Census (2012c), Table 599.

7. U.S. Department of Labor, Bureau of Labor Statistics (2013), p. 21, Table 7.

8. U.S. Department of Labor, Bureau of Labor Statistics (2013), p. 74, Table 20.

9. U.S. Department of Labor, Bureau of Labor Statistics (2013), p. 82, Table 25.

10. Bradbury and Katz (2004), p. 27, Table 1.

11. Edwards (2014), Table 2b.

12. DeNavas-Walt et al. (2013), p. 6, Table 1.

13. Cherlin (2010), p. 404.

14. Cherlin (2010), p. 405.

15. Groves (2011).

16. Lerman (2002); Cherlin (2010); Thomas and Sawhill (2005).

17. For criticism of the redistribution to the wealthy inherent in the spousal benefit, see Biggs (2013a). For data showing the regressive pattern of spousal and widows' benefits, see Meyer (1996), 461, Figure 3 (showing that low earners tend to receive benefits based on contributions, whereas high earners are more likely to receive a noncontributory spousal or widows' benefit).

18. Stone (2007).

19. See Graetz and Mashaw (1999), pp. 227–254 (proposing subsidies for families' purchases of childcare and housing).

20. Alstott (2004), (2008).

21. Social Security Administration (2013), Table 5.B1, Table 5.C2.

22. Favreault et al. (2012), p. 3 (Figure 3), p. 4 (Figure 4).

23. Favreault et al. (2012), p. 5 (Figure 6). See also Butrica and Smith (2012a), p. 6 (Chart 5) (predicting that 71% of late-Boomer wives will claim as retired workers, and only 7% will claim as wives only).

24. Social Security Administration (2012b).

25. For discussions of a minimum benefit as a means of protecting women, see Meyer (1996), pp. 457–458; Sigg and Taylor (2006), p. 214. For a proposed flat benefit to supplement present Social Security, see Lind et al. (2013). For a proposed flat benefit (supplemented by government-subsidized savings accounts) intended to improve adequacy for low earners, see Biggs (2013a). For additional minimum-benefit proposals intended to alleviate poverty, see Reno and Walker (2014); Mermin and Steuerle (2006); Steuerle (2011); Favreault et al. (2007); Favreault (2009a); Weller (2010); Sullivan et al. (2009).

26. Simpson-Bowles Commission (2010). See also the Debt Reduction Commission (Domenici-Rivlin) (2010), proposing a minimum benefit set at 133% of the poverty threshold for workers with a 30-year work history and up to 8 years of childcare credit.

27. Favreault (2009a).

28. Meyer (1996), p. 457. The special minimum benefit is technically on the books still but no longer applies to any workers. See Olsen and Hoffmeyer (2001/2002).

29. For a discussion of just policies toward parents, see Alstott (2004).

30. See Steuerle (2011); Herd (2009).

31. Fultz (2011).

32. Schneller (2012).

33. Brake (2012).

34. Schieber (2012), pp. 340–41. Sigg and Taylor (2006) describe a variety of joint-survivor annuities that exist in other countries.

10 Reforming the Taxation of Retirement

1. Ackerman and Alstott (1999).

2. Ackerman and Alstott (1999).

3. The Joint Committee on Taxation (2013) (predicting that tax expenditures on employer pensions and IRAs will amount to $126 billion in 2014).

4. Graetz and Mashaw (1999), pp. 99–101.

5. Lind et al. (2013), pp. 15–16.

6. Social Security Administration (2014d), Table 2.A6; Lind et al. (2013), p. 3 (Figure 1).

7. Marmor et al. (2014), p. 183.

8. See the studies cited in Gale (2011).

9. Chetty et al. (2013) conclude that price subsidies are less effective as a policy tool than automatic contributions in increasing savings for retirement. See also Vanderhei et al. (2006), pp. 103–107.

10. Sperling (2014).

11. Sperling (2005); Gale (2011). See also Gale et al. (2004) for a discussion of the savers' credit and possible reforms, including refundability).

12. Biggs (2013a).

13. Lind et al. (2013), p. 16.

14. Simpson-Bowles Commission (2010), p. 51 (proposing to increase the wage cap to cover 90% of wages by 2050); Lind et al. (2013), pp. 13–14; Reno and Walker (2014). See also Weller (2010), p. 45 (proposing to eliminate the wage cap on the employer tax only). For opposition, see Biggs (2013b) (opposing raising the payroll tax cap on the grounds that doing so would create a "growing resemblance to a welfare plan").

15. IRC section 1411.

16. For a proposal to tax capital income to fund an expansion of Social Security, see Lind et al. (2013), p. 14.

11 Principles and Politics in Retirement Policy

1. Siegel (2010).

2. Rawls (1993).

3. Rawls (1993), p. xxvii.

4. Rawls (1993), p. 268.

5. Rawls (1993), p. 16.

6. Eskridge and Ferejohn (2013); Ackerman (2014).

7. Rawls (1993), p. 228–229.

8. U.S. Bureau of the Census (2012d) (reporting that 71% of citizens aged 65–74 voted in the November 2012 election, compared with 50% of those aged 25–44).

9. U.S. Bureau of the Census (2012b), Table 1.

10. See Kahan et al. (2013) (describing an experiment that validates cultural cognition theory, which holds that people filter technocratic information through prior cultural worldviews).

11. See http://www.teaparty.org/audit-irs/ and http://teaparty2016.weebly.com /the-platform.html.

12. Franklin D. Roosevelt, "A Social Security Program Must Include All Those Who Need Its Protection," radio address, August 15, 1938, available at http://www.ssa .gov/history/fdrstmts.html#message2.

References

Ackerman, Bruce. 1981. *Social Justice in the Liberal State*. New Haven: Yale University Press.

———. 2014. *The Civil Rights Revolution*. Vol. 3, *We the People*. Cambridge: Harvard University Press.

Ackerman, Bruce, and Anne Alstott. 1999. *The Stakeholder Society*. New Haven: Yale University PRess.

Adams, Scott J. 2004. "Age Discrimination Legislation and the Employment of Older Workers." *Labour Economics* 11: 219–241.

Adams, Scott J., and David Neumark. 2006. "Age Discrimination in U.S. Labor Markets: A Review of the Evidence." In *Handbook on the Economics of Discrimination*, edited by W. M. Rodgers, 187. London: Edward Elgar Publishing.

Alstott, Anne L. 2004. *No Exit: What Parents Owe Their Children and What Society Owes Parents*. New York: Oxford University Press.

———. 2008. "Is the Family At Odds with Equality? The Legal Implications of Equality for Children." *Southern California Law Review* 82: 1.

———. 2010. "Why the Earned Income Tax Credit Doesn't Make Work Pay." *Law & Contemporary Problems* 73: 285.

———. 2013. "Updating the Welfare State: Marriage, the Income Tax, and Social Security in the Age of Individualism." *Tax Law Review* 66: 695.

American Community Survey. n.d. Disability Statistics. Accessed June 15, 2014. http://www.disabilitystatistics.org/reports/acs.cfm?statistic=1.

American Federation of State, Local, County, and Municipal Employees. 2012. "Congress: Hands Off My Social Security." http://action.afscme.org/c/51/p/dia /action3/common/public/?action_KEY=6818.

Anton, Ted. 2013. "The Greedy Geezer Theory," *Slate*, October 28. http://www.slate
     .com/articles/technology/future_tense/2013/10/labor_lump_do_older_workers
     _keep_young_workers_down.html.

Ashenfelter, Orley, and David Card. 2002. "Did the Elimination of Mandatory
     Retirement Affect Faculty Retirement Flows?" *American Economic Review*
     92: 957.

Autor, David, et al. 2011. "Does Delay Cause Decay? The Effect of Administrative
     Decision Time on the Labor Force Participation and Earnings of Disability
     Applicants." Working Paper No. 2011-258, September, University of Michigan
     Retirement Research Center.

Autor, David H. 2011. "The Unsustainable Rise of the Disability Rolls in the United
     States: Causes, Consequences, and Policy Options." Working Paper 17697,
     National Bureau of Economic Research, Cambridge, MA.

————. 2014. "Skills, Education, and the Rise of Earnings Inequality among the
     'Other 99 Percent.'" *Science* 344: 843.

Autor, David H., and Mark Duggan. 2010. *Supporting Work: A Proposal for Modernizing
     the U.S. Disability Insurance System*. Brookings Institution and the Center for
     American Progress, Hamilton Project, Washington, D.C..

Autor, David H., Lawrence F. Katz, and Melissa S. Kearney. 2008, "Trends in U.S.
     Wage Inequality: Revising the Revisionists." *Review and Economics and Statistics*
     90: 300. http://economics.mit.edu/files/586.

Avendano, Mauricio, and M. Maria Glymor. 2008. "Stroke Disparities in Older
     Americans: Is Wealth a More Powerful Indicator Than Income and Education?"
     Stroke 39: 1533.

Baker, Dean, and David Rosnick. 2010. *The Impact of Income Distribution on the
     Length of Retirement*. Issue Brief, Center for Economic and Policy Research.
     http://www.cepr.net/publications/reports/impact-of-income-distribution-on
     -retirement-length.

Banerjee, Sudipto, and David Blau. 2013. "Employment Trends by Age in the United
     States: Why Are Older Workers Different?" Working Paper WP 2013-285,
     Michigan Retirement Research Center (MRRC), http://www.mrrc.isr.umich
     .edu/publications/papers/pdf/wp285.pdf.

Beach, William W., and Gareth E. Davis. 1998. *Social Security's Rate of Return*. Report
     No. 98-01, January 15, Heritage Foundation Center for Data Analysis. http://
     www.heritage.org/research/reports/1998/01/social-securitys-rate-of-return.

Behaghel, Luc, and David M. Blau. 2012. "Framing Social Security Reform:
     Behavioral Responses to Changes in the Full Retirement Age." *American
     Economic Journal: Economic Policy* 4: 41–67.

Berger, Peter, and Hansfried Kellner. 1964. "Marriage and the Construction of
     Reality." *Diogenes* 46: 1–24.

Bianchi, Suzanne M., et al. 2006. *Changing Rhythms of American Family Life*. New
     York: Russell Sage Foundation, 64–67, 111.

Biggs, Andrew G. 2013a. "A New Vision for Social Security." American Enterprise
    Institute. http://www.aei.org/article/economics/retirement/social-security
    /a-new-vision-for-social-security/.
———. 2013b. "Don't Raise or Eliminate the Cap," *New York Times,* April 18. http://
    www.aei.org/article/economics/retirement/social-security/dont-raise-or-eliminate
    -the-cap/.
Biggs, Andrew G., Mark Sarney, and Christopher R. Tamborini. 2009. "A
    Progressivity Index for Social Security." Issue Paper No. 2009-01, January, Social
    Security Administration. http://www.ssa.gov/policy/docs/issuepapers/ip2009-01
    .html
Bingley, Paul, et al. 2012. "Disability Programs, Health, and Retirement in Denmark
    Since 1960." In *Social Security Programs and Retirement around the World:
    Historical Trends in Mortality and Health, Employment, and Disability Insurance
    Participation and Reforms,* edited by David A. Wise, 217. Chicago: University of
    Chicago Press.
Blahous, Charles. 2010. "Fairly Understanding the Simpson-Bowles Social Security
    Proposal." *e21 Economic Policies for the 21st Century at the Manhattan Institute,*
    November 11. http://www.economics21.org/commentary/fairly-understanding
    -simpson-bowles-social-security-proposal.
Bradbury, Katharine, and Jane Katz. 2004. "Wives' Work and Family Income
    Mobility." Public Policy Discussion Paper No. 04-3, Federal Reserve Bank of
    Boston. http://www.bos.frb.org/economic/ppdp/2004/ppdp0403.pdf.
Brake, Elizabeth. 2012. *Minimizing Marriage.* New York: Oxford University Press.
Bramlett, M. D., and W. D. Mosher. 2002. "Cohabitation, Marriage, Divorce, and
    Remarriage in the United States." *Vital Health Statistics* 23: 1. http://www.cdc
    .gov/nchs/data/series/sr_23/sr23_022.pdf.
Braveman, Paula A., et al. 2010. "Socioeconomic Disparities in Health in the United
    States." *American Journal of Public Health* 100: S186.
Burtless, Gary. 2013a. "Life Expectancy and Rising Income Inequality: Why the
    Connection Matters for Fixing Entitlements." Brookings Institution Opinion,
    October 23. http://www.brookings.edu/research/opinions/2012/10/23-inequality
    -life-expectancy-burtless.
———. 2013b. "The Impact of Population Aging and Delayed Retirement on
    Workforce Productivity." Working Paper 2013-11. http://crr.bc.edu/working
    -papers/the-impact-of-population-aging-and-delayed-retirement-on-workforce
    -productivity/.
Business Roundtable. 2013. "Social Security Reform and Medicare Modernization
    Proposals." January 2013. http://businessroundtable.org/sites/default/files
    /legacy/uploads/studies-reports/downloads/BRT_Social_Security_Reform_and
    _Medicare_Modernization_Proposals_-_January_2013_FINAL.pdf.
Butrica, Barbara. 2013. "Retirement Plan Assets." Urban Institute. http://www.urban
    .org/publications/412622.html.

Butrica, Barbara, Karen E. Smith, and Howard Iams. 2012. "This Is Not Your Parents' Retirement: Comparing Retirement Income Across Generations." *Social Security Bulletin* 72: 37. http://www.urban.org/UploadedPDF/This-Is-Not-Your-Parents-Retirement-Comparing-Retirement-Income-Across-Generations.pdf.

Butrica, Barbara A., and Karen E. Smith. 2012a. "The Impact of Changes in Couples' Earnings on Married Women's Social Security Benefits." *Social Security Bulletin* 72: 1. http://www.urban.org/UploadedPDF/1001591-The-Impact-of-Changes-in-Couples-Earnings-on-Married-Womens-Social-Security-Benefits.pdf.

———. 2012b. "The Retirement Prospects of Divorced Women." *Social Security Bulletin* 72: 11. http://www.urban.org/UploadedPDF/1001596-The-Retirement-Prospects-of-Divorced-Women.pdf.

Butrica, Barbara A., Eric J. Toder, and Demond J. Toohey. 2008. *Boomers at the Bottom: How Will Low Income Boomers Cope with Retirement?* Urban Institute Research Report. http://www.urban.org/UploadedPDF/1001217_low-income_boomers.pdf.

Cahill, Kevin E., et al. 2006. "Retirement Patterns from Career Employment." *The Gerontologist* 46: 514–523.

Campbell, Mary, et al. 2005. "Economic Inequality and Educational Attainment across a Generation." *Focus* 23: 11. http://www.irp.wisc.edu/publications/focus/pdfs/foc233b.pdf.

Center on Budget and Policy Priorities. 2012. "Policy Basics: Top Ten Facts about Social Security. November 6. http://www.cbpp.org/cms/?fa=view&id=3261.

Centers for Disease Control and Prevention. 2005. "Racial/Ethnic and Socioeconomic Disparities in Multiple Risk Factors for Heart Disease and Stroke." *Morbidity and Mortality Weekly* 54, Report 113.

———. 2012. "United States Life Tables, 2008." *National Vital Statistics Reports* 61 (3), September 24. http://www.cdc.gov/nchs/data/nvsr/nvsr61/nvsr61_03.pdf.

———. 2013. "Deaths: Final Data for 2010." *National Vital Statistics Reports* 61 (4). http://www.cdc.gov/nchs/data/nvsr/nvsr61/nvsr61_04.pdf.

Cherlin, Andrew J. 2009. *The Marriage Go-Round*. New York: Penguin Random House.

———. 2004. "The De-Institutionalization of American Marriage." *Journal of Marriage and Family* 66: 848.

———. 2010. "Demographic Trends in the United States: A Review of Research in the 2000s." *Journal of Marriage and Family* 72: 403.

Chetty Raj, et al. 2013. "Active vs. Passive Decisions and Crowd-Out in Retirement Savings Accounts: Evidence from Denmark." Working Paper No. 18565, December, National Bureau of Economic Research, Cambridge, MA.

Cohen, Wilbur J. 1957. *Retirement Policies Under Social Security.* Berkeley: University of California Press.

Congressional Budget Office. 2006. "Is Social Security Progressive?" December 15. http://www.cbo.gov/sites/default/files/cbofiles/ftpdocs/77xx/doc7705/12–15 -progressivity-ss.pdf.

———. 2008. "Life Expectancy Differentials." http://www.cbo.gov/publication /24768.

———. 2012. *Raising the Ages of Eligibility for Medicare and Social Security.* Issue Brief, January. https://www.cbo.gov/publication/42683.

Copen, Casey E., et al. 2012. *First Marriages in the United States: Data from the 2006–2010 National Survey of Family Growth.* Report No. 49, National Health Statistics. http://www.cdc.gov/nchs/data/nhsr/nhsr049.pdf.

Costa, Dora. 1999. *The Evolution of Retirement.* Chicago: University of Chicago Press.

———. 2005. "Causes of Improving Health and Longevity at Older Ages: A Review of the Explanations." *Genus* 61: 21. http://www.econ.ucla.edu/costa /genusreviewessay.pdf.

Crimmins, Eileen, et al. 2009. "Change in Disability-Free Life Expectancy for Americans 70 Years Old and Older." *Demography* 46: 627–646. http://www .ncbi.nlm.nih.gov/pmc/articles/PMC2831348/.

Cristia, Julian. 2009. "Rising Mortality and Life Expectancy Differentials by Lifetime Earnings in the United States." *Journal of Health Economics* 28: 984.

Curtis, John W., and Saranna Thornton. 2012–2013. *The Annual Report on the Economic Status of the Profession.* American Association of University Professors (AAUP). http://www.aaup.org/file/2012-13Economic-Status-Report.pdf.

Cutler, David M. 2001. "Declining Disability among the Elderly." *Health Affairs* (November/December): 11–27. http://scholar.harvard.edu/files/cutler/files /declining_disability_among_the_elderly.pdf.

Dalton, Matthew. 2013. "Idling Older Workers to Help the Young—or Not?" *Wall Street Journal,* June 13. http://online.wsj.com/news/articles/SB1000142412788732 4049504578543603704083428.

Daniels, Norman. 1988. *Am I My Parents' Keeper?* New York: Oxford University Press.

———. 2006. "Equity and Population Health: Toward a Broader Bioethics Agenda." *Hastings Center Report* 36: 22. http://www.hsph.harvard.edu/benchmark/ndaniels /pdf/HCRDaniels.pdf.

Daniels, Norman, Bruce P. Kennedy, and Ichiro Kawachi. 1999. "Why Justice Is Good for Our Health: The Social Determinants of Health Inequalities." *Daedalus* 128: 215–251.

Debt Reduction Task Force. 2010. "Restoring America's Future." Bipartisan Policy Institute. http://bipartisanpolicy.org/library/restoring-americas-future/.

DeNavas-Walt, Carmen, Bernadette D. Proctor, and Jessica C. Smith. 2013. *Income, Poverty, and Health Insurance Coverage in the United States: 2012.* U.S. Bureau of the Census. http://www.census.gov/prod/2013pubs/p60-245.pdf.

Diller, Matthew. 1996. "Entitlement and Exclusion: The Role of Disability in the Social Welfare System." *UCLA Law Review* 44: 361.

Duggan, James E., et al. 2008. "Mortality and Lifetime Income: Evidence From U.S. Social Security Records." *IMF Staff Papers* 55: 566.

Duggan, Mark, and Scott A. Imberman. 2009. "Why Are the Disability Rolls Skyrocketing? The Contribution of Population Characteristics, Economic Conditions, and Program Generosity." In *Health at Older Ages: The Causes and Consequences of Declining Disability among the Elderly,* edited by David M. Cutler and David A. Wise, 337. Cambridge, MA: National Bureau of Economic Research.

Dupre, Matthew E. 2007. "Educational Differences in Age-Related Patterns of Disease: Reconsidering the Cumulative Disadvantage and Age-as-Leveler Hypotheses." *Journal of Health and Social Behavior* 48: 1.

Dworkin, Ronald. 2002. *Sovereign Virtue.* Chicago: University of Chicago Press.

Edwards, Ashley. 2014. *Dynamics of Economic Well-Being and Poverty, 2009–2011.* U.S. Bureau of the Census. http://www.census.gov/prod/2014pubs/p70–137.pdf.

Eisner, Mark, et al. 2009. "Socioeconomic Status, Race, and COPD Health Outcomes." *Journal of Epidemiology & Community Health* 65: 26.

Ellin, Abby. 2014. "For Some Retirees, a Second Act Is Easier Than Expected." *New York Times,* June 6. http://www.nytimes.com/2014/06/07/your-money/for-retirees-a-second-career.html?hpw&rref=business&_r=1.

Erikson, Erik. 1959. "Identity and the Life Cycle: Selected Papers." *Psychology Issues* 1 (1).

Eskridge, William N., Jr., and John Ferejohn. 2013. *A Republic of Statutes: The New American Constitution.* New Haven: Yale University Press.

Favreault, Melissa M. 2009a. "A New Minimum Benefit for Low Lifetime Earners." In *Strengthening Social Security for Vulnerable Groups,* edited by Virginia P. Reno and Joni Lavery, 31. City: Washington, DC: National Academy of Social Insurance.

———. 2009b. "Rising Tides and Retirement: The Aggregate and Distributional Effects of Differential Wage Growth on Social Security." Urban Institute, April. http://www.urban.org/uploadedpdf/411872_risingtidesandretirement.pdf.

Favreault, Melissa M., et al. 2007. *Minimum Benefits in Social Security Could Reduce Aged Poverty.* Brief No. 11, January, The Retirement Project, Urban Institute. http://www.urban.org/UploadedPDF/311416_Reduce_Aged_Poverty.pdf.

Favreault, Melissa M., et al. 2012. *Boomers' Retirement Income Prospects.* Brief No. 34, February, Urban Institute. http://www.urban.org/UploadedPDF/412490-boomers-retirement-income-prospects.pdf.

Favreault, Melissa M., and Richard W. Johnson. 2010. "Raising Social Security's Retirement Age." Urban Institute. http://www.urban.org/uploadedpdf/412167-Raising-Social-Security.pdf.

Fendrich, Laurie. 2014. "The Forever Professors." *Chronicle of Higher Education* (November). http://m.chronicle.com/article/Retire-Already-/149965.

Freedman, Marc. 2007. *Encore: Finding Work that Matters in the Second Half of Life.* New York: Public Affairs.

Freedman, Vicki A., et al. 2013. "Trends in Late-Life Activity Limitations in the United States: An Update from Five National Surveys. *Demography* 50: 661.

Freedman, Vicki A., et al. 2014. "Behavioral Adaptation and Late-Life Disability: A New Spectrum for Assessing Public Health Impacts." *American Journal of Public Health* 104 (February): e88.

Fry, Richard, and D'Vera Cohan. 2010. "New Economics of Marriage: The Rise of Wives." Pew Research Center, January 19. http://pewresearch.org/pubs/1466 /economics-marriage-rise-of-wives. (See also BLS Table 25, http://www.bls.gov /cps/wlf-table25–2011.pdf.)

Fuller-Thompson, E., et al. 2009. "Basic ADL Disability and Functional Limitation Rates among Older Americans from 2000–2005: The End of the Decline?" *Journal of Gerontology* 64: 1333–1336.

Fultz, Elaine. 2011. "Pension Crediting for Caregivers: Policies in Finland, France, Germany, Sweden, the United Kingdom, Canada, and Japan." Institute for Women's Policy Research, Washington, DC.

Gale, William G. 2011. "Tax Reform Options: Promoting Retirement Security." Testimony submitted to the U.S. Senate Committee on Finance, September 15. http://www.taxpolicycenter.org/UploadedPDF/901448-Gale-Tax-Reform -Options.pdf.

Gale, William G., J. Mark Iwry, and Peter R. Orszag. 2004. "The Saver's Credit: Issues and Options." Brookings Institution. http://www.brookings.edu/views /papers/gale/20040419.pdf.

Galston, William A. 2007. "Why President Bush's 2005 Social Security Initiative Failed, and What It Means for the Future of the Program." Brookings Institution. http://www.brookings.edu/research/papers/2007/09/21governance -galston.

Geiger, Kim. 2012. "Alan Simpson Pens Scathing Letter to 'Greedy Geezers' Retiree Group." *L.A. Times,* May 23. http://articles.latimes.com/2012/may/23/news /la-pn-alan-simpson-pens-scathing-letter-to-greedy-geezers-retiree -group-20120523.

Ghilarducci, Teresa. 2005. "Americans Should Not Be Required to Work Longer." *In Search of Retirement Security,* edited by Teresa Ghilarducci et al., 36–45. New York: Century Foundation Press.

Goda, Gopi Shah, John B. Shoven, and Sita Nataraj Slavov. 2007. "A Tax on Work for the Elderly: Medicare as a Secondary Payer." Working Paper No. 13383, September, National Bureau of Economic Research, Cambridge, MA.

———. 2009. "Removing the Disincentives in Social Security for Long Careers." In

Social Security Policy in a Changing Environment, edited by Jeffrey R. Brown et al., 21. Chicago: University of Chicago Press.

Gokhale, Jagadeesh. 2013. "Spending beyond Our Means: We Are Bankrupting Future Generations." Cato Institute White Paper, February 13. http://www.cato.org /publications/white-paper/spending-beyond-our-means-how-we-are-bankrupting -future-generations.

Goss, Stephen C. 2010. Letter to National Commission on Fiscal Responsibility and Reform, Office of the Chief Actuary, Social Security Administration, December 1. https://www.socialsecurity.gov/OACT/solvency/FiscalCommission_20101201.pdf.

Government Accountability Office (GAO). 2014. *Retirement Security: Challenges for Those Claiming Social Security Benefits Early and New Health Coverage Options.* GAO-14-311, April. http://www.gao.gov/assets/670/662727.pdf.

Graetz, Michael, and Jerry Mashaw. 1999. *True Security.* New Haven: Yale University Press.

Gray, Harry. 2005. "The Rediscovery of Middle Age." *Res. in Post-Compulsory Education* 10: 57.

Groves, Robert. 2011. "America's Changing Households." Census Bureau presentation. http://www.census.gov/newsroom/cspan/households.html.

Gruber, Jonathan, Kevin Milligan, and David A. Wise. 2010. Introduction and Summary, *Social Security Programs and Retirement Around the World: The Relationship to Youth Unemployment,* edited by Jonathan Gruber and David A. Wise. Chicago: University of Chicago Press.

Gruber, Jonathan, and Peter Orszag. 1999. *What to Do about the Social Security Earnings Test?* Issue Brief. Boston College Center for Retirement Research. http://crr.bc.edu/wp-content/uploads/1999/07/ib_1.pdf.

Hamilton, Brady E., et al. 2011. *Births: Preliminary Data for 2010.* National Vital Statistics Reports, Centers for Disease Control. http://www.cdc.gov/nchs/data /nvsr/nvsr60/nvsr60_02.pdf.

Hamm, Trent. 2010. "What Does an Extended Lifespan Mean in Terms of Retirement Savings?" *Christian Science Monitor,* June 14. http://m.csmonitor .com/Business/The-Simple-Dollar/2010/0614/What-does-an-extended-lifespan -mean-in-terms-of-retirement-savings.

———. 2011. "Retirement at 65? But It's the New 45!" *Christian Science Monitor,* June 10. http://www.csmonitor.com/Business/The-Simple-Dollar/2011/0610 /Retirement-at-65-But-it-s-the-new-45%21.

Han, Shin-Kap, and Phyllis Moen. 1999. "Clocking Out: Temporal Patterning of Retirement." *Am. J. Soc.* 105: 191.

Handler, Joel F. 1995. *The Poverty of Welfare Reform.* New Haven: Yale University Press.

Hannon, Kerry. 2014. "For Many Older Americans, an Enterprising Path." *New York Times,* February 7. http://www.nytimes.com/2014/02/08/your-money/for

-many-older-americans-an-entrepreneurial-path.html?nl=booming&emc=edit_bg_20140211.

Harden, Blaine. 2007. "Numbers Drop for the Married with Children: Institution Becoming the Choice of the Educated, Affluent." *Washington Post,* March 4. http://www.washingtonpost.com/wp-dyn/content/article/2007/03/03/AR2007030300841.html.

Harper, Michael C. 2012. "Reforming the Age Discrimination in Employment Act: Proposals and Prospects." *Employee Rights and Employment Policy Journal* 16: 13.

———. 2013. "A Gap in the Agenda: Enhancing the Regulation of Age Discrimination in Employment." In *Age and Equality Law,* edited by Michael Selmi, 339. Burlington, VT: Ashgate.

Herd, Pamela. 2009. "Crediting Care in Social Security: A Proposal for an Income-Tested Care Supplement." http://www.nasi.org/sites/default/files/research/Pamela_Herd_January_2009_Rockefeller_Project.pdf.

Hicks, Josh. 2014. "Lawmakers Press OPM to Finally Begin Phased Retirement for Federal Workers." *Washington Post,* July 8. http://www.washingtonpost.com/politics/federal_government/lawmakers-press-opm-to-finally-begin-phased-retirement-for-federal-workers/2014/07/08/1206d8a8–06e8–11e4-a0dd-f2b22a257353_story.html.

Hill, Catherine, and Virginia P. Reno. 2005. "The Financial Case for Late Retirement." *In Search of Retirement Security,* edited by Teresa Ghilarducci et al., 9. New York: Century Foundation Press.

Ho, Jessica Y., and Andrew Fenelon. 2013. "Contribution of Smoking to Educational Differences in U.S. Life Expectancy." Princeton University, September. http://paa2014.princeton.edu/uploads/140737.

Hout, Michael, et al. 1993. "Making the Grade: Educational Stratification in the United States, 1925–1989." In *Persistent Inequality: Changing Educational Attainment in Thirteen Countries,* edited by Yossi Shavit and Hans-Peter Blossfeld, 25. Boulder, CO: Westview Press.

Houtenville, Andrew J., et al. 2009. "Complex Survey Questions and the Impact of Enumeration Procedures: Census/American Community Survey Disability Questions. Social Science Research Network (SSRN). https://papers.ssrn.com/sol3/papers.cfm?abstract_id=1444534.

Hoyert, Donna L. 2012. *75 Years of Mortality in the United States, 1935–2010.* NCHS Data Brief No. 88, March, Centers for Disease Control. http://www.cdc.gov/nchs/data/databriefs/db88.htm.

Hoynes, Hilary, Marianne Page, and Ann Huff-Stevens. 2006. "Poverty in America: Trends and Explanations." *Journal of Economic Perspectives* 20: 47–68.

Hulse, Carl. 2014. "Politically, V.A. Scandal Cuts Both Ways." *New York Times,* May 30. http://www.nytimes.com/2014/05/31/us/politics/pressing-va-scandal-holds-political-perils-for-gop.html?_r=0.

Joffe-Walt, Chana. 2013. "Unfit for Work: The Startling Rise of Disability in America." National Public Radio. http://apps.npr.org/unfit-for-work/.

John, David, and Virginia Reno. 2012. "Option: Begin Means-Testing Social Security Benefits." *AARP Perspectives,* June. http://www.aarp.org/content/dam/aarp /research/public_policy_institute/econ_sec/2012/option-means-test-social -security-benefits-AARP-ppi-econ-sec.pdf.

Johnson, Richard W. 2012. *Impact of Federal Policies on an Aging Workforce with Disabilities.* National Technical Assistance and Research Center Report, March. http://www.urban.org/UploadedPDF/1001621-Impact-of-Federal-Policies-on -an-Aging-Workforce-with-Disabilities.pdf.

Johnson, Richard W., Janette Kawachi, and Eric K. Lewis. 2009. "Older Workers on the Move: Recareering in Later Life." AARP Public Policy Institute Research Report, Washington, D.C..

Johnson, Richard W., Gordon Mermin, and C. Eugene Steuerle. 2006. "Work Impediments at Older Ages." The Retirement Project, Urban Institute, May. http://www.urban.org/UploadedPDF/311313_work_impediments.pdf.

Johnson, Richard W., and David Neumark. 1997. "Age Discrimination, Job Separations, and Employment Status of Older Workers: Evidence from Self-Reports." *Journal of Human Resources* 32: 779–811, 782.

Johnson, Richard W., and Janice Park. 2012. "Unemployment Statistics on Older Americans." Urban Institute, September 7. http://www.urban.org/publications /411904.html.

Joint Committee on Taxation. 2013. *Estimates of Federal Tax Expenditures for Fiscal Years 2012–2017.* JCS-1-13. http://www.jct.gov/publications.html?func=startdown &id=4503.

Jönsson, Lisa, et al. 2012. "Disability Insurance, Population Health, and Employment in Sweden." In *Social Security Programs and Retirement around the World: Historical Trends in Mortality and Health, Employment, and Disability Insurance Participation and Reforms,* edited by David A. Wise, 79. Chicago: University of Chicago Press.

June, Audrey Williams. 2012. "Aging Professors Create a Faculty Bottleneck." *Chronicle of Higher Education* (March 18).

Kahan, Dan, et al. 2013. "Motivated Numeracy and Enlightened Self-Government." http://www.culturalcognition.net/browse-papers/motivated-numeracy-and -enlightened-self-government.html.

Kahneman, Daniel, and Amos Tversky. 1984. "Choices, Values, and Frames." *American Psychologist* 39: 341.

Kaplan, Richard. 2012. "Reforming the Taxation of Retirement Income." *Virginia Tax Review* 32: 327.

Keane, Tom. 2013. "Touching the Third Rail of Politics." *Boston Globe,* April 21. http://www.bostonglobe.com/opinion/2013/04/20/social-security-third-rail -politics/YWLU4kyHo6y8ivZJabCRMK/story.html.

Kim, Jungmeen E., and Phyllis Moen. 2001. "Is Retirement Good or Bad for Subjective Well-Being?" *Current Directions in Psych. Sci.* 10: 83.

Klees, Barbara S., et al. 2014. *Brief Summaries of Medicare and Medicaid.* Centers for Medicare and Medicaid Services, November 1. http://www.cms.gov/Research-Statistics-Data-and-Systems/Statistics-Trends-and-Reports/Medicare ProgramRatesStats/Downloads/MedicareMedicaidSummaries2014.pdf.

Klieber, Eric. 2009. "Strengthening Social Security for Workers in Physically Demanding Occupations. In *Strengthening Social Security for Vulnerable Groups,* edited by Virginia P. Reno and Joni Lavery, 49. Washington, DC: National Academy of Social Insurance.

Knoll, Melissa, and Anya Olsen. 2014. "Incentivizing Delayed Claiming of Social Security Retirement Benefits before Reaching the Full Retirement Age." *Social Security Bulletin* 74: 21. http://papers.ssrn.com/sol3/papers.cfm?abstract_id =2520547.

Kopcke, Richard, Zhenyu Li, and Anthony Webb. 2014. "The Effect of Increasing Earnings Dispersion on Social Security Payroll Tax Receipts." Working Paper, Center for Retirement Research at Boston College. http://crr.bc.edu/wp-content /uploads/2014/05/wp_2014–61.pdf.

Kopczuk, Wojciech, Emanuel Saez, and Jae Song. 2010. "Earnings Inequality and Mobility in the United States: Evidence from Social Security Data since 1937." *Quarterly Journal of Economics* 125: 91. http://www.columbia.edu/~wk2110/bin /mobility_final.pdf.

Kronman, Anthony. 1981. "Talent Pooling." *Nomos* 26: 58.

Kuttner, Robert. 2012. "Greedy Geezers, Reconsidered." *American Prospect* (December 3). http://prospect.org/article/greedy-geezers-reconsidered.

Lahey, Joanna. 2006. "State Age Protection Laws and the Age Discrimination in Employment Act." Working Paper No. 12048, National Bureau of Economic Research, Cambridge, MA.

Leonesio, Michael V., Denton R. Vaughan, and Bernard Wixon. 2003. *Increasing the Early Retirement Age under Social Security: Health, Work, and Financial Resources.* Brief No. 7, National Academy of Social Insurance. http://www.nasi .org/research/2004/increasing-early-retirement-age-under-social-security -health.

Lerman, Robert I. 2002. "Marriage and the Economic Well-Being of Families with Children." Urban Institute. http://www.urban.org/url.cfm?ID=410541.

Lester, Gillian. 2011. "Can Joe the Plumber Support Redistribution? Law, Social Preferences, and Sustainable Policy Design." *Tax Law Review* 64: 313.

Liebman, Jeffrey B., and Jack A. Smalligan. 2013. "An Evidence-Based Path to Disability Insurance Reform." Hamilton Project, Brookings Institution. http:// www.brookings.edu/research/papers/2013/02/disability-insurance-reform.

Lind, Michael, et al. 2013. "Expanded Social Security: A Plan to Increase Retirement

Security for All Americans." New America Foundation. http://growth
.newamerica.net/sites/newamerica.net/files/policydocs/LindHillHiltonsmith
Freedman_ExpandedSocialSecurity_04_03_13.pdf.

Lipman, Francine. 2003. "Enabling Work for People with Disabilities: A Post-
Integrationist Revision of Underutilized Tax Incentives." *American University
Law Review* 53: 393.

Lu, Liquin, Andrew J. Rettenmaier, and Thomas R. Saving. 2012. "Lifetime Income,
Longevity, and Social Security Progressivity. Study No. 342, December 11,
National Center for Policy Analysis. *http://www.ncpa.org/pub/st342.*

MacDonald, Bryon R., and Megan O'Neil. 2006. "Being American: The Way Out of
Poverty." World Institute on Disability, City, State.

Manton, Kenneth G., and XiLiang Gu. 2001. "Changes in the Prevalence of Chronic
Disability in the United States Black and Nonblack Population Above Age 65
from 1982 to 1999." *Proceedings of the National Academy of Sciences.* http://
faculty.usfsp.edu/jsokolov/agehlt5manton.htm.

Marmor, Theodore R., Jerry L. Mashaw, and John Pakutka. 2014. *Social Insurance:
America's Neglected Heritage and Contested Future.* Thousand Oaks, CA: CQ
Press.

Marr, Chuck, et al. 2014. "Lone Group Taxed into Poverty Should Receive a Larger
EITC." Center on Budget and Policy Priorities, April 4. http://www.cbpp.org
/research/lone-group-taxed-into-poverty-should-receive-a-larger-eitc.

Martin, Linda G., et al. 2010. "Trends in Health of Older Adults in the United
States: Past, Present, Future." *Demography* 47 (Supplement): S17.

Mashaw, Jerry, and Virginia Reno. 1996. *Balancing Security and Opportunity: The
Challenge of Disability Income Policy.* Report of the Disability Policy Panel,
National Academy of Social Insurance, Washington, DC.

Mastrobuoni, Giovanni. 2009. "Labor Supply Effects of the Recent Social Security
Benefit Cuts: Empirical Estimates Using Cohort Discontinuities." *Journal of
Public Economics* 93: 1224–1233.

Mechanic, David. 2002. "Disadvantage, Inequality, and Social Policy." *Health Affairs*
21: 48–59.

Merline, John. 2012. "The Sharp Rise in Disability Claims." Federal Reserve Bank of
Richmond. http://www.richmondfed.org/publications/research/region_focus
/2012/q2–3/pdf/feature3.pdf.

Mermin, Gordon B. T., and C. Eugene Steuerle. 2006. *Would Raising the Social
Security Retirement Age Harm Low-Income Groups?* Brief No. 19, December,
Urban Institute. http://www.urban.org/UploadedPDF/311413_Raising
_Retirement_Age.pdf.

Meyer, Madonna Harrington. 1996. "Making Claims as Workers or Wives: The
Distribution of Social Security Benefits." *Am. Soc. Rev.* 61: 449, 452.

Milligan, Kevin, and David A. Wise. 2012. Introduction and Summary, *Social*

Security Programs and Retirement around the World: Historical Trends in Mortality and Health, Employment, and Disability Insurance Participation and Reforms, edited by Jonathan Gruber and David A. Wise, 1. Chicago: University of Chicago Press.

Mitchell, Josh. 2014. "Educational Attainment and Earnings Inequality among U.S.-Born Men: A Lifetime Perspective." Urban Institute, April. http://www .urban.org/UploadedPDF/413092-Educational-Attainment-and-Earnings -Inequality-among-US-Born-Men.pdf.

Moen, Phyllis. 2003. "Midcourse: Navigating Retirement and a New Life Stage." In *Handbook of the Life Course,* edited by Jeylan T. Mortimer and Michael J. Shanahan, 269. New York: Springer-Verlag.

Morrissey, Monique, and Natalie Sabadish. 2013. "Retirement Inequality Chartbook: How the 401(k) Revolution Created a Few Big Winners and Many Losers." Economic Policy Institute, September 6. http://www.epi.org/publication /retirement-inequality-chartbook/.

Munnell, Alicia, et al. 2009. *National Retirement Risk Index: How Much Longer Do We Need to Work?* Issue in Brief 9-7, Boston College Center for Retirement Research.

Munnell, Alicia, et al. 2012. "The National Retirement Risk Index: How Much Longer Do We Need to Work?" Boston College Center for Retirement Research. http://crr.bc.edu/wp-content/uploads/2012/06/IB_12-12-508.pdf.

Munnell, Alicia H. 2013. "Social Security's Real Retirement Age is 70." Working Paper No. 13-15, October, Boston College Center for Retirement Research. http://crr.bc.edu/wp-content/uploads/2013/10/IB_13–15.pdf.

Munnell, Alicia H., and Steven A. Sass. 2008. *Working Longer.* Washington, D.C.: Brookings Institution Press.

National Academy of Social Insurance. 2014. "What Is the Social Security Retirement Age? Accessed June 19. http://www.nasi.org/learn/socialsecurity /retirement-age.

National Research Council (U.S.). 2011. *Panel on Understanding Divergent Trends in Longevity in High-Income Countries.* Edited by Eileen Crimmins et al. http:// www.ncbi.nlm.nih.gov/books/NBK62373/.

Neumark, David. 2008. "The Age Discrimination in Employment Act and the Challenge of Population Aging." Working Paper No. 14317, National Bureau of Economic Research, Cambridge, MA.

Neumark, David. 2013. "Did Age Discrimination Protections Help Older Workers Weather the Great Recession?" Working Paper No. 19216, National Bureau of Economic Research, Cambridge, MA.

Neumark, David, and Joanne Song. 2011. "Do Stronger Age Discrimination Laws Make Social Security Reforms More Effective?" Working Paper No. 17467, National Bureau of Economic Research, Cambridge, MA.

Offe, Claus, and Johan de Deken. 2013. "Sabbatical Grants." In *Basic Income: An Anthology of Contemporary Research,* edited by Karl Widerquist et al., 447. London: Wiley-Blackwell.

Office of Management and Budget. 2014. Budget of the United States, FY 2015, Historical Tables. http://www.whitehouse.gov/omb/budget/Historicals.

Old Age, Survivors, and Disability Insurance Trustees. 2013. 2013 OASDI Trustees Report. Social Security Administration. https://www.socialsecurity.gov/OACT/TR/2013/.

Olsen, Anya, and Kathleen Romig. 2013. "Modeling Behavioral Responses to Eliminating the Retirement Earnings Test." *Social Security Bulletin* 73: 1. http://www.ssa.gov/policy/docs/ssb/v73n1/v73n1p39.html.

Olsen, Kelly A., and Don Hoffmeyer. 2001/2002. "Social Security's Special Minimum Benefit." *Soc. Sec. Bull.* 64: 1. http://www.socialsecurity.gov/policy/docs/ssb/v64n2/v64n2p1.pdf.

Olshansky, Jay, et al. 2012. "Differences in Life Expectancy Due to Race and Educational Differences Are Widening, and Many May Not Catch Up." *Health Affairs* 31 (8/August): 1803.

Olson, Elizabeth. 2014. "Of the Right Age, but Can't Seem to Stay Retired." *New York Times,* December 5. http://www.nytimes.com/2014/12/06/your-money/some-prefer-to-quit-retirement-and-return-to-work.html?emc=edit_bg_20141209&nl=booming&nlid=44003240.

Organisation for Economic Cooperation and Development (OECD). 2003. *Transforming Disability into Ability: Policies to Promote Work and Income Security for Disabled People.* Paris: OECD.

———. 2013. *Pensions at a Glance.* Paris: OECD.

Pattison, David, and Hilary Waldron. 2013. "Growth in New Disabled-Worker Entitlements, 1970–2008." *Social Security Bulletin* 73 (4): 25. https://www.socialsecurity.gov/policy/docs/ssb/v73n4/v73n4p25.html.

Pedersini, Roberto. 2001. "Progressive Retirement in Europe." European Industrial Relations Observatory On-Line. http://www.eurofound.europa.eu/eiro/2001/09/study/tn0109184s.htm.

Pezzin, Liliana E., Robert A. Pollak, and Barbara S. Schone. 2013. "Complex Families and Late-Life Outcomes among Elderly Persons: Disability, Institutionalization, and Longevity." *Journal of Marriage and Family* 75: 1084–1097.

Piketty, Thomas, and Emmanuel Saez. 2003. "Income Inequality in the United States, 1913–1998 (updated to 2012)." *Q. J. Econ.* 118: 1. http://eml.berkeley.edu/~saez/pikettyqje.pdf.

Posner, Richard A. 1995. *Aging and Old Age.* Chicago: University of Chicago Press.

Pozen, Robert C. 2005. "A Progressive Solution to Social Security." *Wall Street Journal,* March 15.

Prial, Dunstan. 2013. "Social Security Faces Insolvency in 20 Years." *Fox Business,*

May 31. http://www.foxbusiness.com/personal-finance/2013/05/31/medicare
-outlook-brightens-social-security-outlook-steady/.

Quadagno, Jill. 2008. *Aging and the Life Course*. New York: McGraw-Hill.

Quinn, Joseph F. 2005. "Americans Can Work Longer." In *In Search of Retirement Security*, edited by Teresa Ghilarducci et al., 25–35. New York: Century Foundation Press.

Rawls, John. 1971. *A Theory of Justice*. Cambridge: Belknap Press.

———. 1975. "A Kantian Conception of Equality." *Cambridge Review* (February): 94–99.

———. 1993. *Political Liberalism*. New York: Columbia University Press.

Reno, Virginia P., and Joni Lavery. 2007. "Social Security and Retirement Income Adequacy." Brief No. 25, National Academy of Social Insurance. http://www.ncpssm.org/pdf/nasi-report.pdf.

Reno, Virginia P., and Elisa A. Walker. 2013. "Social Security Benefits, Finances, and Policy Options: A Primer." National Academy of Social Insurance, June. http://www.nasi.org/sites/default/files/research/2013_Social_Security_Primer_PDF.pdf.

Reznik, Gayle L., Dave Shoffner, and David A. Weaver. 2005/2006. "Coping with the Demographic Challenge: Fewer Children and Living Longer. *Social Security Bulletin* 66.

Ruffing, Kathy, and Paul N. Van de Water. 2011. "Bowles-Simpson Social Security Proposal Not a Good Starting Point for Reforms." Center on Budget and Policy Priorities, February 17. http://www.cbpp.org/cms/index.cfm?fa=view&id=3402.

Ruffing, Kathy A. 2012. "Social Security Disability Insurance Is Vital to Workers with Severe Impairments." August 9, Center on Budget and Policy Priorities, Washington, D.C..

———. 2014. "How Much of the Growth in Disability Insurance Stems from Demographic Changes?" Center on Budget and Policy Priorities, January 27. http://www.cbpp.org/cms/index.cfm?fa=view&id=4080.

Rutledge, Matthew S. 2014. *How Long Do Unemployed Older Workers Search for a Job?* Issue Brief No. 14-3, February, Boston College Center for Retirement Research. http://crr.bc.edu/wp-content/uploads/2014/02/IB_14-3-508.pdf.

Rutledge, Matthew S., Norma B. Coe, and Kendrew Wong. 2012. "Who Claimed Social Security Early Due to the Great Recession?" Center for Retirement Research at Boston College. http://crr.bc.edu/wp-content/uploads/2012/07/IB_12-14-508.pdf.

Sauré, Philip, and Hosny Zoabi. 2012. "Retirement Age across Countries: The Role of Occupations. http://www.snb.ch/n/mmr/reference/working_paper_2012_06/source/working_paper_2012_06.n.pdf.

Schieber, Sylvester J. 2012. *The Predictable Surprise: The Unraveling of the U.S. Retirement System*. New York: Oxford University Press.

Schneller, Jonathan. 2012. "The Earned Income Tax Credit and the Administration of Tax Expenditures." *North Carolina Law Review* 90: 719.

Schoeni, Robert F., et al. 2008. "Socioeconomic and Demographic Disparities in Trends in Old-Age Disability." In *Health at Older Ages,* edited by David M. Cutler and David A. Wise, 75.

Shoven, John B., and Gopi Shah Goda. 2010. "Adjusting Government Policies for Age Inflation." In *Demography and the Economy,* edited by John B. Shoven,143. Chicago: University of Chicago Press.

Siegel, Elyse. 2010. "George W. Bush Reveals His Biggest Failure Was Not Privatizing Social Security." *Huffington Post,* October 22.

Siegel, Matt. 2014. "Australia to Raise Retirement Age to 70 by 2035, Treasurer Says." Reuters, May 1. http://www.reuters.com/article/2014/05/02/us-australia -pensionsage-idUSBREA4102D20140502?feedType=RSS&virtualBrandChannel =11563.

Sigg, Roland, and Rebecca Taylor. 2006. "Reforming Social Security for a Long-Life Society: What Impact on Women?" In *Gender and Social Security Reform: What's Fair for Women?* edited by Neil Gilbert, 207. Piscataway, NJ: Transaction Publishers.

Simpson-Bowles Commission. 2010. *The Moment of Truth: Report of the National Commission on Fiscal Responsibility and Reform.* http://www.fiscalcommission. gov/news/moment-truth-report-national-commission-fiscal-responsibility -and-reform.

Skocpol, Theda. 1988. "The Limits of the New Deal System and the Roots of Contemporary Welfare Dilemmas." In *The Politics of Social Policy in the United States,* edited by Margaret Weir, Ann Shola Orloff, and Theda Skocpol, 293–311. Princeton: Princeton University Press.

———. 1991. "Targeting within Universalism: Politically Viable Policies to Combat Poverty in the United States." In *The Urban Underclass,* edited by Christopher Jencks and Paul Peterson, 411–436. Washington, D.C.: Brookings Institution Press.

Slear, Tom. 2014. "I'm an Army Veteran, and My Benefits Are Too Generous." *Washington Post,* June 6. http://www.washingtonpost.com/opinions/im-an-army -veteran-and-my-benefits-are-too-generous/2014/06/06/5e8db2ec-eb35-11e3 -9f5c-9075d5508f0a_story.html.

Social Security Administration. 1983. Social Security Fact Sheet, Increase in Retirement Age. https://www.socialsecurity.gov/pressoffice/IncRetAge.html.

———. 2012a. *Social Security Bulletin,* Annual Statistical Supplement.

———. 2012b. Women and Dual Entitlement, 2025–2080. http://www.social security.gov/retirementpolicy/projections/women-dual-2025.html

———. 2012c. Measures of Central Tendency for Wage Data, Office of the Chief Actuary. http://www.ssa.gov/oact/cola/central.html.

———. 2013. Social Security Bulletin, Annual Statistical Supplement. https://www
.socialsecurity.gov/policy/docs/statcomps/supplement/2013/index.html.

———. 2014a. Benefit Formula Bend Points. Accessed July 3. http://www.ssa.gov
/oact/cola/bendpoints.html.

———. 2014b. Effect of Early or Delayed Retirement on Retirement Benefits.
http://www.socialsecurity.gov/OACT/ProgData/ar_drc.html.

———. 2014c. Exempt Amounts under the Earnings Test. https://www.social
security.gov/OACT/COLA/rtea.html.

———. 2014d. Income of the Population 55 or Older, 2012. http://www.social
security.gov/policy/docs/statcomps/income_pop55/.

———. 2014e. Primary Insurance Amount. Accessed July 3. http://www.ssa.gov
/oact/cola/piaformula.html.

———. 2014f. OASDI and SSI Program Rates and Limits. http://www.ssa.gov
/policy/docs/quickfacts/prog_highlights/index.html.

———. 2014g. Retirement Planner: Benefits By Year of Birth. https://www
.socialsecurity.gov/retire2/agereduction.htm.

———. 2014h. Social Security Benefit Amounts. Accessed July 3. http://www.ssa
.gov/oact/cola/Benefits.html.

———. 2014i. Social Security History. http://www.ssa.gov/history/lifeexpect.html.

———. 2015. Research Note #12: Taxation of Social Security Benefits. Accessed May.
http://www.ssa.gov/history/taxationofbenefits.html.

Sperling, Gene. 2005. "A Progressive Framework for Social Security Reform." Center
for American Progress, Washington, D.C.

Sperling, Gene B. 2014. "A 401(k) for All." New York Times, July 22. http://www
.nytimes.com/2014/07/23/opinion/a-401-k-for-all.html.

Spletzer, James R. 2014. Inequality Statistics from the LEHD, Center for Economic
Studies. U.S. Census Bureau, June 5. http://www.census.gov/fesac/pdf/2014
–06–13/Spletzer_Background.pdf.

Stapleton, David C. 2009. "Employment Support for the Transition to Retirement:
Can a New Program Help Older Workers Continue to Work and Protect Those
Who Cannot?" Center for Studying Disability Policy, Mathematica Research,
Inc. http://assets.aarp.org/rgcenter/econ/2009_05_transition.pdf.

Steuerle, C. Eugene. 2011. Restoring Solvency and Improving Equity in Social
Security: Benefit Options. July 8. http://www.urban.org/uploadedpdf/901435
-Improving-Equity-in-Social-Security.pdf.

———. 2013. Statement before the House Ways and Means Committee,
Subcommittee on Social Security, May 23. http://www.urban.org/UploadedPDF
/904585-Reforming-Social-Security-Benefits.pdf.

Steuerle, C. Eugene, Adam Carasso, and Lee Carasso. 2004. "How Progressive Is
Social Security and Why?" Urban Institute, May 1. http://www.urban.org
/publications/311016.html.

Steuerle, C. Eugene, and Caleb Quakenbush. 2012. "Social Security and Medicare Taxes and Benefits over a Lifetime." Urban Institute. http://www.urban.org /UploadedPDF/412660-Social-Security-and-Medicare-Taxes-and-Benefits-Over -a-Lifetime.pdf.

Steuerle, C. Eugene, and Stephanie Rennane. 2011. "Social Security and Medicare Taxes and Benefits over a Lifetime. Urban Institute, June 20. http://www.urban .org/publications/412281.html.

Steuerle, C. Eugene, Karen E. Smith, and Caleb Quakenbush. 2013. "Has Social Security Redistributed to Whites from People of Color?" Brief No. 38, November, Urban Institute. http://www.urban.org/UploadedPDF/412943-Has -Social-Security-Redistributed-to-Whites-from-People-of-Color.pdf.

Stone, Pamela. 2007. *Opting Out? Why Women Really Quit Careers and Head Home.* Oakland: University of California Press.

Strauss, Robert. 2015. "Easing into Leisure, One Step at a Time." *New York Times,* January 2. http://www.nytimes.com/2015/01/03/your-money/slowing-down-in -stages-on-gradual-path-to-full-retirement.html?emc=edit_bg_20150106&nl =booming&nlid=44003240&_r=0.

StrengthenSocialSecurity.org. 2012. "The Bowles-Simpson Plan Would End Social Security as We Know It." http://www.strengthensocialsecurity.org/sites/default /files/B-S%20Fact%20Sheet%20Updated_May%202012_0.pdf.

Struble, Laura M., and Barbara-Jean Sullivan. 2011. "Cognitive Health in Older Adults." *Nurse Practitioner* 36: 24. http://journals.lww.com/tnpj/Fulltext /2011/04000/Cognitive_Health_in_Older_Adults.7.aspx.

Sullivan, Laura, et al. 2009. "Enhancing Social Security for Low-Income Workers." In *Strengthening Social Security for Vulnerable Groups."* National Academy of Social Insurance, edited byVirginia P. Reno and Joni Lavery, 27. Washington, D.C.: National Academy of Social Insurance.

Sweeney, Megan M. 2002. "Two Decades of Family Change: The Shifting Economic Foundations of Marriage." *American Sociological Review* 67: 132.

Tanner, Michael D. 2011. "Social Security, Ponzi Schemes, and the Need for Reform." Policy Analysis No. 689, Cato Institution, November 17. http://www .cato.org/publications/policy-analysis/social-security-ponzi-schemes-need -reform.

———. 2012. *Still a Better Deal: Private Investment vs. Social Security.* Policy Analysis No. 692, Cato Institute, February 13. http://www.cato.org/publications /policy-analysis/still-better-deal-private-investment-vs-social-security.

Tavernise, Sabrina. 2012. "Life Spans Shrink for Least-Educated Whites in the U.S." *New York Times,* September 20. http://www.nytimes.com/2012/09/21/us /life-expectancy-for-less-educated-whites-in-us-is-shrinking.html?pagewanted =all&_r=0.

Thaler, Richard, and Cass Sunstein. 2008. *Nudge.* New York: Penguin Books.

Thomas, Adam, and Isabel Sawhill. 2005. "For Love and Money? The Impact of Family Structure on Family Income." *Future of Children* 15: 57. http://www.eric.ed.gov/PDFS/EJ795851.pdf.

Titmuss, Richard. 2006. "Commitment to Welfare" (1968). Republished as "Universalism versus Selection," in *The Welfare State Reader*, 2nd ed., edited by Christopher Pierson and Francis G. Castle, 40. London: Wiley.

Tungodden, Bertil, and Peter Vallentyne. 2006. "Who Are the Least Advantaged?" In *Egalitarianism: New Essays on the Nature and Value of Equality,* edited by Nils Holtug and Kasper Lippert-Rasmussen, 174–195. London: Oxford University Press.

UBS Investor Watch. 2013. "Eighty Is the New Sixty." http://www.ubs.com/us/en/wealth/research/Investor-Watch-Research-Archives/_jcr_content/par/textimage_4.1878809578.file/bGluay9wYXRoPS9jb25oZW50L2RhbS9XZWFsdGhNYW5hZ2VtZW50QW1lcmljYXMvZG9jdW1lbnRzL2ludmVzdGdoyLXdhdGdGNoLTRRMjAxMy1yZXBvcnQucGRm/investor-watch-4Q2013-report.pdf.

Urban Institute. 2014. Price Indexing. http://www.urban.org/retirement_policy/sspriceindexing.cfm.

U.S. Bureau of the Census. 2009. Number, Timing, and Duration of Marriages and Divorces: 2009. http://www.census.gov/hhes/socdemo/marriage/data/sipp/2009/tables.html

———. 2010. Social Explorer, American Community Survey 2010 Summary File: Technical Documentation. http://www.socialexplorer.com/data/ACS2010_5yr/documentation/

———. 2010–2012. American Community Survey, Selected Population Profile. http://factfinder2.census.gov/faces/tableservices/jsf/pages/productview.xhtml?pid=ACS_12_3YR_S0201&prodType=table.

———. 2011. America's Families and Living Arrangements. http://www.census.gov/hhes/families/data/cps2011.html.

———. 2012a. Households and Families: 2010. http://www.census.gov/prod/cen2010/briefs/c2010br-14.pdf.

———. 2012b. The Older Population in the United States: 2012. http://www.census.gov/population/age/data/2012.html.

———. 2012c. Statistical Abstract of the United States. http://www.census.gov/compendia/statab/cats/population/marital_status_and_living_arrangements.html.

———. 2012d. Voting and Registration in the Election of November 2012. http://www.census.gov/hhes/www/socdemo/voting/publications/p20/2012/tables.html.

———. 2014. CPS Historical Time Series Tables. Accessed June 30. http://www.census.gov/hhes/socdemo/education/data/cps/historical/index.html.

U.S. Department of Education. 2012a. Higher Education: Gaps in Access and Persistence Study. National Center for Education Statistics, August. http://nces.ed.gov/pubs2012/2012046.pdf.

————. 2012b. Profile of 2007–08 First-Time Bachelor's Degree Recipients in 2009, National Center for Education Statistics, October. http://nces.ed.gov/pubs2013 /2013150.pdf.

U.S. Department of Labor, Advisory Council on Employee Welfare and Pension Benefit Plans. 2008. Report on Phased Retirement. http://www.dol.gov/ebsa /publications/2008ACreport2.html.

U.S. Department of Labor, Bureau of Labor Statistics. 2013a. Civilian Labor Force Participation Rates by Age, Sex, Race, and Ethnicity. http://www.bls.gov/emp /ep_table_303.htm.

————. 2013b. Women in the Labor Force: A Databook. http://www.bls.gov/cps /wlf-databook-2012.pdf.

————. 2014a. Employment Status of the Civilian Noninstitutional Population by Age, Sex, and Race. http://www.bls.gov/cps/cpsaat03.htm.

————. 2014b. News Release: Employment Status of the Civilian Population 25 Years and Over, July 3. http://www.bls.gov/news.release/empsit.t04.htm.

U.S. Department of the Treasury. 2008. Social Security Reform: Strategies for Progressive Benefit Adjustments. Issue Brief No. 5. http://www.treasury.gov /resource-center/economic-policy/ss-medicare/Documents/ssissuebriefno .%205%20no%20cover.pdf.

VanDerhei, Jack. 2012. "Is Working to Age 70 Really the Answer for Retirement Income Adequacy?" *EBRI Notes* 33: 10.

VanDerhei, Jack, et al. 2006. "Retirement Security in the United States." *EBRI.* http://www.ebri.org/publications/books/index.cfm?fa=rsus.

Van de Water, Paul N., Arloc Sherman, and Kathy Ruffing. 2013. "Social Security Keeps 22 Million Americans Out of Poverty: A State-By-State Analysis." Center on Budget and Policy Priorities, October 25. http://www.cbpp.org/cms/?fa =view&id=4037.

Van Parijs, Philippe. 1998. *Real Freedom for All.* London: Clarendon Press.

Waldron, Hilary. 2007. Trends in Mortality Differentials and Life Expectancy for Male Social Security-Covered Workers, by Socioeconomic Status. *Social Security Bulletin* 67 (3). http://www.ssa.gov/policy/docs/workingpapers/wp108.html.

————. 2013. "Mortality Differentials by Lifetime Earnings Decile: Implications for Evaluations of Proposed Social Security Law Changes." *Social Security Bulletin* 73: 1. http://www.ssa.gov/policy/docs/ssb/v73n1/v73n1p1.html.

Wasik, John F. 2014. "Social Security at 62? Let's Run the Numbers." *New York Times,* May 14. http://www.nytimes.com/2014/05/15/business/retirementspecial /social-security-at-62-lets-run-the-numbers.html?_r=0.

Weatherford, Roy C. 1983. "Defining the Least Advantaged." *Philosophy Quarterly* 33: 63–69.

Weir, David R. 2007. "Are Baby Boomers Living Well Longer?" In *Redefining*

Retirement: How Will Boomers Fare? edited by Brigitte Madrian et al., 95. Philadelphia: Pension Research Council.

Weller, Christian E. 2010. "Building It Up, Not Tearing It Down: A Progressive Approach to Strengthening Social Security." Center for American Progress, December. http://cdn.americanprogress.org/wp-content/uploads/issues/2010/12/pdf/social_security.pdf.

Whitman, Kevin, and Dave Shoffner. 2011. *The Evolution of Social Security's Taxable Maximum.* , Policy Brief, Social Security Administration. http://www.ssa.gov/policy/docs/policybriefs/pb2011–02.html.

Williams, Alan. 1997. "Intergenerational Equity: An Exploration of the 'Fair Innings' Argument." *Health Econ.* 6: 117–132.

Woolf, Eliza. 2010. "A Bleak Market." *Inside Higher Ed* (August 13). https://www.insidehighered.com/advice/on_the_fence/woolf5

Yale University Faculty Phased Retirement Plan, as amended January 1, 2012. http://www.yale.edu/hronline/resources/docs/faculty-phased-retirement-plan-document-FPRP.pdf.

Yamaguchi, Kazuo, and Yantao Wang. 2002. "Class Identification of Married Employed Women and Men in America." *American Journal of Sociology* 108: 440, 441.

Yoder, Eric. 2012. "Phased Retirement Authority a Work in Progress." *Washington Post*, August 14. http://www.washingtonpost.com/blogs/federal-eye/post/federal-employee-phased-retirement-details-emerge/2012/08/13/8b9ab244-e56a-11e1-8741-940e3f6dbf48_blog.html.

———. 2013. " 'Phased Retirement' Policy for Federal Workers Unveiled." *Washington Post*, June 4. http://www.washingtonpost.com/blogs/federal-eye/wp/2013/06/04/phased-retirement-policy-for-federal-workers-unveiled/.

Zhivan, Natalia, et al. 2008, *An "Elastic" Earliest Eligibility Age for Social Security.* Issue in Brief No. 8-2, Boston College Center for Retirement Research, February. http://crr.bc.edu/briefs/an-qelasticq-earliest-eligibility-age-for-social-security/.

Acknowledgments

THIS BOOK REFLECTS the altruism of colleagues and friends who contributed their time and intellectual energy to my project. Al Klevorick, Dan Halperin, Michael Graetz, Teresa Ghilarducci, Bill Sage, Kris Collins, and Rory Van Loo offered valuable comments. Anonymous reviewers for Harvard University Press provided me with excellent questions and suggestions. Conversations with Noah Zatz and Bruce Ackerman confirmed—and challenged—my thinking in productive ways. And I learned a great deal about the sociology of the family from Vicki Schultz as we cotaught our Family, State, and Market courses at Yale in 2012 and 2013.

Yale Law students Jordan Bryant and Julian Polaris brought intellectual rigor to the work of reading and correcting the last draft. Jesselyn Friley provided first-rate research assistance early on.

My assistant, Patricia Spiegelhalter, has been invaluable in supporting my research and writing. She retired in 2015, and I miss her very much.

I owe so much to my longtime friends Phoebe Leith and Joan Leonard, who are always there when I need them. You help more than you know!

I am grateful to Robert Post and to the Yale Law School for the generous leave and summer funding that permitted me to concentrate on this project in 2013 and 2014.

Last but not least are David and Johanna. Together, we can make our society a fairer and better place.

Index